NARRATIVES OF CRISIS

HIGH RELIABILITY AND CRISIS MANAGEMENT

Series Editors: Karlene H. Roberts and Ian I. Mitroff

NARRATIVES OF CRISIS

Telling Stories of Ruin and Renewal

Matthew W. Seeger
and Timothy L. Sellnow

STANFORD BUSINESS BOOKS

An Imprint of Stanford University Press

Stanford, California
Stanford University Press

Special discounts for bulk quantities of Stanford Business Books are available to
corporations, professional associations, and other organizations. For details and
discount information, contact the special sales department of Stanford University
Press. Tel: (650) 736–1782, Fax: (650) 725–3457

Printed in the United States of America on acid-free,
archival-quality paper

Library of Congress Cataloging-in-Publication Data

Names: Seeger, Matthew W. (Matthew Wayne), 1957- author. | Sellnow,
Timothy L. (Timothy Lester), 1960- author.
Title: Narratives of crisis : telling stories of ruin and renewal / Matthew W.
Seeger and Timothy L. Sellnow.
Other titles: High reliability and crisis management.
Description: Stanford, California : Stanford Business Books, an imprint of
Stanford University Press, 2016. | Series: High reliability and crisis management
| Includes bibliographical references and index.
Identifiers: LCCN 2015044864 (print) | LCCN 2015050239 (ebook) |
ISBN 9780804788922 (cloth : alk. paper) | ISBN 9780804799515 (pbk. : alk.
paper) | ISBN 9780804799522 (ebook)
Subjects: LCSH: Communication in crisis management. | Crisis management. |
Narration (Rhetoric)
Classification: LCC HD49.3 .S44 2016 (print) | LCC HD49.3 (ebook) |
DDC 363.34/5--dc23
LC record available at http://lccn.loc.gov/2015044864

.
CIP data for 9780804788922
I

Contents

Acknowledgments

CRISES AND DISASTERS hold a unique fascination for us in part because of our personal experiences, but more broadly because of the impact these events have on society. Crises are transformational at a personal, institutional, and societal level, and as we argue in this book, they are among the most powerful forces of change. Despite this fact, the study of crises is fragmented and overly narrow. Distinct disciplinary traditions make creating a unified understanding of the research difficult, and only recently have crisis scholars begun to develop and use theory in an intentional and systematic way.

As communication researchers, we focus our work on the process of exchanging messages and creating meaning within the context of risks and crises. We believe this process is central to understanding crises because meaning influences the actions taken in anticipation of and response to risks and crises. Communication is epistemic and is particularly critical in a high-uncertainty condition such as a crisis.

Our work for more than thirty years has been directed toward broadening the parameters of crisis communication inquiry. Thus, we have sought to extend work beyond postcrisis image repair research to encompass precrisis work in risk communication. We have also focused on the potentially positive outcomes of crises through the theory of crisis and renewal. Whenever possible, we have brought an interdisciplinary focus to our work, including sociology, political science, and anthropology. And we are also very interested in the application of crisis communication to contexts such as public health, food safety, product recalls, engineering, and law, as well as organizations.

The application of narrative inquiry to crisis and risk communication is a natural extension of our work and again reflects our own experiences with crisis. We have heard hundreds of personal, group, and organizational stories of loss, destruction, and struggle, but also of renewal, spiritual strength, and growth. Stories are how we humans come to understand and make sense of uncertain situations, and they are important vehicles for encoding and communicating emotions, understanding, and lessons.

We set out to write a book that carved new territory and was accessible to a number of audiences. The systematic extension of crisis communication inquiry using narrative is a natural next step. Moreover, because we are all storytellers and because we have all experienced crisis—some larger, some smaller—we believe many people will relate to our analysis.

The world is becoming more complex and chaotic, and large-scale social, technological, economic, and environmental forces will create more crises and disasters in the future. Effective communication and storytelling is critical to avoiding these threats whenever possible and managing them when they erupt.

We have many people to thank for their patience and support, including our spouses, Beth and Deanna, and our children, Maggie, John, and Henry and Debbie, Scott, and Rick. We also wish to acknowledge a new addition, Seneca. Many colleagues, friends, and current and former students allow us to share, refine, and develop ideas. Our work builds on the work of others, and for this we are grateful. These include, in no particular order, Marsha Vanderford, Barbara Reynolds, Joel Iverson, Dennis Gouran, Bill Benoit, Tim Coombs, Sherry Holladay, Andreas Swartz, Claudia Auer, Dan O'Hair, Kevin Barge, Robert Littlefield, Robert Heath, Lee Wilkins, Finn Frandsen, Keith Hearit, Robert Rowland, Ron Arnett, Donyale Padgette, Julie Novak, Mary Henige, Bill Nowling, Lisa Vallee Smith, Louise Smith, Michael Palenchar, Deanna Sellnow, Steven Venette, Patric Spence, Ken Lachlan, Kimberly Parker, Bobi Ivanov, Derek Lane, Jeff Brand, Robert Ulmer, Melvin Gupton, Laura Pechta, Colleen Ezzeddine, J. J. McIntyre, Shari Veil, Alyssa Millner, Elizabeth Petrun, Kathryn Anthony, and Bethney Wilson. We are also grateful to Marshall Scoot Poole for his recommendation and to Karlene Roberts and Ian Mitroff for their willingness to include this book in the High Reliability and Crisis Management series at Stanford University Press. The anonymous reviewers of this proposal were gracious, detailed, and insightful in their critique. The staff at Stanford University Press, Margo Beth Fleming, and James Holt have provided critical help, encouragement, and support.

Nathan Stewart, Stephanie Church, Melissa Landon, Paige Moorhead, and Emily Helsel provided critical editorial and research assistance to this project. We also recognize Laura Pechta, Elizabeth Petrun, and Morgan Wickline-Getchell for their editorial assistance on previous projects that paved the way for this book. We dedicate this work to the next generation of scholars and practitioners and the stories they will tell about crisis.

NARRATIVES OF CRISIS

CHAPTER I

Narratives of Crisis

THE MARCH 11, 2012, Fukushima Daiichi crisis was a catastrophic failure of complex, high-risk technology following the magnitude 9.0 Great East Japan Earthquake. This crisis was so profoundly disruptive that Japanese officials and members of TEPCO, the Daiichi nuclear power plant owners, were deeply confused and unclear about how to respond and what to tell the public. The Japanese Nuclear Regulatory Authority originally classified the event leak as a level 1 or "anomalous" event according to the International Nuclear Event Scale. In response to international pressure, the regulatory authority revised the classification to a level 3: "serious radiation incident." The technical and engineering response might best be described as trial and error as technicians and emergency managers sought solutions for containing the damage. The communication response was also confused, resulting in incomplete and inaccurate information, which ultimately undermined public trust and compounded the harm. Even months after the initial accident was under control, TEPCO continued to minimize the risk and deny that radioactive water was leaking from the damaged facility into the Pacific Ocean. Fish caught hundreds of miles from the facility show high levels of contamination, but little information has been available about the potential risk to human health.

Within this context of high uncertainty, an ongoing crisis that is rapidly changing, and official channels that are limiting their response, media, watchdog groups, and members of the community began filling the informational void. The story was also closely followed by international media organizations. The leak has the potential to affect Japan's neighbors and international events, including the 2020 Olympics. Environmental groups such as EcoWatch and Greenpeace have also participated in the Fukushima narrative, calling for action and warning of widespread environmental harm. In addition, the disaster led to the development of event-specific groups such as Fukushimaresponse.org and fukushima-diary.com. These and many other groups have added to the larger Fukushima story and offer competing stories. These narratives of what is probably the worst nuclear accident in history are complex and dramatic.

Hurricane Katrina slammed into New Orleans, Louisiana, on August 27, 2005. Initially the community appeared to have managed the storm's impact, using well-established technologies and approaches such as levees, pumps, evacuations from low-lying areas, and family emergency kits. As the storm progressed, however, several key levees failed, resulting in catastrophic flooding of more than 80 percent of the city. The devastation was so widespread that it overwhelmed response capacity, which was further crippled by bureaucratic and governmental infighting and general lack of preparedness. In the end, Katrina was the most expensive disaster in U.S. history, costing over $108 billion and resulting in more than seven hundred deaths. The storm has become a powerful symbol of lack of preparedness, the disproportional impact of crises on poor and minority communities, and broader beliefs about government's role in disaster response. Hurricane Katrina was also a significant event for larger social, political, and economic issues in the United States. It brought up issues of race and class, and failures with the subsequent response undermined the administration of President George W. Bush. The widespread destruction in a major American city shocked the nation.

Communication allows feedback and adjustment, and during a crisis, these adjustments can help refine a response or correct mistakes. The media-produced feedback of the Hurricane Katrina response is an example of this. Media, serving their traditional watchdog function, identified deficiencies in the government response through posts on blogs and other electronic media, prompting government correction. Despite being forced to abandon their offices due to flooding, many journalists, photographers, and editors of the New Orleans–based *Times Picayune* remained in the surrounding area to report on the aftermath of Katrina. With their presses inoperable, they published online editions until temporary offsite presses could be set up.

Journalists at the Mississippi *Sun Herald* also used electronic media to provide coverage of Hurricane Katrina before, during, and after by posting updates and stories on the blog Eye of the Storm. In addition to providing essential information regarding Katrina's progress and subsequent instructions for citizens, they attempted to confirm or dispel various rumors and unconfirmed reports that began circulating as a result of the mass confusion and communication breakdown. One of the more interesting functions that blogs served during and after the storm was relating personal stories of not just the journalists who remained to cover the storm but also of emergency responders and regular citizens coping with the trials that Katrina brought.

While the ability to provide these journalistic functions in a non-traditional format during a crisis is interesting in itself, blogs provide a unique opportunity for rebuilding connections and empowering crisis participants. For a blog dedicated to a crisis, such as Eye of the Storm, posts range from real-time information and updates to personal accounts of ordinary people in extraordinary circumstances and even observations about the quality of the response. These posts then become communication hubs for further information and elaboration related to the topic. Readers who are also experiencing the crisis can add their individual experiences, thus creating a rich narrative accounts of the situation from a variety of perspectives. For those not directly experiencing the crisis, these posts provide opportunities to connect and empathize with individuals and communities they have no prior exposure to.

The luxury ocean liner RMS *Titanic* sank on April 15, 1912, after colliding with an iceberg in the North Atlantic. The ship, on its maiden voyage from Southampton in the United Kingdom to New York City, was carrying many of the nation's powerful and elite, including John Jacob Astor and Benjamin Guggenheim. More than 1,500 of the 2,224 passengers and crew died. The disaster shocked the world in terms of the scale of the loss and the fact that the most technologically advanced vessel of its time could suffer such a catastrophic failure. The *Titanic* has taken on almost mythic proportions in popular culture and has been the subject of numerous motion pictures and several museum exhibitions. The 1997 film *Titanic* is one of the highest-grossing film ever, at over $2 billion. The hundredth anniversary of the sinking in 2012 spawned several events, including the concert performance of *The Titanic Requiem*, candlelight vigils, and interfaith memorial services. The touring exhibition *Titanic: The Artifact Exhibition* featured more than three hundred objects recovered from the disaster site. The RMS *Titanic* has become a broad cultural symbol of risk, tragedy, loss, and arrogance.

Like many other disasters, the *Titanic* tragedy promoted official inquiries in both Great Britain and the United States. The U.S. Senate Commerce Committee conducted an extensive inquiry that included eighteen days of testimony from more than eighty witnesses. The committee concluded that design, operation, and regulatory failures were compounded by failures in response, including the iceberg warnings, the ship's speed, distress calls, and the evacuation as the ship sank. The committee also specifically noted a lack of preparation for a potential disaster and, most important, inadequate numbers of lifeboats and life preservers. The investigations initiated the creation of the 1914 International Convention for the Safety of Life at Sea. The provisions recognized the power of the *Titanic* tragedy and the need for action:

> The High Contracting Parties undertake to give effect to the provisions of this Convention, for the purpose of securing safety of life at sea, to promulgate all regulations and to take all steps which may be necessary to give the Convention full and complete effect. Having recognized the desirability of determining by common agreement certain uniform rules with respect to the safety of life at sea, have decided to conclude a Convention to that end, and have appointed as their plenipotentiaries who, having been duly authorized to that effect, have drawn up by common consent the following Convention. (Safety of Life at Sea, 1914)

The longevity and popularity of the RMS *Titanic* story may be attributed to a number of factors. The story appeals to many larger themes of culture, class, and hubris. Passengers were segregated according to economic class: the wealthy in first class, professionals and middle-class passengers in second class, and primarily poor immigrants in steerage. Thus, the disaster struck all classes of society and created a kind of social equality of tragedy and loss. The disaster's theme of hubris is reflected in the failures of the industry and ship operators to invest in appropriate safety equipment. The safety of the passengers was compromised in favor of economic considerations. At the same time, some crew members and passengers gave up their seats in lifeboats to women and children and thus became heroes of the *Titanic* story. The Men's Titanic Society, a group of television producers and directors, meets annually on the anniversary of the sinking at the Washington, DC, memorial, where they offer toasts to the men who gave up their seats in the lifeboats to women and children.

These and many other examples illustrate the power of large-scale crises and disasters to shape our culture, beliefs, lives, and institutions. Disasters and the stories told about them carry meaning, encode lessons, and frame larger public and societal understanding of risks, warnings, and potential harm. In some cases, crises take on mythic status and are commemorated in public ceremonies and memorials as ways of reifying specific meaning and lessons.

Disasters create significant confusion. Often leaders, members of the public, and those experiencing a crisis are unable to make sense of what is happening. This paralysis often compounds the damage. The loss of individual sense-making capacity following a crisis has been described as a cosmology episode by Karl Weick (1993). Cosmology episodes occur when "people suddenly and deeply feel that the universe is no longer a rational, orderly system." In normal circumstances, "people . . . act as if events cohere in time and space and that change unfolds in an orderly manner. These orderly cosmologies are subject to disruption. And when they are severely disrupted, I call this a cosmology episode" (Weick 1985, pp. 51–52). Moreover, "What makes such an episode so shattering is that both the sense of what is occurring and the means to rebuild it collapse together. Stated more informally, a cosmology episode feels like vu jàdé—the opposite of déjà vu: I've never been here before, I have no idea where I am, and I have no idea who can help me." Many crises create profound confusion and disorganization for those experiencing the event firsthand as normal conditions are radically and rapidly disrupted. The fundamental sense of personal meaning may be lost as a person's life story takes a sudden and unexpected turn.

Sorting out the long network of intersecting factors, decisions, variables, and mistakes that cause a crisis like the Fukushima Daiichi accident or the *Titanic* tragedy is often a slow, tedious, and inevitably incomplete process. A crisis is always the consequence of multiple factors and decisions interacting in complex ways, often without being fully observed or understood. Katrina may be explained by decades of development and environmental policies. The Fukushima Daiichi disaster can be attributed to engineering practices, growing energy demands, and social norms that dissuade questioning of authority. During the postcrisis stage, various stakeholders advocate for specific explanations and may seek to shift blame and responsibility in strategic ways to restore or defend their image (Benoit, 1995). Various explanations and accounts of crises can lead to very different structures of liability, understandings of risk, and policy decisions. Moreover, crises often disrupt, overwhelm, and, in some cases, destroy established channels of communication, including television, print, and community-based networks. This strains communication capacities at the very time when more capacity and information are needed to tell the story. Natural disasters such as hurricanes and floods often disrupt local media as well as cell phone and Internet capacity. This reduced capacity may further impede the ability of crisis participants to tell the story of the crisis and make sense of what happened. This information vacuum can create particularly fertile conditions for the development of rumors. Stories of rapes and murders at the New Orleans Superdome were widely reported in the media but later were found to be incorrect.

Often this extreme disruption, loss, and general confusion result in a loss of ability to make sense of the events, contextualize them, and then create and connect with larger systems of meaning. The sudden loss of highly valued processes, possessions, and relationships often creates existential questions not easily answered. These losses may continue to affect individuals and communities for years. Seeing one's entire home consumed in a fire, facing the cleanup from floodwaters contaminated with chemicals and sewage, or losing family members and friends in a disaster can create deep psychological and social harm. The economic impact can be quite extreme as well, with businesses destroyed, supply chains disrupted, and employees lost. These losses often leave individuals and communities struggling not just to recover but, more fundamentally, to make sense of what has happened. This meaning deficit may be manifest in psychological problems, social struggles, and larger disruption of communities and institutions.

Crises can create the need, perceived or real, for significant social, economic, and political change. In fact, crises are arguably the most powerful force in social change contributing to ongoing systemic adaption and evolution. The events of 9/11 precipitated a wholesale rethinking of security norms and procedures, resulting in the most extensive overhaul of U.S. federal bureaucracy in decades through the creation of the Department of Homeland Security. Hurricane Katrina called into question fundamental assumptions about development, the environment, and social equality. Katrina also helped change basic assumptions and approaches to disaster response and a movement from centralized to decentralized "whole community" frameworks.

One of the most important features of crises and disasters is the increasing frequency and expanding impact of these events. According to normal accident theory, crises are often systemic failures involving complex interactive subsystems that are tightly coupled such that failures are compounded. Failures may become cascading events, with each step compounding the harm. Charles Perrow, the theory's founder, also argued that such failures may be programmed into many large, technologically intensive systems such that complexity and tight coupling are dominant characteristics of these systems (Perrow, 1984). Many modern high-risk systems such as transportation, energy, and food are characterized by both complexity and tight coupling. Moreover, aging infrastructure; growing, aging, and mobile populations; greater centralization and technological dependence; more reliance on high-risk technologies; and environmental changes, including climate change, all contribute to a greater probability of crises creating more harm for more people.

Few social phenomena are as complex, multifaceted, and dynamic and carry as much potential impact as large-scale crises and disasters. These events bring together psychological, social, economic, political, technological, and environmental factors within the context of high uncertainty, high risk, and severe harm. The subsequent tapestry of stories, accounts, and explanations of these events is a narrative process necessary to make sense and determine actions. All crises generate these narratives, and within them are patterns and relationships that can help explain their larger impact.

CRISIS AS A COMMUNICATIVE SPACE

The lack of clarity and the existence of a communication vacuum and meaning deficit of a crisis create a discursive space that is filled by narratives, often multiple and conflicting. The stories of loss, heroes, victims, hubris, blame, responsibility, recovery, and risk form the basis for a larger structure of sense making and meaning woven around large-scale disasters and crises. Through narratives, events are ordered in a sequential manner to create larger meaning structures that may be rooted in patterns of association such as cause and effect (Jasinski, 2001). Robert Heath (2004) notes that through the crisis narrative, "the world and people's actions reflect a logic that explains what happens, why it happens, who makes it happen, when it happens, and how people should respond to these events" (p. 171). These narratives often compete with one another in support of the larger lessons of the crisis and ultimately for the social changes that may occur as a consequence. Various narratives may order events or activities in different sequences, include different associations between elements, and reach different conclusions about meaning. Characters may be shifted, taking on different roles in the narrative, and different lessons may emerge. Specific social, political, and cultural changes are supported by these competing narratives of loss, responsibility, and blame. A narrative that grounds a crisis as a technological failure, for example, may lead to greater regulation of technology. Narratives that describe a crisis as a natural disaster caused by natural forces suggest that nothing could be done to avoid the harm; therefore, no human agent is responsible.

Narratives are influenced by the physical, psychological, cultural, and ideological standpoint of the narrator. These issues are distinct from how a narrator intends to construct the narrative. While crisis narratives often function in an instrumental capacity to fill the absence of meaning in response to a specific event, they also have unintended or secondary constitutive consequences. The constitutive function of narrative relates or positions itself with respect to a culture's social world (Jasinski, 2001). Because narratives function to help shape our perception of the world around us and narrators are responsible for those perceptions, it makes sense that their particular views, perspectives, life experiences, social standpoints, and deeper ideological views would influence how they interpret and organize the narrative. What is important to note is that these instrumental and constitutive functions of narratives are not mutually exclusive within the same larger narrative.

New technology allows us to see or experience a crisis in a new and sometimes very personal way. In essence, the larger public can become vicarious participants in a crisis. This is exemplified in the case of the apprehension of the surviving Boston Marathon bombing suspects. The search created an opportunity for the public to participate as approximately 2.32 million people listened to a live Internet broadcast of the police scanner during the apprehension of Dzhokhar Tsarnaev (Ngak, 2013). When the police started to move in on Tsarnaev, people began not only to post links to the live broadcast on Twitter, but also to post status updates with closely paraphrased excerpts of the police and FBI radio chatter. Twitter users began to "report" the events taking place even faster than the news channels could get and report "confirmed" information. Some of the major news networks, including CNN, began reporting on Twitter posts. As the events were unfolding, Twitter users began speculating on the status of the apprehension and what would happen next. The most powerful moment occurred when Twitter users were able to vicariously experience the relief of law enforcement officials when police scanners confirmed the suspect was in custody. A sequence of police officers and dispatchers expressed their relief, gratitude, and congratulations. The public was able to experience all of this as if they were actually there at that moment. For many, it was a powerful and gratifying conclusion to what had been an extremely emotionally charged crisis.

Much of the meaning, power, and ultimate impact of a crisis are functions of the ensuing network of narratives. In most instances, these crisis narratives cluster around a handful of meaning systems. The form, structure, storyteller, audience, channel, and frequency, as well as probability and fidelity of the content, influence the meaning, lessons, and the larger outcomes.

WHAT IS A CRISIS?

While scholars from various fields have debated the meaning of *crisis*, they have largely agreed that the term is filled with significance. The term is used widely to denote a disruption or threatening circumstance usually within a specific context, such as an environmental, economic, or political event. Sociologists view crises as extreme events arising from the interaction of a hazard, such as an earthquake, hurricane, tornado, or technological risk, with a social system (Burton, Kates, & White, 1978; Kaplan & Garrick, 1981). Robert Heath described crisis as the manifestation of a risk (1995), that is, the probability of a negative outcome or consequence. *Crisis* denotes some abnormal event or events that threaten values, goals, and resources. As a consequence, describing an event as a crisis is a rhetorical act that calls for some immediate action to alleviate the potential threat. A disease outbreak that is described as routine, such as seasonal flu, carries a different level of urgency than does an event described as a pandemic.

In Western use, the term *crisis* derives from the Greek *krisis*, a medical term that the physician Hippocrates used to describe the turning point in a disease, and *Krinein* which means to judge, separate, or decide. In its Eastern etymology, a crisis is a moment where a judgment is necessary. The Chinese symbol for crisis is *wēijī*. The symbol *wēi* roughly translates to danger, dangerous, endanger, jeopardize, perilous, precipitous, precarious, high, fear, afraid. The symbol *jī* may sometimes mean "opportunity" and may also mean "a crucial point" (Mair, 2010). Both Greek and Chinese translations suggest that a crisis is a point or time of threat and danger requiring some decision, choice, judgment, or action (Sellnow & Seeger, 2013).

These translations are largely consistent with the view that crises are characterized by three general attributes: surprise, high uncertainty, and threat (Hermann, 1963; Seeger, Sellnow, & Ulmer, 2003). Crises are generally unanticipated or violate expectations in surprising ways, creating high levels of uncertainty and sometimes creating cosmology episodes.

Most often, they are a radical departure from the status quo and a violation of general assumptions and expectations, disrupting normal activities and limiting the ability to anticipate and predict. The severe violation of expectations is usually a source of uncertainty, psychological discomfort, and stress. In retrospect, however, warning signs and signals of a crisis are often evident. Crises almost always threaten some high-priority goals such as health, personal or family safety, property, economic security, and psychological stability. Finally, these events require relatively rapid response to reduce, contain, or mitigate the potential harm. Slow responses usually compound the level of harm or the scope of the damage. Crisis responses are often accompanied by the human stress hormone adrenaline, which produces several physical responses, including increased heart rate and dilated air passages. These responses develop the physical capacity to respond to a threat. Accounts of exceptional physical feats during crisis are common. In 2013, two daughters, aged fourteen and sixteen, lifted a 3,000-pound tractor off their father after it overturned on him. These reports of amazing strength in the face of a crisis are part of the larger hero narrative (McClam, 2013).

Given these characteristics, a general working definition of a *crisis* is a specific, unexpected, nonroutine event or series of events that create high levels of uncertainty and a significant or perceived threat to high-priority goals (Seeger et al., 2003). A crisis is generally concentrated in a particular space or locations at a specific defined time. As described earlier, crises precipitate a meaning deficit by disrupting the processes and patterns of sense making. During a crisis, communication channels—newspapers, television, personal networks—are often cut off. Established patterns and routines cannot be maintained. Personal possessions, physical objects, even buildings that carried social meaning may be gone. There is a need, therefore, to tell stories and offer accounts and explanations to reduce the uncertainty and find perspective and create or recreate meaning. In many ways, the human and social experience of crisis encoded in narratives and crises cannot be separated from the stories told about them.

From yet other perspectives, the question of what constitutes a crisis is a function of individual, community, or cultural experience. Events that occur frequently, even if they carry high risk, tend to be perceived as routine, and strategies for mitigating the risks have typically been developed and refined. Coombs (2010), for example, described crisis as a function of perceptions based on a violation of some strongly held expectation. Social or cultural expectations therefore create a kind of baseline of normalcy, and the violation of these expectations will be judged as a crisis. Risk theorist Vincent Covello (2009) has demonstrated that novel risks, which are invisible and seen as exotic or unfair, increase the perception of risk. Radiological events are considered riskier than secondhand cigarette smoke even though the latter causes many more deaths.

Other definitions have emphasized the relationship between crisis and risk. Heath and O'Hair (2009) describe a crisis as the outcome and manifestation of a risk such that crisis and risk are counterpoints. When a risk is inappropriately managed, it erupts into a crisis. The idea that a crisis involves the incubation or interaction of risks is widely accepted (Fink, 1986; Smart & Vertinsky, 1977). A risk incubates in the sense that it goes unaddressed or even unrecognized. A comparatively small flaw in the design of an aircraft may become exacerbated over time though normal stress. A risk may interact with other risk factors to create the kind of dramatic failure that triggers the onset of a crisis. The small flaw in an aircraft may interact with the wind shear caused by a thunderstorm and lead to the crash of an airplane.

Closely related to the term *crisis* is the term *disaster*, the term favored by those approaching these events as sociological phenomenon (Kreps, 1984; Quarantelli, 1984). According to sociology, a disaster is a social phenomenon with broad sociological and psychological consequences that creates severe damage and disrupts all or some of the essential functions of the society (Fritz, 1961). It is "a potentially traumatic event that is collectively experienced, has an acute onset, and is time delineated; disasters may be attributed to natural, technological or human causes" (McFarlane & Norris, 2006, p. 4). Disasters are typically conceptualized as a function of some general hazard, usually in the form of physical agents like earthquakes, tornadoes, or hurricanes or technological factors that threaten a community or region and require a community-based response (see Perry, 2007). The distinctions between a disaster and a crisis are largely ones of emphasis: a crisis is often contained in its scope and impact, and a disaster is more often described as a community- or society-wide event.

Whether described as a crisis, disaster, calamity, or catastrophe, these events have profound social, economic, and political impact. They often create fundamental changes in social and governmental structures, beliefs about risk, and the social norms associated with risk management. The associated crisis stories can take on mythic status, as with the *Titanic* disaster. They encode fundamental social truths, such as the Hurricane Katrina disaster. Crises also influence and frame basic understandings regarding risks, such as followed the Fukushima Daiichi nuclear disaster.

DESCRIBING THE CRISIS NARRATIVE

This exploration conceptualizes crisis as a deeply disruptive and abnormal event with largely, although not exclusively, negative outcomes. Crisis creates a narrative space, a communication vacuum, or a meaning deficit that will be filled by stories told by those who experienced the crisis, crisis managers, journalists, and observers. These stories create a complex, always incomplete, and often conflicting set of frames for making sense of these events. These narratives come from particular physical, political, and philosophical places such that the standpoint of the narrator influences the story. Beyond seeking to make sense of a complex and confusing event, crisis narratives serve a variety of other purposes. They fulfill a rhetorical function advocating for specific social, economic, and political changes. Crisis narratives encode larger lessons regarding risk, its management, and its manifestation. Among the most important functions is to assess and affix blame and responsibility. These narratives also serve an important psychological function, creating a kind of communicative catharsis for those who have experienced the crisis. In addition, cognitive processes often favor a narrative structure. Narrative-based comprehension is among the earliest cognitive capacity to develop in children and the most universal form of cognition for organizing human experience (Bruner, 1991).

The analysis of crisis narratives outlined in this book is based on the identification of recurring themes and characteristics such that general narrative types are evident. The crisis account, for example, is a narrative designed to sort out what exactly happened to cause the crisis. A crisis is always associated with many factors or causes and is subject to interpretation. The account is also used to determine blame and responsibility and ultimately fix accountability. The blame narrative is a ubiquitous feature of many postcrisis contexts. The rhetorical goal is to repair or restore the image of those who may be responsible. In contrast, the renewal narrative privileges plans for future recovery, growth, and restoration over questions of who is to blame for the crisis. Renewal is therefore prospective rather than retrospective and draws heavily on the reservoir of goodwill that may develop following a crisis. As such, these narratives construct the crisis as the starting point for a compelling vision of the future. Almost all crises create harm to individuals, groups, communities, and organizations. Those harmed are usually referred to as victims, although this term carries political meaning and implications that are stigmatizing and may actually compound the harm. Stories told by victims are among the most compelling narratives following a crisis and are usually widely reported. They may include stories of struggle, hardship, and loss, as well as recovery. Closely related to the victim narrative is the hero narrative. The hero character in the crisis story usually makes some personal sacrifice or takes some personal risk in response to the crisis. The hero may be an individual, an everyman who steps up in the face of the crisis; a leader who is tasked with managing the crisis; or a group such as firefighters or first responders. Hero stories carry unique political and rhetorical significance and may position the central character for much wider notoriety.

Together the various narratives create a larger network of meaning around a crisis event, sometimes in separate texts and sometimes within the same text. These narratives compete in the public space for dominance and general social acceptance. It is through this process that crises and disasters fundamentally shape culture, beliefs, norms, policies, and institutions. By understanding the shape, form, and function of these narratives, we can more accurately anticipate the postcrisis meaning-creation process and the social changes that follow.

TELLING THE STORY OF CRISIS

A crisis story may be told in many different ways. Epic poems such as Beowulf provide accounts of heroic responses to threats. The biblical story of Noah and the Great Flood recounts a response to an antici-pated risk. Newspapers have provided detailed journalistic accounts of disasters almost since their development, and film provided a way to record events as they developed. On May 6, 1937, the explosion of the German passenger airship *Hindenburg* was captured on film. Televi-sion and radio have been particularly useful as systems for distributing contemporaneous information about risks, including warnings, evacu-ations, and shelter-in-place notices. The initial broadcast alert system, CONELRAD (Control of Electromagnetic Radiation), was established in 1951 as part of larger preparation for possible nuclear attack. It was replaced in 1963 with the Emergency Broadcasting System. The develop-ment of the twenty-four-hour news channel associated with the develop-ment of cable news created more news space, which forced journalists to increase their coverage of crises, even those that were more local. Digital technology has expanded crisis coverage even more with live updates through platforms such as Twitter and Facebook. These channels and technologies of communication have all expanded the opportunities to tell the stories of crises.

Many different narrators may tell the story of a single crisis from their own perspectives. Those who experience the crisis directly, the victims and community members, have direct, albeit often limited, views of the crisis. Journalists and first responders bring a particular set of professional frames to a crisis story. Politicians and community, business, religious, and cultural leaders also have specific perspectives and standpoints re-garding these events. Significantly, crises often become the subject of of-ficial reports and legal proceedings and eventually become the subject of historical accounts. Some crises, such as the Great Flood, take on mythic proportions. In some cases, a crisis is picked up in popular literature or film, where the stories are retold with the addition of artistic license. At a more personal level, crises often become the stuff of family stories, passed on from generation to generation. Sometimes the narratives of crisis complement one another, and sometimes they compete. Taken together, these narratives can provide rich insight into how individuals, groups, and society respond to the high levels of crisis-induced uncertainty, threat, and short response time.

CONCLUSION

Crises happen and will continue to happen with more frequency and greater levels of harm as society becomes increasingly complex and dynamic. They have profound impacts and are forces of individual and social change. Individuals who survive a major crisis often report that their outlook and sense of meaning have been forever altered. In many cases, these events fundamentally alter how people see themselves and the world. Crises change geography, disrupt economies, and influence larger understandings of risk. The stories told about crisis encompass both individual and larger social understandings of these events.

Despite the increasing frequency of these events and their power as forces of change, comparatively little effort has been directed toward understating the crisis story. Rather, crises are usually seen as events to be managed through the allocation of resources—human, technological, and informational—and through appropriate human vigilance. The stories of crisis, however, determine the larger meaning of crises and ultimately the lessons learned and the larger institutional and social and responses.

CHAPTER 2

Humans as Storytellers

NARRATIVES are fundamental processes that humans use to shape meaning, understanding, and action. Sharing personal narratives through storytelling "is a vital part of the human experience; it transmits knowledge, assists in problem solving, and is thought to have been used since the dawn of humankind" (Badger, Royse, & Moore, 2011, p. 577). A focus on narratives contests the view that people typically form opinions and make decision through a discourse based on formal reasoning (Fisher, 1987). Instead, a more practical discourse, based on storytelling, is the natural means through which we comprehend our world. Although the "rational-world paradigm is an ever-present part of our consciousness because we have been educated into it, the narrative impulse is part of our very being because we acquire narrative in the natural process of socialization" (Fisher, 1987, p. 65). Those who share this view assume that we are by nature storytelling beings, making the exchange of stories the process through which we best understand our world. This understanding, however, is not passively achieved through the spontaneous emergence of objective narrative accounts. Instead, narratives are far more than a mere "descriptive recounting of events" involving selected "characters, actions, and settings" (Heath, 2004, p. 171). Rather, individual narratives serve as arguments for seeing the world in a distinct way. This argumentative dimension resides in observable objectives of the narrative. A credible narrative "performs an action of some kind, it produces outcomes or consequences, or it does a certain kind of rhetorical work" (Foss, 2009, p. 310).

In this manner, multiple narratives can actually compete against one another (a topic we address in Chapter 10). Martin (1986) vividly characterizes this competition: "Narrative, considered as a form of entertainment when studied as literature, is a battleground when actualized in newspapers, biography and history" (p. 8). The expansion of social media in the past decade has widened this battlefield extensively. The multiple interpretations and objectives competing for public acknowledgment or agreement reflect the natural means by which people interpret their world. Rather than a rational debate through which a single truth is confirmed, the narrative perspective sees human reasoning as pluralistic, accounting for multiple viewpoints that structure our reality (Fisher, 1987; Perelman & Olbrechts-Tyteca, 1969).

The interpretation of a crisis resides in the narratives that represent it. As multiple stories are shared, those seen as the most consistent or believable take hold in the minds of observers, creating a dominant view of the crisis: its impact, inception, blame, and demand for meaningful change. All parties touched by the crisis have the opportunity to participate in the narrative. Organizational spokespersons may attempt to create a narrative that offers a more positive view of their role in the crisis. Regulatory agencies may assign blame while defending the policies in place to prevent such crises. Consumers harmed by the crisis may demand compensation or express grief over losses ranging from human lives to valuable property. Other organizations within the industry may seek to distance themselves from the afflicted organization by creating narratives differentiating their products and procedures from those created and enacted by the organization facing the crisis. Selected aspects from all of these narratives weave together to form a dominant view and, often, a less dominant, alternate view of the crisis.

In this chapter, we discuss the means by which narratives comprise dominant views in the communicative space created by crises. To do so, we discuss the multiple, inherent functions of narratives during and after crises, including emotional expression and information seeking. Next, we delineate the component parts of a narrative. Finally, we discuss the criteria by which observers ascertain the consistency or believability of narratives.

MEANING AND IDENTITY DEFICIT
IN CRISIS NARRATIVES

The inherently novel and shocking nature of narratives causes a momentary lapse in or loss of understanding. As we discussed in Chapter 1, this loss of comprehension creates a communicative space that can be characterized as a loss of understanding that leads to "existential denarration" (Richardson, 2008, p. 101). The shock and threat of crises often challenge existing narratives of safety, security, competence, and camaraderie. Existential denarration acknowledges that crises can initiate "a person's loss of life story" (Richardson, 2008, p. 101). Denarrated people feel "lost, dangerous, out of control and susceptible to the forces of randomness" (Coupland, 1996, p. 179). As a consequence of momentary denarration, those facing crises must rebuild, repair, or recreate narratives that better account for the unexpected circumstances. This rekindling of comprehension begins with the narrative process. As meaning is restored, those experiencing crises subconsciously ask themselves, "How can I know what I think until I see what I say?" (Weick, 1995, p. 18).

The creation of new or revised narratives accounting for crisis circumstances must account for the complexity of the situation. People, particularly members of an organization, "are thrown into challenging situations, often without what was considered adequate preparation," and they respond with narratives rich in circumspection (Browning & Morris, 2012, p. 147). Those responding to these unfamiliar events, including crises, "do the best they can under the circumstances, and reflect upon what the narrated incident means for their identity as an organization member" (Browning & Morris, 2012, p. 147). Circumspection in narratives acknowledges the complexity of the situation and recognizes "that valuable information can emerge from anywhere" (Browning & Morris, 2012, p. 148). This narrative response to crisis allows people to both express their painful emotions and fill gaps in understanding caused by the loss of their familiar narrative.

Crisis Narratives as Emotional Expression

Those who have lived through crises have a story to tell. Telling that story is such a natural part of the human psyche that failure to express stories of personal tragedy or crisis can be emotionally harmful. In his extensive body of work on narrative expression, Pennebaker (1990) found that

> holding back or inhibiting our thoughts and feelings can be hard work. Over time, the work of inhibition gradually undermines the body's defenses. Like

other stressors, inhibition can affect immune functions, the action of the heart and vascular systems, and even the biochemical workings of the brain and nervous systems. In short, excessive holding back of thoughts, feelings, and behaviors can place people at risk for both major and minor diseases. (p. 13)

By contrast, the narrative expression of crisis experiences has the potential to aid in emotional recovery and physical healing. For example, Badger et al. (2011) argue that storytelling "organizes thinking, aids the process of making meaning from experiences, and assists with reconnecting the story-teller socially with others through the releasing of thoughts and feelings" (p. 578).

Narrative expression enables individuals to more fully engage their minds in reflecting on an experience. Kahneman (2011) identifies a tendency for people to think superficially or lazily about complex issues. He explains that when we think superficially, we frame issues narrowly, making "decisions as problems arise," rather than considering them from a situational perspective (p. 366). From a narrative viewpoint, this tendency would cause individuals to express momentary thoughts or emotions without considering the broader context of the situation. Pennebaker (1990) sees a similar tendency. When individuals experience painful circumstances such as crises, they are inclined to think superficially or at a lower level, which allows them to avoid the painful circumstance briefly. Both Kahneman (2011) and Pennebaker (1090) see this lower-level thinking as detrimental to both human productivity and recovery. Both advocate a more complex narrative that considers the larger context.

Pennebaker (1990) specifically advocates the mindful thinking that Ellen Langer espouses. Langer's (2009) more recent work on mindfulness makes a direct connection between higher-level thinking and health. She explains that we tend to favor "certainty over a more complex understanding of what health is" (p. 25). She then argues that the mindless pursuit of such certainty blinds us "to alternative ways of understanding that would have made just as much sense and could turn out [to] be far more useful" (p. 22). She offers considerable evidence that individuals who optimistically engage in higher-level, mindful thinking are better equipped for managing their health. Narratives, by their nature, command this higher level of thinking. They require the simultaneous consideration of multiple events, organized in time, with causal relationships that are organized in a unified manner. Expressing narratives in this manner invokes psychological and physiological benefits identified by Pennebaker (1990) and Langer (2009). Where lower-level thinking discounts pluralism and multiplicity, narratives require us to interlace multiple experiences in time and context to find meaning.

Badger et al. (2011) offer a compelling example of the benefits that narratives composed at a higher level of thinking can have on physical and psychological health. They analyzed the stories shared by burn survivors as part of their recovery. The rationale for their study was based on previous studies that found that those who disclosed details of their trauma had a lower tendency to experience persistent anxiety after a traumatic burn. Conversely, those who internalized their trauma and were unable to share their burn story with others did not share the same level of recovery. Badger et al. found that storytelling is "an integral part of the burn community and represents an intervention that is very accessible" (p. 590). They contend that social workers can help patient recovery by encouraging burn victims to articulate their burn story—not just as past-tense reflection on their injury but also in a present-tense description of how they are coping and reconnecting with others. This healing potential for storytelling is also recognized in the communication discipline. Health communication scholars have observed the healing power of storytelling when individuals can share their stories of pain, loss, and recovery (Sharf, Harter, Yamaski, & Haidet, 2011). This expression through storytelling plays a vital role in health care.

Seeking to Fill Gaps through Crisis Narratives

The meaning deficit created by crises creates gaps or "discontinuities or problematic situations that constantly arise in our lives" (Johnson & Case, 2012, p. 124). This information seeking is complicated, however, by the fact that all the major players in the crisis are likely to put forward information that reflects favorably on themselves and the actions of their organizations. The information we seek in crisis situations is typically revealed to us in the form of stories, including characters and motives following plot lines of either tragedy or comedy. These crisis narratives interact or compete with one another, answering questions focused on three general categories: evidence, intent, and responsibility (Sellnow & Ulmer, 2004; Ulmer & Sellnow 2000).

Questions of evidence. The evidence surrounding crisis events is not unlike that presented in public debates or trials, where the relevance or applicability of some evidence may be questioned. Evidence that is acknowledged by the parties who are generating crisis narratives is often interpreted differently among the various parties in the debate. Consideration of evidence surrounding a crisis often produces two or more plausible interpretations, thereby introducing ambiguity to the narrative (Sellnow & Ulmer, 2004). This interpretation process is typically done in a manner that reflects favorably on the narrator. We are not suggesting that this interpretation process is inherently deceitful and are certainly not implying that individuals and organizations involved in crises should remain passive as evidence is shared publicly. Rather, we are observing that the questions of evidence answered by multiple narratives in response to a crisis can actually increase rather than decrease ambiguity and uncertainty.

Questions of intent. Questions of intent in crisis narratives ask, "What were the true intentions behind the actions that preceded the crisis?" Individuals and organizations have difficulty responding to narratives that portray their actions as unethical or illegitimate. For example, organizations experience reputational crises when their "stakeholders perceive an incongruity to exist between a corporation's values, as evidenced in its acts, and those of the social system" (Hearit, 2006, p. 13). Conversely, an organization or individual may be responsible for a crisis despite having the best of intentions. In such cases organizations and individuals argue that the actions and events causing a crisis or causing failure to prepare for a crisis "occurred accidentally" (Benoit, 1995, p. 73). Questions of intent can continue in later stages of the narrative, assigning motives to those responsible for recovery efforts. The sincerity and sufficiency of the recovery efforts and compensation for victims may be questioned or affirmed in these stages of crisis narratives. Overall, crisis narratives typically devote considerable time and space to speculating about the intentions of all parties.

Questions of locus. Ultimately, crisis narratives identify a locus of responsibility for the crisis, a complex and often imprecise process. The complexity of our society tends to fragment responsibility for crises (Sellnow & Ulmer, 2004,). Layers of decision making in organizations make identifying an individual for blame difficult or impossible. The fact that no one was arrested for improper behavior on Wall Street in the wake of the collapse of the banking industry in 2008 is a powerful example of the difficulty in assigning responsibility. Despite these legal limitations, crisis narratives typically speculate on who is to blame.

Human Need to Tell Stories and Reflect

The perceived need for information following a crisis reflects a desire to see the story completed (Heath, 2004). Questions that typically make up the foundation of a news story are paramount in the public's need to know. For example, questions such as who is affected, who is responsible, what happened, where the primary harm is, when this started, and why it happened dominate discourse about crises. Thus, storytelling as a process is part of crisis response. In fact, stories of the risks of tsunamis have been passed down in the oral history of many cultures in Southeast Asia. These stories help people living today understand the risks and manage them.

The interpretation of crises through storytelling is also central to learning from crises. For example, organizations are represented by an accumulation of stories that may culminate in an organizational saga (Bormann, 1983). These organizational sagas feature "narratives of achievements, events, goals, and ideal states of an entire organization" (p. 115). Stories create lessons learned and are retained as memory by families, communities, and organizations. Communities and organizations can observe the crisis and use the story as a form of vicarious learning.

EMERGENCE OF CRISIS NARRATIVES

The many interpretations of evidence, intentions, and responsibility surrounding crisis events complicate the narrative process. Over time, however, stories coalesce to form a more central narrative. As individuals consider the narrative fragments that emerge from a crisis, they assign credibility to the elements that provide the clearest justification for being believed

(Venette, 2008). In this section, we identify the component parts of narratives and provide more detail for how these justifications or warrants for narrative are weighed and selected by audiences.

Consistent Components of Crisis Narratives

Although all narratives are composed of characters, settings, plots, and themes, there is a distinction between literary and rhetorical narratives (Rowland, 2009). Literary narratives do not need an overt purpose beyond entertaining the audience. By contrast, rhetorical narratives, continues Rowland, have "explicit or clearly implied" themes that seek to persuade audiences to "believe a conclusion or reinforce an audience that already has a given perspective" (p. 121). Crisis narratives are rhetorical. They assign blame, distill lessons learned, memorialize victims, anoint heroes, and instruct audiences about how to protect themselves, to name only a few. Any of these functions involve some degree of persuasion. Literary and rhetorical narratives do, however, share the consistent components of characters, setting, plot, and theme (Rowland, 2009).

Characters. As in any other narrative, the primary characters of crisis narratives are the protagonist and antagonist. The protagonist struggles to overcome the threats introduced by the antagonist. In crisis narratives, the protagonist and antagonist are not typically represented as individuals. Rather, entire communities may be protagonists as they seek to recover from a flood, earthquake, tornado, hurricane, or some other crisis. In some cases, an individual hero may emerge as a protagonist. Antagonists may be individuals, but they may also be organizations, industries, any level of government, entire countries, natural forces, hazardous environmental practices, or any other source that threatens safety and security. Crisis narratives pit the protagonist against the antagonist in a struggle to restore order from the chaos of crisis.

The narrator, or source, in crisis narratives is important. Typically we think of traditional media as sorting through the characters of narratives and telling their stories. For example, the *Grand Forks Herald* newspaper won a Pulitzer Prize for maintaining coverage of a flood that decimated the city in 1997. Residents relied on the newspaper to locate friends and family, learn where and when to obtain government assistance, and follow progress on the city's plans for cleaning up. In the nearly two decades since that flood, new media have become common. During Superstorm Sandy, New York and New Jersey residents made consistent use of social media sources, including Twitter and Facebook, to seek information and narrate their plight. A growing number of citizens also list independent blogs as major sources of information during crises. More than any other aspect of crisis narratives, the source and form of narration have evolved over the past twenty years.

Most narratives also feature supporting characters who interact with the protagonist and antagonist. These supporting characters are often victims or potential victims. Protagonists seek to rescue victims from harm and share messages or offer physical protection to stop the spread of destruction and injury. Supporting characters, however, do not necessarily need to be in harm's way. Rather, some characters may simply show empathy to those who are threatened. For example, many observers are inspired by crises to donate to the Red Cross or UNICEF or to travel to storm-ravaged communities as volunteers in response to hearing or seeing crisis narratives. In doing so, they become part of the narrative.

Setting. Setting refers to the place or places where the crisis occurs. The setting can be as narrow as a single organization or city or as broad as a multinational company's distribution of a contaminated product worldwide. For example, in 2008, Sanlu, a dairy products company in China, distributed milk power that was contaminated with melamine and created a crisis setting that spanned the globe. Narratives are most compelling when the reader or viewer identifies or sees personal relevance in the narrative (Rowland, 2009). This personal relevance is not limited to those who are directly connected with the setting. Those who are directly affected by the crisis usually do so through physical proximity. They are made ill, injured, have lost property, or are emotionally influenced by what they have experienced directly. Naturally this form of proximity enhances identification with the crisis narrative. Those who observe the crisis narrative from a distance may experience psychological proximity, which occurs in crisis narratives when those who observe the narrative have a high level of community or emotional commitment for those whose lives are hit by the crisis (Mencl & May, 2009). This emotional commitment often influences the decisions people make as they contemplate crisis narratives (Ghorbani, Liao, Caykoylu, & Chand, 2013). From a narrative perspective, those who experience psychological proximity are transported mentally to the setting of the crisis and empathize with and have a desire to care for those who are harmed or wronged by the crisis (Rowland, 2009).

Plot. In its simplest sense, the plot is a series of events ordered in relation to one another in a way that creates a story. Langer (1953) characterizes life as a sequence of intensity and release patterns. These patterns are characterized in symbolic accounts of life, including music, theater, literature, and social narratives (Sellnow, 2014). In following this intensity release pattern, plots in crisis narratives align closely with the essential characteristics that distinguish crises from other day-to-day life experiences. Crises are characterized by threat, surprise, and short response time (Hermann, 1963). Thus, for a narrative to be considered a crisis narrative, some sort of sudden event must occur that threatens the physical, financial, or emotional well-being of an organization or community. This sudden event represents intensity. The plot is intensified by the fact that the trouble will get worse before it gets better if the protagonists do not act quickly. As the immediate crisis is resolved and the urgent threat passes, the narrative moves toward release or resolution.

Theme. Themes of crisis narratives arise from the interaction of characters, settings, and plots. Crisis narratives are rhetorical in purpose, and the theme is generally persuasive. The ultimate objective of the crisis narrative is to provide an explanation of what happened to whom and to establish and advocate for lessons, recommendations for response, or a particular meaning. Themes of crisis narratives generally concern risk and danger. If the cause of the crisis is believed to originate with conscious decision making and actions, the theme is based on future decision making and the associated risks. By contrast, if the crisis originates outwardly—by a natural disaster, for example—the plot's theme generally emphasizes danger and how to cope with it in the future (Luhmann, 2008). The recommendations endorsed by the theme of the crisis may be broad aphorisms such as the perils of greed or dissuading residents from building homes in areas that are highly vulnerable to natural disasters like hurricanes or wildfires.

CONSISTENT CRITERIA FOR EVALUATING
AND ADOPTING CRISIS NARRATIVES

The believability or persuasiveness of a crisis narrative depends on whether listeners believe the narrative presents a coherent and rational set of good reasons that account for the situation. Narratives are tested against the principles of "probability (coherence) and fidelity (truthfulness and reliability)" (Fisher, 1987, p. 46). Audiences naturally employ these criteria as they consider "rival stories" (p. 14). In other words, audiences employ the criteria of probability and fidelity to choose which version of a crisis narrative is accurate. Table 2.1 provides a summary of the process of testing narratives against the criteria of probability and fidelity. Fisher (1987, p. 64) summarizes the function of narratives or stories in five presuppositions, each of which is useful for understanding crisis narratives:

Humans are essentially storytellers.

The paradigmatic mode of human decision making and communication is good reasons, which vary in form among situations, genres, and media of communication.

The production and practice of good reasons are ruled by matters of history, biography, culture, and character.

Rationality is determined by the nature of persons as narrative beings—their inherent awareness of narrative probability (what constitutes a coherent story and their constant habit of testing narrative fidelity, whether or not the stories they experience ring true with the stories they know to be true in their lives).

The world as we know it is a set of stories that must be chosen among for us to live life in a process of continual recreation.

Probability

We assess stories by asking if they are probable. Audiences realize that as multiple narratives explaining a crisis arise, "some stories are better than others, more coherent, more 'true' to the way people and the world are—in fact and in value" (Fisher, 1984, p. 10). The perceived truth is based in part on whether the story appears coherent and probable (Fisher, 1987). There are three forms of probability in narratives: argumentative or structural coherence, material coherence, and characterological coherence (Fisher, 1987).

Argumentative or structural coherence. A story is considered to have argumentative or structural coherence when it is complete and internally consistent. According to Jasinski (2001), this determination is based largely on the arrangement and plot, and, in this case, plot establishes "both wholeness and unity of action" (p. 390). The elements of the story are interconnected, and they unfold to reveal a conclusion. If a plot fails to reflect the assumptions and values of its culture, then it most likely will be judged unsatisfactory (Jasinski, 2001). For example, General Motors and Chrysler executives were rebuked by members of a congressional committee in 2008 for flying to Washington, DC, in private jets to plead for government-sponsored financial assistance during the financial crisis (Congress members criticize, 2008). The committee found the fact that the executives of the ailing companies continued with luxurious travel created a structurally incoherent component of their stories.

Material coherence. Audiences determine material coherence by comparing and contrasting stories with other stories told in other contexts (Fisher, 1987). A story may follow a plot that is internally consistent, "but important facts may be omitted, counterarguments ignored, and relevant issues overlooked" (p. 47). A story that shows bias by ignoring relevant facts and opposing points of view is not materially coherent. For example, in his reflections on the AIG government bailout, economic analyst David Fiderer (2013) argued, "The popular narrative—that Tim Geithner needlessly favored the interests of banks over those of taxpayers—does not withstand close scrutiny" (para. 1). Geithner, serving as secretary of the treasury during the economic crisis of President Obama's first term, oversaw the government takeover of AIG, one of the world's largest insurers. Critics of Geithner ignored the laws that constrained him and failed to recall the realistic fear that AIG's collapse would have had a devastating impact on the U.S. economy. The material coherence of the narrative is questionable.

Characterological coherence. Characterological coherence is "one of the key differences between the concept of narrative rationality and traditional logics," and from this perspective, whether a story is believable or not depends on the reliability of characters both as narrators and actors" (Fisher, 1987, p. 47). The actions that the narrators and characters take "form an organized set of actional tendencies" that reflect character values (p. 47). Thus, "coherence in life and in literature requires that characters behave characteristically" (p. 47). However, if a character's or narrator's actional tendencies "contradict each other, change significantly, or alter in strange ways, the result is a questioning of character and a loss of characterological coherence" (p. 47). For example, reporter Lara Logan and CBS were forced to retract a story broadcast on the network's news program *60 Minutes* in 2013. Logan reported a story questioning previous accounts of what happened in 2012 when four Americans, including the U.S. ambassador, were killed during an uprising at the U.S. diplomatic compound in Benghazi, Libya. The major source for the story, Dylan Davies, created a journalistic sensation by providing an account for what went on during the attack that differed dramatically from other explanations (Youseff, 2013). In the days following the story, however, Davies's claims were exposed as highly inconsistent with what he reported to the FBI in the days following the attack. Ultimately Logan and CBS had to retract the story and apologize publicly due to the characterological incoherence of Davies's claims in the story.

Fidelity

Probability and fidelity differ in that narrative probability focuses on the story as a whole while fidelity focuses on the individual components. As Fisher defines it, "The principle of fidelity pertains to the individuated components of stories—whether they represent accurate assertions about social reality and thereby constitute good reasons for belief or action" (1987, p. 105). Two primary components of fidelity in crisis narratives are reasonableness and plurality.

Reasonableness. A narrative is considered reasonable if it is based on what the audience believes are good reasons for seeing the situation from the perspective advocated by the narrator. Good reasons are "to some extent fixed by human nature and to a very large extent by generally accepted principles and practices which make social life, as we understand it, possible" (Wallace, 1963, p. 248). From this perspective, good reasons are "conceived as those elements that provide warrants for accepting or adhering to advice fostered by any form of communication that can be considered rhetorical" (Fisher, 1984, p. 107). Reasonableness, then, is determined contextually from the perspective of the audience. A narrative appears reasonable if the explanations and conclusions are fitting with the norms and standards that the audience practices or values. By contrast, if the narrative derives conclusions that violate these expectations, it is less likely to be accepted. As Fisher (1980) clarifies, "The logic of good reasons entails a concept that is self-perpetuating, non-manipulative, bilateral, deliberative, reflexive, and attentive to data" (p. 121).

From a crisis communication perspective, reasonableness is typically linked to social legitimacy. For example, organizations are expected to "establish congruence between the social values associated with or implied by their activities and the norms of acceptable behavior in the larger system of which they are a part" (Dowling & Pfeffer, 1975, p. 122). In a practical sense, organizations are typically seen as legitimate when their actions are consistent with widely held values such as honesty and environmental protection (Hearit, 2006). Thus, an organization's crisis narrative can be seen as a means for reestablishing social legitimacy after a major failure. To do so, the explanation must align with dominant public values or it will not be seen as reasonable.

Pluralism. Pluralism allows multiple perspectives and generally supports reasonableness through acknowledging multiple views of the world (Fisher 1980). If a narrative appears to be based on good reasons or to be reasonable, we can move to the criterion of pluralism. A pluralism of values allows for a "multiplicity of ways of being reasonable" (Dearin, 1969, p. 214).

The rhetorical theorist Chaïm Perelman was a Jew living under the chaos and threat of Nazi-occupied Belgium and saw firsthand the failures of classic rationalism during this crisis. At the war's end, Perelman "played a significant role in the recovery of the Jewish world and joined efforts to rescue European philosophy from its failure to establish the moral and intellectual anchors necessary to prevent genocide" (Frank, 2011, p. 246).

His approach was in opposition to classical rationalism and its search for truth and certitude. Perelman sought to expand the "domain of reason to encompass a rhetorical rationalism allowing for a pluralism of values and a multiplicity of ways of being reasonable" (Dearin, 1969, p. 214). The goal of pluralism is to avoid allowing any individual or specific group, regardless of position, the exclusive right to determine what is valid and appropriate (Perelman, 1979). Thus, the practical reasoning process functions best when a broad audience hears and considers multiple narratives .

CONCLUSION

By nature, crises create both uncertainty and an immediate desire for information. Crises create confusion, disorientation, and psychological discomfort. Emotional expression of pain, disappointment, and remorse is also characteristic of crises. Crisis narratives emerge to counter uncertainty and to fulfill this emotional need for expression. They also provide cognitive schemas, scripts, and mental models to help people make sense of what they are experiencing. Key questions emerging from crises focus on how the available evidence should be interpreted, the intentions of those involved in the crisis or crisis management, and the locus of responsibility for the crisis. Crisis narratives have characters, settings, plots, and themes that interact to establish warrants for why a an audience should believe a given narrative. In assessing the believability of crisis narratives, audiences consider the probability and fidelity of the stories. Probability focuses on the coherence of the narrative as whole and is divided into argumentative or structural coherence, material coherence, and characterological coherence. Fidelity concentrates on the individual arguments within the narrative. Ultimately, fidelity is established in narratives that offer good reasons and an inclusive presentation in their accounts of a crisis.

The larger function of crisis narratives is to create understanding and meaning and to share that meaning. In Chapter 3, we explore this meaning-making function and many of the ways crises disrupt, dislocate, and reframe established meaning and generate new, sometimes more complex and nuanced understandings. These crisis stories have an important function not only for the individuals, groups, and communities experiencing the crisis but for others observing and trying to make sense of the event.

CHAPTER 3

How Stories Disrupt
Our Sense of Meaning

CRISES CREATE profound social, political, and economic change. They have been described as evolutionary forces that lead to chaos and fundamentally reshape larger, complex systems. They shift the public agenda, focus attention and resources on risk factors, and have an impact on larger systems of meaning. Crises have the potential to fundamentally alter strongly held beliefs about the world, what is important and what might be considered normal. In Chapter 2, we examined the way crises create spaces and a need to tell the story of what happened. These events challenge established systems of meaning and require that understanding and meaning be reconstituted. The specific ways in which crises affect established systems of meaning and sense making are the focus of this chapter.

MEANING

Meaning is an abstract concept that has been examined from a variety of philosophical and discipline-based perspectives. Religion, family, personal identity, place, history, and culture are all sources of meaning. In its most general form, meaning refers to a concept's or object's larger significance, importance, or value. An object salvaged from a house fire may take on larger value and significance because it represents a life before the fire and stands in for other things that were lost in the flames. Meaning occurs at the group or organizational level and the social and cultural level.

Existentialism is the philosophical tradition that focuses on questions of human meaning. The founder of existentialism, Danish philosopher Søren Kierkegaard, suggested that individuals must create their own meaning for their lives and that that is an essential part of the human experience. The lack of meaning creates a sense of confusion and disorientation. An existential crisis occurs when individuals are forced to confront the foundational meaning of their lives and is often provoked by events such as psychological trauma, a major loss, or a life-threatening experience.

Philosopher and Holocaust survivor Viktor Frankl (1985) provided detailed and compelling accounts about how concentration camp prisoners survived, made sense of their circumstances, and created meaning. He suggested that meaning was associated with purpose, doing, and creating; encountering, experiencing, and interacting with others; and the attitudes chosen in the face of adversity and suffering. Even within the inhuman conditions of the Nazi concentration camp, Frankl argued that humans could find meaning; in fact, meaning was essential to survival. Life was meaningful or could be given meaning under even the most horrific circumstances. Creating meaning is thus both a human need and a personal choice. Humans may choose to create meanings and, according to Frankl, this choice of meanings is the most fundamental human freedom.

In communication, meaning is usually defined as the intentionality of an expression or message that is conveyed by a sender to a receiver. Storytellers create meaning by relating their stories to audiences in a way that allows the audience to share in the storyteller's understanding. Meaning therefore arises between people through communicative processes, through sharing symbols, and in this way, it is cocreated through sharing. Linguistic theorists such as Ogden and Richards (1927) described meaning as a process of relating symbols, thoughts or references, and referents such as objects or concepts. It is thus the product of these associations, and the symbols themselves become meaningful. A powerful event such as a crisis may fundamentally change the meaning associated with a symbol or infuse a relatively innocuous symbol with meaning. The Triangle Shirtwaist Factory fire of March 25, 1911, for example, was a deadly industrial disaster that claimed the lives of some 146 garment workers. The fire became a symbol of irresponsible corporate conduct and every year is memorialized by a march of the Remember the Triangle Fire Coalition, an alliance of more than two hundred organizations. This tragedy has taken on much larger symbolic meaning for these organizations and represents other cases of abuse by organizations. The Newseum in Washington, DC, has on display a large twisted antenna salvaged from the wreckage of the World Trade Center. The antenna itself is a chaotic and distorted mass of metal and wires with little intrinsic value, but it symbolizes both the attack and the role communication and journalism played in the crisis.

Psychologists have defined meaning in a variety of ways, including as a general life orientation, the basis of personal significance, and a structure of attributions and causalities that explains events and outcomes (Park & Folkman, 1997). Global meaning involves a relatively stable system built up of experiences, beliefs about the world, fundamental assumptions, and expectations. People may believe, for example, that their world is basically safe, stable, and predictable. Situational meaning concerns how a person's experiences and circumstances interact with global meaning. People may expect to be able to acquire safe food and water and have safe and comfortable shelter, a stable job, and secure surroundings for themselves and their families. Over time, individuals create a sense of place based on family, community, job, and relationships. These fundamental beliefs and expectations are often compromised in the face of a crisis situation where individuals may experience a world that is neither safe nor stable. During a crisis, people may become physically and psychologically dislocated and lose the meaning taken from their positions.

Those who have experienced a crisis, that is, the victims, must reconcile the event with other meaning systems and cope with what is often an existential crisis. Victims must reconcile, come to terms with, and contextualize the crisis. Often this requires a process of psychological counseling, grieving, interacting with others, remembering some aspects of the crisis and forgetting others, using other meaning systems such as family and faith, and moving on to focus on rebuilding and recovery.

Memorializing is an important part of the meaning-creation process and may involve actual physical monuments, commemorative publications, websites, songs, and stories. An example of how memorials function to create symbolic meaning out of crisis situations is how people reacted in the wake of the Oklahoma City bombing in 1995. Shortly after the incident, improvised memorials sprang up around the actual site. People began spontaneously memorializing the 168 people who died in the blast with common items of remembrance such as flowers and cards. However, more mundane items, such as key chains, name badges, and clothes, were also included. These "spontaneous, informal memorials develop from the simple need to communicate the pain that those left behind feel, and to let others see and share in the grief" (Veil, Sellnow, & Heald, 2011, p. 167). Recognizing the need to memorialize the event and the loss of life, a task force of 350 individuals was appointed to develop a permanent and appropriate site of remembrance. This task force was charged with developing words, symbols, and themes for the permanent memorial that not only served as a source of public memory and grief but also functioned as a source of renewal of meaning—a way to facilitate the grieving process while remembering the tragedy itself (Veil et al., 2011). Similar memorials are created for almost all major crises.

CRISIS AND THE DISRUPTION OF MEANING

Crises share three general attributes. First, they are largely unanticipated or surprising and violate basic routines and taken-for-granted expectations and assumptions. They are almost always unanticipated by those who experience them, although there are usually warning signs and cues. Most often, they are a radical departure from the status quo and a violation of general assumptions and expectations such that "normal" is disrupted and the ability to anticipate and predict is very limited. Established, dominant narratives are disrupted through the process of denarration (discussed in Chapter 2). The severe violation of expectations is usually a source of uncertainty as well as psychological discomfort and stress. Sometimes occurrences are so confusing that people simply do not know what to do and experience extreme psychological dislocation. Weick (1988) has described this response as a cosmological episode: "When people suddenly feel that the universe is no longer a rational, orderly system. What makes such an episode so shattering is that people suffer from the event and, at the same time, lose the means to recover from it" (p. 52). Meaning is recreated or reassembled through various communication processes. Weick notes that people must hear what they are saying (or what is being said) to know what to think. According to this view, narratives generated after a crisis event serve to precede the ability to make sense of what happened.

This process is problematized during a crisis when established channels of communication are disrupted, people are displaced and can no longer interact in familiar ways, and the communication agenda is radically shifted. One of the most significant examples of this loss of communication channels occurred as a result of the terrorist attacks on the World Trade Center in 2001. Beyond the media telecommunication equipment that was lost, creating difficulty in maintaining the flow of information about the event, the attacks left much of New York without basic telephone service. "The 2,200 Verizon employees who were situated in the vicinity of the Center were involved in running the densest knot of cables and switches anywhere in the world. The attack knocked out 300,000 voice access lines and 4.5 million data circuits and left ten cellular towers inactive, depriving 14,000 businesses and 20,000 residential customers of service" (Argenti, 2011). The resulting devastation at this one location was enough to create a communication vacuum and left many in Manhattan and the surrounding area with no way to get basic information or check on loved ones or for family and friends elsewhere to check on their loved ones.

A crisis is also surprising because it stands in contrast to the normal conditions that existed before the crisis. The sudden shift from normal, predictable, and routine to abnormal, uncertain, and unpredictable may be profoundly shocking and deeply psychologically disruptive. Routines that provide order for life, taken-for-granted assumptions, even physical landmarks may be gone along with possessions, jobs, friends, and family. According to Kammerer and Mazelis (2006), "Without familiar places and rhythms even those who have not previously experienced trauma have difficulty sustaining internal equilibrium and external relationships. In the wake of disaster, domestic violence, child neglect and maltreatment, drug and alcohol use, suicide, and divorce all increase."

A second defining characteristic of crises and disasters is the threat to high-priority goals, such as personal and family health and well-being, financial security, and property. Death and injury are common features of so-called natural disasters such as earthquakes, hurricanes, and tornadoes. Earthquakes are the most deadly events, particularly when they intersect with inadequate building codes in highly populated areas. Many earthquakes have caused hundreds of thousands of deaths. The 1976 Tangshan, China, earthquake was a magnitude 7.5. The official casualty figure is 255,000 deaths, but unofficial estimates place the death toll at over 650,000. While such events are the consequence of naturally occurring phenomena, they become disasters because of their impact on human built systems and structures. Human-caused crises, including explosions, shootings, and terrorist events, can also create high levels of death and injury. The worst mass shooting in the United States occurred in 2007 on the campus of Virginia Tech University when thirty-two people were killed by a single gunman, who then committed suicide. Twenty-seven deaths occurred in 2012 at Sandy Hook Elementary School. Among the dead were twenty six- and seven-year-olds and six adults. In addition to the physical harm, psychological harm, including posttraumatic stress disorder (PTSD), is a common feature of crisis. Crisis is associated with a range of both short- and long-term psychological disorders for those who have experienced a crisis. Rates of PTSD have been estimated to average about 20 percent for the victims of crises but may range much higher.

The loss of property in many crises is also extreme, with damages from some events reaching into the billions of dollars. The U.S. National Oceanic and Atmospheric Administration estimated that costs associated with 2006's Hurricane Katrina could run as high as $125 billion. The cost of Superstorm Sandy was estimated at $50 billion. Crisis may also permanently reduce the financial stability or viability of a community and wipe out or cripple entire industries and even regions. The physical damage from crises will grow as infrastructure ages and disasters become more intense.

Finally, crises usually require a relatively rapid response to contain or mitigate the damage (Hermann, 1963; Seeger, Sellnow, & Ulmer, 2003). While a crisis is generally seen as an event, something that *happened*, crises are more accurately described as processes that evolve over time through a series of overlapping stages or phases (Reynolds & Seeger, 2005; Seeger, Sellnow, & Ulmer, 2003). Crises are time bound, time sensitive, and evolutionary in the sense that what happens at earlier points in the crisis affects later developments. This is most evident immediately after a crisis erupts. Timely decisions about evacuations, warnings, or recalls have a direct impact on levels of harm. Failure to act in a timely way may also complicate the process of creating meaning by raising questions about the adequacy of the response.

MEANING MAKING AFTER CRISIS

Events that are threatening and traumatic, such as crises, tend to create vivid memories. These flashbulb memories are particularly vivid recollections that retain many of the characteristics of the time the event occurred (Law, 2011). The memories of a crisis are often denser and thicker and can include the intense emotional responses experienced during the crisis, including fear and sadness. As these events are recalled, the vivid nature of the memories may create the impression that the event lasted much longer that it actually did. These detailed memories are retained with such clarity because they were laid down during moments of high stress and emotion and are frequently told and retold. Like all other memories, flashbulb memories are not always accurate but seem to be highly influenced by the information learned after an event. These memories increasingly tend to project universal feelings and perceptions as stories are shared and retold. Memories of a crisis tend to become homogenized over time, and the collective memory of an event becomes a universal and generalized meaning. In some cases, the collective meaning becomes almost mythic and may take on the status of a metanarrative. For example, the story of the *Titanic* tragedy has been told and retold in books, film, and museum exhibitions. The crisis has become part of the larger metanarrative regarding human hubris and the frailty of human construction in the face of natural forces.

Meaning making is a complex psychological process that incorporates the construction of global, fundamental, and relatively stable beliefs, assumptions, and expectations about the world. Systems of global meaning, beliefs, values, cognitive schemes, and mental models are built up from a lifetime of events and experiences. In most day-to-day experiences, events are integrated into existing meaning systems with little or no need for significant reappraisal of global meaning. In some cases, events that do not fit into established meaning systems may be ignored or discounted. A crisis, however, is typically too dramatic and significant to simply ignore, and individuals may be forced to question the viability of their world and self-views (Park & Folkman, 1997). These events often require appraisals of basic beliefs and, in many, cases a reconstruction of a personal meaning system.

These appraisals refer to an assessment of the situational meaning of an event and its implications for global systems of meaning. For example, people may appraise a flood based on their personal capacity to manage, cope, recover, or soldier through the rising water. The experience of the flood and of water rising rapidly and incessantly and the consequence for property and livelihood, however, may create a breakdown in global meaning systems. Floodwaters are often powerful, and efforts to control the force of rising floodwater are physically demanding and overwhelming. People who live next to a river may have come to know it as ideal and relaxing scenery with pastoral meaning. Following a flood, those same individuals may report they now see the river as a sinister threat and a source of significant risk to property and life.

One of the fundamental changes in meaning that arises from a crisis is a new understanding of risks. Anthropologist Mary Douglas's work on culture and risk, for example, argues that risks and associated harms arise with a social context. These risks intersect with a dominant view of the natural environment and "a view that that influences its choices of dangers worth attention" (Douglas & Wildavsky, 1983, p. 8). As new risks present themselves in sometimes dramatic ways, new cultural understandings of risk emerge. Moreover, society tends to associate risk-related harms with some social, moral, or normative transgression. A flood, for example, may be attributed to faulty weather forecasts, engineering practices, or climate change (Sellnow & Seeger, 2001). In this way, societies develop a broad-based understanding of what is dangerous and how to mitigate or even avoid risk. This tendency is also associated with questions of blame and responsibility, which often dominate postcrisis discourse.

One typical postcrisis narrative encoding new understanding of risk is the cautionary tale. This tale concerns some potentially risky or threatening act, location, or process. The interaction of stakeholders with the risk factor leads to some usually significant harm that may involve ignoring the risk, failing to understand or perceive the risk, or incompetently managing the risk. The cautionary tale usually ends with some general precautionary principles reflecting a greater understanding of risks and appropriate methods for risk avoidance. Cautionary tales are told and retold as a way of transmitting a lesson about a risk and the potential losses that may occur when a risk is ignored. They are widely represented in children's stories, but also take the form of folk stories, urban legends, and journalistic accounts.

CRISIS AS LOSS

Crisis is almost always associated with some loss, but the nature of that loss can vary significantly. So far we have noted that crisis often results in a loss of meaning, disruption of global meaning, and loss of dominant life narratives. The loss of sense making and meaning described earlier can undermine global systems of meaning regarding the world and a person's relationship to it. The extreme disruption, loss, and general confusion of a major crisis results in an inability to make sense of the events, contextualize them, and reappraise, recreate, and connect with larger systems of meaning. These existential losses, however, are usually the consequence of many more tangible and physical losses.

The psychological impacts of crisis, well documented, include a variety of symptomatic disorders: sleeplessness, generalized and specific anxiety, depression, PTSD, drug and alcohol abuse, and a variety of social problems such as family conflict and higher divorce rates. In addition, victims of a crisis are likely to suffer higher rates of stress-related diseases like hypertension and heart attacks (Norris et al., 2002). One study of the behavioral and psychological impacts of the 9/11 terrorist attacks found that 16 percent of US adults had persistent distress, including lost work, avoiding public gathering places, and some level of alcohol, medication, or drug dependency (Stein et al., 2004). Research also found that prior experience with a crisis provides some inoculation against these psychological impacts (Norris & Murrell, 1988).

Specific losses are associated with the nature and scope of a crisis. Loss of life occurs in many crises and, in the case of natural disasters, can be devastating. Significant costs in terms of damaged property, infrastructure, and economic disruptions are quite common, and with large-scale crises, expenses can run into the billions of dollars. On the individual level, loss of a home, property, and possessions can create a sense of deep personal loss, confusion, and despair that far exceed the economic value of possessions. The loss of a home results in a state of homelessness that compounds uncertainty and the psychological impact. The loss of possessions, pictures, family heirlooms, and records may break a connection with personal history. The devastating floods that ravaged Fargo, North Dakota, in 1997 also resulted in a downtown fire that consumed many businesses, including the *Grand Forks Herald*, the town's newspaper. Among the losses was the newspaper's archive of historical documents, including photographs. Despite these losses, the paper continued to publish and document the community's historic floods.

Many organizations are not so fortunate, and one of the losses that often follows a crisis is the closing of businesses. The U.S. Federal Emergency Management Administration estimates that 40 percent of small businesses never recover from a major natural disaster. The popular restaurant chain Chi-Chi's never recovered from a crisis involving foodborne hepatitis A in 2003. Many small businesses associated with the tourism industry, including restaurants and hotels, were adversely affected when Superstorm Sandy devastated the Jersey shore. Much of the seafood industry in the Gulf states closed following the Deepwater Horizon oil spill. The industry suffered losses from the contamination of fish and fishing grounds and from public perception that fish from the Gulf were not safe. The loss of these businesses translates into lost jobs, wages, and, in some cases, the very viability of the community.

One comprehensive investigation of crisis and community focused on the 1972 Buffalo Creek flood, which involved the catastrophic failure of a coal slurry impoundment sending a 30-foot wall of slurry over the town of Buffalo Creek, West Virginia. The town had an estimated population of 5,000 before the crisis. There were 125 deaths and 1,121 injuries, and more than 4,000 people were left homeless. The town was essentially wiped away. Those who did survive suffered severe emotional trauma and the loss of community. The anthropologist Kai Erickson (1976) noted :

> Human relationships in [Buffalo Creek] had been derived from traditional bonds of kinship and neighborliness. When forced to give up these long-standing ties with familiar places and people, the survivors experienced demoralization, disorientation, and loss of connection. Stripped of the support

they had received from their community, they became apathetic and seemed to have forgotten how to care for one another. This was apparently a community that was stronger than the sum of its parts, and these parts—the survivors of the Buffalo Creek flood—are now having great difficulty finding the personal resources to replace the energy and direction they had once found in their community. (p. 302)

Similar results have been experienced in many crises where victims were forced to evacuate or relocate. Hurricane Katrina evacuees were relocated across the United States. One study found that more than half the households in New Orleans were displaced entirely, and as many as two-thirds saw at least one member displaced (Rendall, 2006). One factor in the high rate of displacement was the prominence of multigenerational and extended families. Many reported losing their fundamental sense of family, community, cultural connections, traditional foods, and sense of identity and normalcy.

A crisis such as the Buffalo Creek flood or Hurricane Katrina can disrupt a sense of normalcy in several ways. During a crisis, established routines of life no longer occur. These routines create a sense of predictability, order, and structure and are associated with a sense of personal stability and control. For many people, everyday routines permeate our lives, and it is not until those routines are disrupted that we realize how prevalent and important they are. These routines can include simple rituals such as listening to music while getting ready for the day, grabbing the newspaper off the front step in the morning, or stopping at the corner coffee shop. Power outages can limit the ability to play music. A disaster can interrupt newspaper delivery. The corner coffee shop may be inaccessible, closed, or destroyed.

A crisis also disrupts general and specific orientations. A crisis may destroy physical landmarks that promote mobility, familiarity, and predictability. Extreme weather events, fires, and earthquakes often destroy buildings, roadways, and natural features used to mark both physical and psychological orientations. Travel patterns and access to work, home, or family may be disrupted when bridges and roadways are destroyed. In some cases, the destruction of landmarks leaves people lost, as occurred with the destruction of the prominent Twin Towers of the World Trade Center:

> Say you've lived in New York for a while. Ten years. Twenty years. Maybe your whole life. You're coming out of the subway, in almost any borough (besides Staten Island). You're on your way to an appointment, or a party, and you're a little turned around when you get to the street. You're not sure which way is north, and which is south. Without thinking about it, you gaze around for the one landmark (or rather, the two landmarks) that always helped orient you in the past—those enormous, companionable markers that silently indicated, at a glance: This is south. This is Lower Manhattan. Get your bearings. (Cosgrove, 2013)

Finally, orientation and normalcy are disrupted when sources of information and networks of communication are broken. Sets of interactions and contacts across time and space create communication networks among people, groups, and organizations. A person's location within this network contributes to personal identity: "I work here." "I belong to this church." "These are the friends I socialize with." Patterns of communication constitute routines that create order, predictability, identity, and community. The morning paper or the radio news reports during commutes are patterns that provide predictable sources of information. Information and stories shared through these networks create a common experience and narrative necessary for community. These networks provide information, support, and identity and when they are disrupted, uncertainty and a sense of dislocation occur.

It is hard to imagine how comprehensive and overwhelming the losses from a crisis can be. Homes, family, jobs, community, and psychological stability are all at risk in a major crisis. The consequences of these losses can be so devastating the survivors never fully recover. The suicide rate in New Orleans nearly tripled in the ten months after Katrina. A suicide rate of 9 per 100,000 residents jumped to almost 27 per 100,000 residents (Saulny, 2006). While the losses can be devastating, crises may also be additive.

CRISIS AS ADDITION

While a crisis is most often associated with significant losses, it also has the potential to be additive in the sense that experiences, perspectives, capacities, insights, relationships, and channels of communication are created. In addition, both situational and global systems of meaning may be enriched and expanded through the experience of a crisis. Crisis in most cases also creates a new and often compelling story. For most people, the experience of a major crisis, flood, fire, chemical spill, or industrial accident is a relatively new experience, as are the high levels of uncertainty, threat, and short response times. In cases where communities are vulnerable to recurring natural disasters such as floods or hurricanes, these experiences develop a kind of familiarity, and people and communities develop methods and strategies for coping. Rarely, however, can they be described as routine.

Consequently, these experiences create new insights and new crisis response capacities. As noted earlier, when people experience a crisis, they often come to perceive risks in a new way. What they perceived as routine, normal, and generally safe they might now see as risky and threatening. In this way, a crisis creates insights into relative levels of risks that may also give rise to new risk avoidance strategies, including risk avoidance norms and management procedures. Prior to the Fukushima Daiichi disaster, the Japanese public saw nuclear power as relatively safe and certainly the most viable option for an energy-hungry economy. Networks of safeguards and technical measures, according to popular wisdom, had made a major accident impossible. Following the disaster, nuclear plants were perceived as very risky, and associated public policy has imposed severe restrictions on the industry. Prime Minister Naoto Kan, in office at the time of the disaster, wrote about how the crisis changed his perception of the safety of Japan's nuclear industry:

> Before the Fukushima accident, with the belief that no nuclear accident would happen as long as the safety measures were followed properly, I had pushed the policy of utilizing nuclear power. Having faced the real accident as Prime Minister, and having experienced the situation which came so close to requiring me to order the evacuation of 50 million people, my view is now changed

180 degrees. Although some airplane crashes may claim hundreds of casualties, there are no other events except for wars that would require the evacuation of tens of millions of people. (Kan, 2013)

Public understandings of risks are largely driven by crises. As media tell the story of the crisis and publicize the causes, calls for public policy, regulations, and additional checks and balances often follow. Regulations of transportation, manufacturing facilities, food production, building codes, and many other areas have been driven by public outrage over a crisis. The sinking of the *Titanic* gave rise to new standards for passenger ships. The terrorist attacks on 9/11 resulted in new standards for air travel. The 1971 Bon Vivant botulism outbreak in canned vichyssoise helped create modern food safety regulations. We have also noted that a crisis often adds to or changes the existing public policy agenda. In fact, crises often become turning points in the development of public policy agendas.

A crisis also generates insights and lessons about how to respond to future crises. One of the best predictors of evacuation during hurricanes, for example, is a previous history of evacuations. As an event unfolds, both preestablished procedures and improvisational responses are implemented. New response methods are sometimes developed through trial and error. Specific response capacities may be learned, such as evacuation routes, techniques for sandbagging, or how to keep refrigerated food safe during power outages. Some observers point to 2010 when a 7.0 earthquake struck Haiti as the first crisis when social media were fully deployed. In this case, social media served as an improvisational response to the event that allowed for much more efficient response in a country with a poorly developed infrastructure.

Learning may occur directly as individuals, groups, and organizations develop new coping mechanisms based on experiences or indirectly through observations or accounts about how others have responded. This indirect or vicarious learning depends on storytelling. Fictional film accounts of disasters, for example, can provide both useful and potentially deadly advice about how to respond to a crisis. Popular portrayals of tornadoes, such as in the movie *Twister*, often suggest it is possible to outrun a tornado. Most experts argue, however, that outrunning a tornado is almost always impossible and seeking shelter is much safer (Centers for Disease Control and Prevention, 2012). In addition to new insights about risk and coping mechanisms, crisis may also promote more general disaster resilience. New psychological, relational, and physical response capacities can be added. Following floods, residents may choose to buy pumps and generators. Those who have experienced a severe case of seasonal influenza may choose immunization. Following the 1989 *Exxon Valdez* oil spill, many oil companies reexamined their crisis response plans.

New levels of organization and organizational structures are sometimes created by crises. One of the primary ways floods are managed is by building temporary barriers with sandbags, a strenuous and labor-intensive process requiring many people working in cooperation. Materials must be provided and staged. Bags must be filled and moved to the location. They must then be stacked in an interlocking pattern to a desired height. This crisis response requires a high level of coordination and organization. Following the 2011 attack on the World Trade Center, occupants organized evacuation teams to transport the injured and disabled out of the towers. This required moving the injured down stairwells that were often dark and filled with smoke. Many of the residents had learned how to evacuate from an earlier attack of the World Trade Center. In 1993, the World Trade Center was attacked when a truck bomb was detonated in a parking garage below the North Tower. This attack disrupted electrical supplies, cut off elevators, and filled many floors with smoke. Six people died and one thousand were injured, primarily during the chaos of the evacuation. Ironically, this earlier attack probably saved many lives during the 2011 attack. The occupants of the World Trade Center learned how to respond.

A crisis also creates new identities or adds to existing ones. Those who have experienced a major event often refer to themselves as survivors, and stories of their survival often dominate news reports. In crises where survivors may be trapped in collapsed buildings, the ongoing reports of survivors found alive may go on for days. Reshma Begum, a young garment worker, survived under rubble for seventeen days following the 2013 collapse of the Rana Plaza in Bangladesh. In some cases, survivors are entitled to compensation funds, ongoing health care, and access to jobs.

Those who have experienced a major event may also come to think of themselves as victims, particularly when the crisis was caused by negligence or malice. Seeing oneself as a survivor will likely create a different notion of empowerment and control versus those who see themselves as victims. In still other cases, those who have been relocated as a consequence of an event sometimes come to think of themselves as evacuees, or even refugees.

Finally, crises and disasters create stories: accounts about what happened, narratives of victims and heroes, cautionary tales about morality and hubris, and stories of recovery, resilience, and renewal. People tell stories to affix blame, pass on lessons, and create meaning. We believe that the crisis story dominates a significant part of our public narrative and is a major social, political, and economic force.

CONCLUSION

Meaning as life orientation, the basis of personal significance, and a structure of attributions and causalities helps create personal order and understanding. Crises can disrupt individual, group, community and social meaning. They alter a sense of personal identify, create a sense of dislocation and disorientation, and disrupt established notions of personal significance. They may change strongly held beliefs about the world— what is important and what might be considered dangerous and risky. They disrupt established life narratives but create new ones. Psychologists suggest the keys to crisis recovery are a search for meaning, regaining mastery over the situation, and the ability to restore self-esteem. The process of creating and sharing the story of the crisis is necessary to make sense of these events, determine how to respond, and frame the lessons learned from the crisis.

Through both losses and additions, crises are fundamental forces of personal, social, and even cultural change. These changes are often supported by and encoded in the stories that are told about crises—what happened, when, to whom, and why. Crisis stories encode the meaning of what happened, including the outcomes and the larger lessons.

CHAPTER 4

Making Sense through Accounts

SYSTEMS OF GOVERNANCE, production, service, and transportation are increasingly complex and interdependent. They involve many inputs including individuals, groups, technologies, processes, energy, and materials and stakeholders to produce outputs (Jackall, 1988). When a product is dangerous and creates harm, or where a system collapses in a dramatic and destructive way, such as an industrial accident, basic questions are asked about what went wrong, why, and who is accountable. These post-crisis narratives portray a stream of events and factors that may explain or account for what happened. Fundamentally, these account narratives take the form of retrospective sense making, allowing people to give meaning to the crisis experience by identifying the accountable agents (Weick, 1979, 1995). By identifying what happened when and describing who or what is accountable, these narratives also have implications for the larger understanding of responsibility and liability.

This chapter first addresses accounts and accountability and then examines three forms of account narratives: the experiential first-person account, the responsibility account, and the third-person/party account. The various functions of the account narratives are described as they relate to narrative structure, form, and outcomes. Accounts as the basic ordering of a string of events in ways that construct narrative coherence form the basis of many other crisis narratives. An account answers basic questions as to what happened. Because accounts ultimately translate into lessons learned and subsequent policies and actions, these narratives are particularly powerful.

ACCOUNTS AND ACCOUNTABILITY

An account in its simplest form is a story of what happened. It is an explanation or report of some event or occurrence that usually addresses basic questions about how the event developed over time (Ray, 1999; Boudes

& Laroche, 2009). Accounts typically follow a chronological order and are usually an exposition of the sequential events, reasons, and causes. In other cases, accounts may follow a topical order or may order events based on the individuals experiencing the crisis. These individual accounts are sometimes assembled into official reports and may subsequently have implications for public policy.

Crises are by definition high-uncertainty events that suspend notions of normalcy, creating a need to sort through the events and make sense of them through narratives such as accounts. In one form, the account is simply a story of what an individual or group experienced. Those experiencing a crisis, for example, are often asked to report what they saw, experienced, and felt, as well as how they responded. These narratives are common in media reports following a crisis. As a first-person account, these descriptions and explanations are often seen as the most direct and credible narratives surrounding a crisis or disaster, and the increasing use digital media has made these accounts more immediate and vivid.

In a second form of account, these explanations are grounded in the association between accountability and responsibility. These accounts seek to connect what happened to those decisions, people, organizations, groups, agencies, or larger social, economic, or environmental factors that caused the events. This second form is typically offered by the person, organization, or agency required or expected to justify the actions or decisions. Through a narrative, persons, organizations, or agencies are held accountable.

In the third form, a neutral and credible third party, such as an investigative board or agency, offers a formal or definitive account of what happened. These agency narratives typically seek to answer questions about what happened, whether it was foreseeable, who is responsible, and what can be done to ensure that similar events do not occur (Boudes & Laroche, 2009). Thus, the accountability narrative is both the manner by which responsibility is uncovered and the communicative manifestation of responsibility. Beyond this, the accountability narrative is a way to encode lessons for subsequent learning and actions.

An account in its most basic form is a story of what happened, when it happened, and what consequences resulted. It is offered by a communicator as a form of explanation or exposition of events. Accounts are most often structured in a longitudinal form, following a chronology of events. In the first-person account, the most common form, events are typically relayed both as they have been experienced and recalled. As a recitation of events as they have been experienced, they are as closely related to the direct experience as possible. Accounts can take the form of diaries, letters, testimony, documentaries, and autobiographies. First-person accounts are generally seen as the most credible and accurate descriptions of events because the narrator experienced them directly. However, such accounts often follow the structure of flashbulb memories and may be influenced by subsequent reports and stories.

Accounts and accountability derive from a larger social context. People are accountable because they belong to some larger community—a group, organization, or society that has values, rules, norms, and guidelines members are expected to follow. When members act in a manner inconsistent with those guidelines and in ways that are negative or harmful, they are expected to explain or account for their actions (Buttny, 1993). These explanations are directed toward the authority of the community, often through the legal system or more generally in the court of public opinion. Sometimes these explanations take the form of an apology, as we will describe in Chapter 5. As Lerner and Tetlock (1999) suggest, those who are able to provide satisfactory explanations may be able to avoid or mitigate some of the negative consequences associated with their role in a crisis.

The concept of accountability has expanded greatly to encompass a broad set of ethical standards and expectations for individuals, organizations, and institutions. In common everyday use, *accountability* has become shorthand for a range of obligations and duties for ethics, social responsibility, and moral conduct. The general notions of accountability are based on the fact that organizations, governments, and individuals exist within a larger network of social obligations and that communication is necessary to explain what happened when those obligations are not met.

Accounts are an essential form of communication because they allow a communicator to influence how others will see the actions and events and the kinds of assessments and evaluations they will make (Buttny, 1993). In this way, accounts serve an impression management function, a goal-directed social behavior whereby communicators try to influence how others see people, events, or things. Accounts influence impressions through the strategic portrayal of events, attribution of cause, omission of details, emphasizing some elements of the story over others, and connections to other elements and events. The meaning of the event is influenced and in some cases modified by the account. This process is reflected to some degree in all three forms of account we describe next.

FIRST-PERSON ACCOUNTS

First-person accounts are personal representations of lived and recalled experiences. They are seen as the most direct evidence of self and self-consciousness whereby people speak for and about themselves and their experiences. They are offered from the position, perspective, and values of the narrator. Sharing of a lived crisis experience often includes cognitive and emotional elements, decision processes, time line, and consequences. Taken together, these become a story of what I saw, what I did, how I felt, and what consequences occurred. The first-person perspective creates a unique window into an individual's experiences, cognitions, and emotional state. These accounts also represent a view from a specific and personal perspective and standpoint. This may involve the individual's physical location ("I was at the back of the plane when THE disruption started"), position within a system ("I was the captain of the ship when the fire occurred"), or the standpoint of a particular physical, emotional, or psychological state ("I was very afraid."). The audience then sees the event from the perspective of the narrator. The first-person account may be limited in the sense that the person might have a limited perspective of the event. Standing at the front of the plane would mean a witness cannot easily see what is happening at the back.

Novel, unique, or extreme experiences are often recorded as a way to preserve and share the experience. Disease, struggle, travel, discovery, and crises are examples of relatively unique events often described in personal narratives. Others who have not had these experiences can come to understand and learn from the experiences of others. Learning in this case is vicarious because accounts allow for people who have not experienced the disease or the crisis to learn from those who have. Personal narratives are often used as a way to record an experience for prosperity so future generations may learn from the event. These accounts often make up a significant part of the recorded history of events.

First-person accounts are also generally considered the most accurate and direct form of evidence regarding how an event developed. In legal proceedings, for example, eyewitness testimony has been privileged over other forms of evidence, although studies of memory have consistently shown that such accounts may not be reliable. Following an event, the witness may hear other accounts, see media reports, or respond to questions in ways that change the original memories. Psychologists have demonstrated that misinformation presented to an eyewitness may be integrated with the original memory (Loftus, 1980). Eyewitness accounts recorded as close to the event as possible are therefore usually considered more credible. These contemporaneous accounts are generally less subject to the integration of misinformation. Accounts also are generated at a particular point in time and may persist over time. A crisis account, such as the account written by *Titanic* passenger Mabel Francatelli, can then reconnect an audience with an event that occurred far in the past.

MISS MABEL FRANCATELLI of 72 Strathbrook Road, Streatham Says:–

I am Secretary of Lady Duff Gordon and accompanied her to New York.

I was a passenger on Titanic.

My cabin being on "E" deck which I believe was about 20 feet above the water line.

After the collision I stood in the corridor outside my cabin.

At last the water started to make it in so I went to the cabin of Lady Duff Gordon who was on "A" deck, the top.

A man came to me and put a life preserver on me assuring me it was only taking precautions and not to be alarmed

When we got to the top deck, the life boats were being lowered on the starboard side.

I then noticed that the sea was nearer to us than during the day, and I said to Sir Cosmo Duff Gordon, "We are sinking" and he said "Nonsense, come away."

The men wished to put Lady Duff Gordon and myself in a lifeboat but we refused to leave Cosmo Gordon. Sir Cosmo then said to me "Here Ms. Franks, you must go" or words to that effect but I refused again, saying I would not leave Lady Duff Gordon. Other lifeboats were then lowered.

As they were letting down the last lifeboats on our side there was a call for "Any more women" and they pulled at Lady Duff Gordon and myself, but we again refused to go and they lowered the lifeboat without us. It was the last lifeboat.

Everyone then seemed to rush away to the other side of the ship and left our side quite empty but we remained there as Sir Cosmos Duff Gordon said we must wait for orders. Presently, an officer started to swing out a little boat, quite an ordinary little rowing boat and ordered some stokers to man it.

There were no other women there by that time. The officer saw us and ordered us in and we said we would go if Sir Cosmos could come also. The officer said to Sir Cosmos "I would be pleased if you would go." We were dropped into this boat and lowered into the sea. Just as they were lowering the boat two American Gentlemen came along the deck and got in also. The office gave orders for us to row away from the ship.

There were seven sailors in the boat, Lady Duff Gordon, Myself, Sir Cosmos, and the two American gentlemen. Twelve in all.

The boat was not a lifeboat but quite a small ordinary rowing boat and not too safe. It could not have lived in high waves for five minutes, in fact it was of so little use that when the Carpathia picked us up they let our boat go and did not trouble to take it aboard the Carpathia. (Daily Mail Reporter (2010)

Accounts like those offered by Francatelli can be rich in subtle details and represent the narrator's view, emotional state, and thinking at various points in the event. These crisis accounts also represent the life-and-death elements of the scene. The *Titanic* account emphasizes the critical role that support of others provided and what may be interpreted as simple luck that led to Francatelli's survival.

The disaster participant account also makes up a significant proportion of the initial media coverage of these events. The extended use of social media and handheld devices has made these narratives much more common, more personal, and more closely connected to the primary elements of the events. First-person YouTube videos of crisis, for example, provide a direct window into the experience of living through a crisis. Videos taken by cell phones or other mobile devices can be easily uploaded to the Internet. Video accounts of extreme weather events, such as the rising water levels from 2012's Superstorm Sandy (Dawes, 2012) or the 2013 explosion of a fertilizer plant in West Texas (RT, 2013), document the experience of the crisis.

Social media has created a powerful outlet for the first-person account of "what I saw from my perspective." In a dramatic case documented in a YouTube video, an observer recounts what he saw when a father rescued his two-year-old daughter from a river (Nature's Beauty, 2010). This account also ended up as a journalistic narrative when the reporter interviewed the man who made the video. Initial media reports of major crises, described in Chapter 8, are usually built around these first personal narratives. In the first moments following the attacks on 9/11, broadcast coverage consisted primarily of witnesses calling in on their cell phones and reporting what they had observed as first-person accounts.

Mainstream news outlets have capitalized on the prevalence of mobile devices that disaster participants use to help contribute to initial journalistic narratives. In August 2006, CNN launched a citizen journalism initiative dubbed "iReport." Specific to disasters, CNN acknowledges the importance of first-person accounts to help the media shape the initial narratives. "iReporters have stolen the spotlight here at CNN whenever a natural disaster occurs. They are the first people on the scene, so naturally they are the first people we turn to when we need information" ("Top Five," 2011). As part of its five-year anniversary, the iReport website recounted the substantial contributions of iReporters during five of the most memorable natural disasters. Not only did these first-person accounts of the devastation contribute to the overall narrative, but they also produced some of most memorable and iconic images and videos that helped those narratives come to life.

While first-person accounts provide a unique and significant perspective that fundamentally shapes other crisis narrative, it is only one part of the larger story. Personal narratives are usually privileged in initial media reports and certain legal proceedings. However, understanding the subjective nature of individuals' experiences is also important. The more objective third-person account may help create intersubjective understanding in crisis narratives (Varela & Shear, 1999). Third-person/party accounts often incorporate subjective first-person accounts and more objectively collected observations and data to further evaluate and analyze these narrative components—thus constructing its own part of the larger narrative.

RESPONSIBILITY ACCOUNTS

The account narrative establishing responsibility is an explanation of the events that typically seeks to strategically portray the level and form of responsibility assigned to key parties. These narratives manage impressions through a strategic portrayal of attribution for causing the crisis or contributing to the harm. Most crisis events have a number of factors that may be described as causing or being associated with a crisis. In most crises, the interaction of many factors is what *causes* the crisis. An airline disaster, for example, might involve weather, pilot error, mechanical failures, maintenance issues, air traffic controller error, or the interaction of several of these factors. There are opportunities following a crisis for narratives to strategically portray various parties as more or less accountable for the crisis. These forms of accounts are also closely associated with the blame narratives (described in Chapter 5). The blame narrative is typically supported or preceded by a strategic account of the chronology or scene of the event, then followed by a strategy designed to repair or restore a positive image. The two forms of narrative function as "this is what happened" and "this is why it's not my fault." As described earlier, "accountability refers to the implicit or explicit expectation that one may be called on to justify one's beliefs, feelings, and actions to others" (Lerner & Tetlock, 1999, p. 255). Moreover, the social principle of accountability means that people who do not provide a satisfactory justification will likely be held accountable.

For individuals to be accountable, they must have some level of personal control over the actions. For example, young children have limited capacity to make rational decisions and therefore are typically not accountable for their actions in the same way as adults. The same principle applies for any person with diminished mental capacity. This diminished capacity concept has created room for a number of novel legal defenses, including a variety of explanations grounded in a person's psychological abuses, defenses based on the diet of the responsible party, and defenses associated with larger social conditions. The abuse account was used in the infamous 1989 trial of Lyle and Erik Menendez for the murder of their parents. The defense claimed the defendants were driven to murder by years of parental abuse and did not fully comprehend their actions. Despite this defense, they were convicted of first-degree murder. Another well-known case involved what has come be known as the Twinkie defense, used in the 1978 murder trial of San Francisco Mayor George Moscone and city supervisor Harvey Milk by a disgruntled employee, Dan White. The defense claimed White was not responsible for the murder because his capacity to understand what he was doing was diminished by his diet of junk food, including the packaged cakes known as Twinkies. This defense helped White receive a sentence of voluntary manslaughter rather than the much more punitive premeditated murder sentence (Dershowitz, 1994).

Accountability for crises often comes down to legal proceedings where liability for harm is established. In the U.S. legal system, liability may be civil or criminal. Civil liability concerns the responsibility for paying monetary damages or other court-enforcement costs arising from a civil lawsuit. Criminal liability means a party is open to punishment for committing a crime. Both forms of liability occur with many crises. For example, Exxon Corporation paid $1.9 billion in fines, penalties, and interest for the 1989 *Valdez* oil spill. This was in addition to about $2 billion it paid in cleanup costs. These penalties will likely be overshadowed by the liability incurred by British Petroleum for the 2010 Deepwater Horizon spill, which released an estimated 4.9 million barrels of oil into the Gulf of Mexico. By December 2013, BP had already agreed to pay nearly $13 billion in claims to businesses, individuals, and the government. Litigation over civil and legal liability will go on for years and will involve a variety of competing narratives about what happened and who is at fault.

The responsibility account is a primary part of the overall postcrisis narrative as basic questions are asked and answered about what happened and who or what caused the crisis. As we describe in Chapter 5, the responsibility account is closely associated with the larger blame and the responsibility narrative. Accounts of responsibility may precede the blame narrative or be woven into it. The responsibility account, or most often many such accounts, becomes part of the larger efforts to sort out complex questions of responsibility. In addition, questions of blame and responsibility are sometimes the focus of the larger third-party/person account.

THIRD-PERSON ACCOUNTS

The third-party account is most often the outcome of a formalized process designed to provide an official report on the crisis. These forms are typically more process driven to ensure the credibility of the final product. Often the third party is a higher authority—the courts, governments, a commission, or an independent agency—and follows an investigatory logic (Mulgan, 2000). The process is usually governed by well-established steps and procedures. Legal proceedings described earlier may become third-party accounts as court decisions are made and entered into the public record. In addition, formal after-action reports, inquiry reports, commission reports, and lessons-learned documents all share the general narrative structure of understanding how the crisis developed. The 9/11 Commission, the Rogers Commission of the 1986 *Challenger* Space Shuttle Disaster, and the National Transportation Safety Board's (NTSB) investigation into air, rail, and shipping disasters all function to answer the basic question: "What happened?"

The third-party/person account is distinct because of the unique resources and perspectives brought to the process of creating the account. The third-party account emphasizes a credible and thorough process to ensure an objective public accounting of the facts. These reports typically begin with an event chronology to establish time lines and associated starting and ending points (Boudes & Laroche, 2009). They usually identify four possible main plots: the fate plot, the human factor plot, the bureaucratic hydra plot, and the system collapse plot. The fate plot makes sense of the event as a fatalistic occurrence that could not be avoided. Such events are described as "acts of God" or natural occurrences. Weather is a common factor in the fate plot. The human factor plot is the human-caused event most often described as a function of human action, such as error or oversight. In the bureaucratic hydra plot, the organization is the villain, vilified for its inability to operate in a logical and coordinated manner or because the organization is too concerned about profits and not enough about the welfare of others. Finally, systems collapse involves human and bureaucratic failures in some combination.

The NTSB uses expert teams and an established structure for its independent investigations of civil airline disasters. Traveling to each crash site is the NTSB "Go Team," which is divided into several specialized areas: operations, which examines flight and crew members' duties; structures, which examines airframe wreckage and the accident scene; power plants, which focuses on engines; and systems, which studies components of the plane's hydraulic, electrical, pneumatic instrumentation. Teams also investigate the function of the air traffic control, including radar data and transcripts of radio transmissions between controller and pilot, weather at the time of the crash, and human performance. Human performance studies crew performance and behavior before the accident as factors that might be involved—for example, human error, fatigue, medication, alcohol, drugs, medical histories, training, workload, equipment design, and work environment. Finally, survival factors examine impact forces and injuries, evacuation, community emergency planning, and all crash-fire-rescue efforts.

Third-party accounts sometimes take their final form as lengthy and detailed public reports. The 9/11 Congress and President George W. Bush created the 9/11 Commission, formally the National Commission on Terrorist Attacks on the United States, on November 27, 2002. The commission was composed of ten senior political and national security officials—half Democrats, half Republicans. This makeup helped contribute to the credibility of the investigation as a nonpartisan effort. The commission was charged broadly to investigate the facts and circumstances related to the terrorist attacks of September 11, 2001. The final report, which was published online and in paperback form, is 450 pages and includes both an account of what happened and broad recommendations for how to manage terrorists' threats and risks (9/11 Commission, 2004). The commission used a wide variety of investigative techniques to create this official account, including hearings, expert testimony, and review of classified and public documents. The members continued to function as an informal advocacy group after the formal report was issued.

The third-party account serves several purposes. As described previously, these accounts become the official public assessment of many crises. They therefore serve as the historical record of the crisis. Many third-party accounts are compilations of other accounts, including first-person accounts, through hearings and testimony. One of the key features of these accounts is the objectivity and credibility of a third-party, independent assessment of what happened in a crisis. The credibility of the final account is important in larger narratives about blame and responsibility, the determination of how future crises can be avoided, and reestablishing legitimacy. The NTSB, for example, often issues recommendations for improving safety as part of its reports. This is important to reassure the public that air travel is safe. It also creates an ongoing improvement process whereby each crisis is a learning opportunity. In other cases, such as the 9/11 Commission, the Rogers Commission investigating the space shuttle *Challenger*, or even the Warren Commission investigating the assassination of President John F. Kennedy, these third-party accounts address controversial aspects of the crisis.

CONCLUSION

In its most basic form, the account is simply a story of what happened. Accounts portray a stream of events and factors that may explain or account for what happened, usually in a strategic way. They usually form the basic structure of other crisis narratives because the most fundamental question to be answered following a crisis is, What happened? Accounts, then, are one general narrative form that may be manifest in several more specific forms such as the blame narrative, the hero narrative, or the victim narrative. These other narrative forms are described in subsequent chapters.

Accounts serve a variety of functions including describing, documenting, learning, impression management, and determining blame and responsibility. Larger social systems, communities, and structures rely on these postcrisis accounts as a way of creating formalized consensus regarding what happened. This understanding is often documented in a formal report. Fundamentally these account narratives take the form of retrospective sense making, allowing people to give meaning to the crisis and allowing others to understand what happened, when, and why.

CASES TO CONSIDER

The two account narratives that follow offer the descriptions generated by individuals to understand and make sense of the shocking crises they experienced. These accounts in many ways are simple descriptions of what happened during a turbulent and threating experience. Beyond this, these narratives order events in a specific way, infer causation and blame, and describe outcomes. They also describe personal actions and emotional responses.

Two first-person accounts of individuals who endured the damage and aftermath of Superstorm Sandy are presented first. The second case involves a CEO's initial efforts to manage impressions about a mining tragedy. Although both cases provide informative accounts of the crises they describe, the content and focus of first-person accounts and responsibility accounts differ dramatically. The first-person superstorm accounts include expressive and emotional information. Conversely, the responsibility narrative displays how critical precise language and word choice were to the efforts of the mining company's CEO to maintain control of the narrative.

First-Person Accounts of Superstorm Sandy

These accounts are first-person narratives by two people who experienced Superstorm Sandy, which made landfall in Brigantine, New Jersey, early on October 29, 2012. Sandy was directly responsible for seventy-two deaths and is the second costliest hurricane in U.S. history at $65 billion in damage. These accounts describe both the storm and the aftermath as experienced by individuals in New York and New Jersey. As we discussed in the chapter, personal values influence first-person accounts. These accounts order events in a developmental way. Note how values of community and compassion for others make their way into these narrative accounts.

HURRICANE SANDY BEACHFRONT EXPERIENCE

by Kira Brodskaya

My Monday night—the night Hurricane Sandy came ashore—was spent in my fourth floor apartment on Manhattan Beach. On one side, I watched the ocean waves cover the roofs of the homes on the beach. On the other side, I watched the Sheepshead Bay canal waters rush in over cars and through buildings. As I saw all this I was wishing I had packed an inflatable boat in my "to go" bag.

Our first night after the storm I watched cars attempting to drive—but mostly floating—away, and firefighters making attempts at evacuations. That's when I realized the unintended effect that my last text message could have had on all my friends who still had access to news: "I'm really scared. The garage across the street is already fully covered, and it hasn't even made landfall yet."

On the morning after the first night, it didn't take long for the streets of Manhattan Beach and Brighton Beach to fill with people—familiar faces—happy to find each other, happy to find out some news, happy (and in line with the Russian tradition) to find an open liquor store.

It has now become clear that we will be seeing the effects of Hurricane Sandy in our neighborhood for a long time to come. What's interesting, however, is that while writing this, it was the first time since Monday that I actively thought about it. The overwhelming community activity to gather and help each other has filled up my Facebook feed, phone, and pushed out any other conversations. Groups of friends and neighbors in all parts of New York City have mobilized to help—even if it has meant spending that last, hard-to-come-by gas in order to bring clothes and volunteers to a shelter.

Personal Narrative: How Twitter Helped Me Help Others

Posted by Natalie Castillo

When the storm had finally settled down and people started to go outside because there was nothing else to do, it felt chaotic. People ran to hardware stores to buy red tanks to store gas, the lines for gas were blocks long and not all of the gas stations were open because they didn't have electricity. For the first time I saw trucks from the National Guard in my town, it felt like a scene from War of the Worlds and I was half expecting to see Tom Cruise. But we managed to get through those five days and all I could think about was the people who lived down the shore and how the memories of my last summer spent there suddenly weren't the same.

So when the lights came back on I knew I had to do something to help. Since it was five days after, many shelters weren't taking clothing donations and we couldn't donate food because all of the stores were practically empty. Thanks to Twitter, I found out that a small church in Staten Island needed clothing donations. After packing two big laundry bags with coats, my dad's old Levi's, sweaters, scarves and sneakers we drove to Staten Island. During the storm I stayed updated on the news and what was going in my city through Facebook on my smartphone that I had to charge in our car and I saw how towns nearby were really coming together and it wasn't really happening where I lived. Neighbors checked on each other, but that was about it. We didn't get a shelter till three to four days afterwards and we never even saw our mayor. We got flyers about places to seek shelter and advice on how to keep warm, etc. but he never made an appearance. What I learned from this hurricane is that you should always be prepared and if others aren't always as willing to give or help, it's okay because I know I always will.

K Brodskaya. (2013, May 12). Hurricane Sandy beachfront experience. [Web log post]. Retrieved from http://www.tronviggroup.com/hurricane-sandy-beach front-experience/. Reprinted with permission from Tronvig Group.

N Castillo. (2012, November 19). Personal narrative: How Twitter helped me help others. [Web log post]. Retrieved from http://pauwwow.com/viewpoints /personal-narrative-how-twitter-helped-me-help-others. Reprinted with permission from the Pauw Wow.

Initial Responsibility Account of Murray Energy Corporation

This responsibility account is drawn from the mine collapse that left six miners trapped in the Crandall Canyon Mine in Utah on August 6, 2007. Active rescue efforts continued until August 16, when another collapse killed three rescue workers and injured six others. The six miners trapped in the initial collapse were never found. As discussed in this chapter, when organizations are suspected of acting in a manner inconsistent with established guidelines or in ways that are negative or harmful, they are expected to account for their actions. Murray Energy Corporation did so by insisting that an earthquake or earthquakes, not questionable safety procedures, caused the collapse.

MURRAY ENERGY CORPORATION'S RESPONSE.

Despite having agreed to a 2012 settlement with the U.S. Labor Department in which Murray Energy Corporation was fined $949, 351 for
violations of mine safety related to the Crandall Canyon Mine Collapse,
the company never publicly accepted responsibility for the tragedy (Berkes, 2012). Instead, it firmly reemphasized its commitment to miner safety.
For example, in response to a 2013 Fox News article that was critical of
the corporation's actions leading to the Crandall Canyon Mine collapse,
Murray Energy Corporation reiterated its commitment to miner safety.
After explaining that continuing research points to seismic activity rather
than unsafe mining practices as the cause of the tragedy, the corporation
restated its consistent safety mantra: "All 3,300 Murray Energy employees
know that, when we address our miners' health and safety, there is no other
priority until that subject has been exhausted" (Murray Energy Corporation, 2013, para. 9).

Murray Energy Corporation insisted from early on in the disaster that
seismic activity was responsible for the mine tragedy. A study completed
by the University of Utah several years after the collapse revealed "up to
2,000 tiny, previously unrecognized earthquakes before, during and after" the mine collapsed (Oskin, 2013, para. 3). Murray further advanced
its longstanding insistence that the company was not negligent based on
the content of this study.

CHAPTER 5

Blame Narratives

A POSTCRISIS NARRATIVE consistently tries to answer the question, "Who is to blame?" Blame and responsibility for a crisis are fundamental issues that communicators must address. In some circumstances, the process of assigning blame dominates the postcrisis narrative. Naturally, those who feel they are blamed unfairly object and offer their own narratives countering the accusation. The blaming process creates considerable narrative space surrounding crises, which is played out in the media, legal proceedings, and the court of public opinion. The result is often a contentious public display of competing stories of blame. For example, Exxon aggressively argued they could have removed the oil from the *Valdez* spill much more efficiently and limited the environmental damage if the local government had simply allowed them to use chemical dispersants. By contrast, the local residents accused Exxon of having an outdated and unrealistic crisis management plan that left the company unprepared for a major spill in the area. They also insisted the choppy waters made the use of dispersants an unrealistic option (Johnson & Sellnow, 1995). This debate over who was responsible for the harm was never fully resolved.

Accusations are central to blame narratives. An attacker, manifest as an individual, ad hoc group, formal organization, or government agency, seeks to focus or compound public outrage toward an organization or agency that is seen as causing the crisis. Thus, the attacker is the "persuasive prime mover" in a blame narrative (Ryan, 1988, p. xviii). The ultimate goal of the attacker is to create an image of the adversary that draws public scorn and demands it be held accountable. This may involve sanctions, such as demotion or incarceration, or restitution for harm caused. Blame narratives projected by accusers generally leave no doubt about the adversary's guilt (Kelley-Romano & Westgate, 2007). In addition, once an individual or organization is publicly accused, the accusations themselves become part of the story for that individual or organization. In fact, individuals may be charged with no crime or formally acquitted of a crime but remain convicted in public sentiment, based on an extensive blame narrative. For example, Walmart and other large retail outlets are often blamed by community and human rights watchdog groups for contributing to low wages and the loss of small mom-and-pop stores and the decay of downtown shopping districts. Although these retailers are not charged with crimes, accusers often encourage consumers to boycott these large chains, oppose new stores, and advocate for new regulations regarding salary and health care for workers.

In this chapter we review the narrative function of persuasive attacks, emphasizing the concept of accusation of wrongdoing, or what scholars term *kategoria*. We also review the response strategies often used to reduce blame, sometimes referred to as *apologia*. Specifically, we discuss strategies of victimage, mortification, and transcendence. These attacks and defenses are connected narratives that sort out the blame for a crisis.

BLAME AS PERSUASIVE ATTACK

Researchers describe blame narratives as kategoria or persuasive attacks (Benoit & Dorries, 1996; Ryan, 1988). An attack is considered persuasive when it generates public interest to a level where the credibility of the subject under attack is widely questioned. Several efforts have been made to systematically analyze the strategies used for initiating these blame narratives. Benoit and Dorries (1996), for example, organize these strategies under two key objectives: increasing perceived responsibility of the accused and increasing perceived offensiveness of the act (see table 5.1).

In a blame narrative, the perceived responsibility for a crisis is heightened in the public's eyes by claims that the actions leading to the crisis were repeated in the past, premeditated, done with a knowledge the acts would cause harm, or enacted with the intent of deriving some benefit. For example, Rupert Murdoch's News Corporation was accused of bribery and improper manipulation and news gathering in the United Kingdom, and some of its employees were convicted. This was a crisis for Murdoch's media empire, which was seen as engaging in ongoing illegal behaviors for financial gain at the expense of others. As a result, critics

TABLE 5.1 *Persuasive Attack Strategies Based on Benoit and Dorries*

Increasing the target's perceived responsibility for the act
- Accused committed the act previously
- Accused planned the act
- Accused knew likely consequences of the act
- Accused benefited from the act

Increasing the perceived offensiveness of the act
- Extent of the damage
- Persistence of negative effects
- Effects on the audience
- Inconsistency
- Victims are innocent or helpless
- Obligation to protect victims

SOURCE: Benoit, W. L., & Dorries, B. (1996). Dateline NBC's persuasive attack on Wal-mart. *Communication Quarterly*, 44, 463–477.

held up Murdoch's corporation as a prime example of what is wrong with consolidated news organizations worldwide. The perceived offensiveness of these actions was advanced by claims in the blame narrative that the organization or individual being blamed caused extensive harm to innocent victims who should have been protected. The offensiveness of the actions was heightened in this case by the perception that Murdoch's corporation had consistently violated existing laws and policies put in place to protect the privacy of citizens.

Blame narratives are distinct from other crisis narratives because they begin with attacks in an effort to assign blame. Whether or not those being singled out for blame believe they are responsible, they are often forced to publicly acknowledge these attacks with a narrative of self-defense that is both informative and persuasive. The informative element emphasizes events and facts favorable to the person or group being accused. These are often represented in the various forms of accounts discussed earlier. The persuasive dimension overtly argues that the claims are false and the accused is innocent or the claims are distorted and that although the accused is responsible, the accusations should be viewed in a more favorable light. Narratives of blame try to reduce, limit, or explain responsibility in a way that is favorable to one group or individual.

RESPONDING TO BLAME

Another view of blame narratives is based on theories of dramatism. According to Kenneth Burke (1984), our experiences are reflected in a hierarchical order of things. Once that hierarchy is violated in any way, guilt or blame will be assigned. The individuals or groups burdened with guilt must engage in acts of purification if they hope to achieve redemption from the guilt. This pattern of behavior is observable in all aspects of life. On an individual level, those who commit crimes are expected to accept their punishment and rehabilitate their problematic behavior. Having done so, they have paid their social debt and are granted a second chance to live as honorable citizens. Similarly, organizations that sell faulty products are expected to learn from their mistakes, correct their problems, and improve their procedures so similar problems will not arise in the future. Toxic spills, transportation accidents, industrial disasters, corporate misconduct, disclosure of customer data, and many other kinds of corporate crises can create guilt and blame and the need for redemption.

The assignment of guilt or blame is central to these narratives. A party is assigned responsibility for a crisis, and that party must either accept the blame or provide a justification for an alternate view of who is responsible. When an accused challenges the view of responsibility established by an attacker, the accused is actually confronting the accusations on an existential level. In other words, unless those accused are willing to accept full responsibility for a crisis, they must provide an alternate meaning and explanation for it. Burke (1961) described how an explanation of blame can be interpreted from multiple perspectives. Blame may be distinguished by its external versus internal origination. Guilt or blame assigned by external agents is referred to as victimage or scapegoating. Guilt assigned and accepted internally by the accused is seen as mortification. Finally, guilt recast from a completely different point of view by the accused, typically in a larger context, is characterized as transcendence (Benoit, 1995).

Victimage

Victimage involves rule-breaking behaviors by others (Sellnow, 2014). In these cases, those accused have two general options in developing narratives to deny the accusations: outright denial and shifting blame (Benoit, 1995). Outright denial can be quite simple: the accused simply insists the accusations are false. This response does not necessarily deny that a crisis occurred. Rather, denial is a story that contests the assignment of responsibility for the crisis. Denial is common in lawsuits where those accused insist they are innocent. As in the Walmart example, the company consistently denies responsibility for the economic and community harm it is accused of causing. In fact, the corporation claims it actually creates community jobs and gives consumers greater value for their money.

In some cases, groups or organizations seek to avoid or relieve responsibility by shifting blame to an individual, subgroup, or organization. This is a scapegoating strategy and is quite common in stories of blame. The goal of a scapegoating narrative is to preserve the organization's integrity by creating a story that places blame elsewhere. Sometimes blame is shifted to another individual or to some small and isolated segment of the organization. The story may paint the picture of a single rogue employee or group of employees while suggesting that the larger organization is blameless. The scapegoating option is common in blame narratives because "the public is quick to demand a scapegoat or responsible party when problems or difficulties arise" (Littlefield & Quenette, 2007, p. 29). Accused parties, particularly organizations, can oblige this public desire by shifting blame early in the narrative to another party either inside or outside the organization (Benoit, 1995).

Unfortunately, preoccupation with scapegoating or assigning a face to an organizational injustice can allow organizations to avoid addressing systematic problems that perpetuate risks. The problem with scapegoating is that the strategy promotes a failure to see beyond the actions of an individual to better comprehend the complex, often recurring series of events preceding crisis. For example, in the aftermath of Hurricane Katrina, residents of the Mississippi Gulf Coast blamed national media and its obsession with New Orleans for the fact that hurricane survivors in Mississippi were initially overlooked in the recovery effort (Anthony & Sellnow, 2011). At the same time, media reports criticized the Department of Homeland Security, President George W. Bush, and local governments for problems with their inadequate response to Katrina (Littlefield & Quenette, 2007).

On a broader scale, public guilt and remorse for shameful acts can be scapegoated onto a few selected perpetrators. For example, national print coverage of the vicious murder of Matthew Shepard in an antigay hate crime in 1998 focused on the savage, inhuman brutality of the two killers (Ott & Aoki, 2002). A cyclist who discovered Shepard as he lay dying in rural Wyoming said that his "face was completely covered in blood, except where it had been partially washed clean by his tears" (Knittel, 2013, para. 15). The emerging blame narrative transferred guilt away from community responsibility to the larger metanarrative of how sexual orientation is viewed throughout the United States (Ott & Aoki, 2002). In addition, the perpetrators were described as bad people who did not represent how the rest of the community acted. The murderers were described as so extremely evil they could not reflect any notion of public sentiment. As these examples illustrate, systematic problems are often overlooked in blame narratives due to a prevailing need by those observing or experiencing the crisis to personalize blame.

Mortification

Mortification is a story of acceptance and redemption. Unlike victimage, it involves a story of an inner struggle: an individual or organization looks within to recognize violations of acceptable standards for behavior. Thus, whereas victimage is a form of attack, mortification involves self-analysis, recognition, and correction or repentance (Burke, 1961). Profound failures and the ensuing blame narrative often initiate the mortification process. Mortification is distinct, however, in that the accused accepts blame and sincerely sees the crisis as an opportunity for learning and improvement.

In 2014 General Motors faced what was the largest recall in history due to faulty ignition switches on several models of its cars. But it ignored the problem and failed to take action even after the switches were associated with several deaths. When the crisis finally resulted in federal investigations, CEO Mary Barra offered a sincere apology and pledged to use this case as a learning opportunity to create a new corporate culture of safety. (We expand on this distinction between mortification and other responses is in Chapter 6 when we discuss narratives of renewal.)

Organizations also have the opportunity to engage in mortification by learning from minor failures before they become full-blown crises. When organizations experience events that come very close to causing major hardship for others, they have the opportunity to learn and take appropriate steps. This response contributes to a narrative of vigilance that potentially establishes a reservoir of goodwill for countering blame narratives if a crisis occurs in the future. For example, high-reliability organizations such as aircraft carriers and nuclear power plants regularly monitor minor failures in an effort to constantly address risk. The primary assumption of such organizations is, "Danger disguised as safety is a stronger sign of vulnerability than safety disguised as danger" (Weick & Sutcliffe, 2007, p. 152). Unfortunately, much research indicates that organizations often learn the wrong lesson from these near misses. In other words, they frequently see near misses as evidence that their safety standards and practices are sufficient (Dillon & Tinsley, 2008). Specifically, "managers may, in certain situations, adopt inappropriate feelings of invincibility or control because, having once survived a near-miss, they discount the probability of the negative outcome" (Dillon & Tinsley, 2005, p. 29). In reality, many near misses are the result of luck, not because safety standards are sufficient. As we discuss later in this chapter, years of transporting oil through the pristine but precarious waters of Alaska created a false sense of confidence that was shattered by the *Exxon Valdez* oil spill.

Once a full-blown crisis occurs, those accused of blame may engage in mortification through apology, change, and restitution. Mortification embodies an extreme act of self-control in which an individual or organization rejects a part of themselves as unfit and replaces it with more socially acceptable behavior (Burke, 1961). For example, individuals may engage in mortification by admitting they have a substance abuse problem that caused the crisis and then taking action to curb the problematic behavior. From the perspective of mortification, blame narratives serve as a stimulus for positive change. Offering restitution to those harmed by the culpable behavior of the accused is another form of mortification.

Willingly compensating victims, paying fines, making generous donations to communities disrupted by the crisis, and providing other forms
of public service are all forms of mortification when they are enacted
without the external pressure of regulatory agencies, pressure groups,
or the legal system.

Transcendence

On occasion, assigning guilt extends beyond a single person, organization, or even government to address a larger problem on the industrial or
macrosocial levels. In this way, the blame narrative transcends the crisis at
hand to align with greater issues for which a macronarrative already exists.
In these cases, blame is directed toward an entire industry or linked to a
greater problem or controversy plaguing society. When blame narratives
take on this kind of macrofocus, they typically attract a third party. As
we discussed in Chapter 4, third-party accounts often provide an official
assessment of the crisis in the form of an objective, investigative report.
When blame narratives take on a macrofocus, however, third-party accounts often manifest as statements made by spokespersons on behalf of
an industry, community, or society. Such spokespersons may be members
of the industry, a trade or industry association, a government entity, a
sanctioned nongovernment organization, a special interest group, or a
group with a spiritual or religious orientation. Ideally these larger narratives can address recurring and systematic failures or threats common in
an industry. Unfortunately, blame narratives more often attach responsibility to individuals. Nevertheless, macronarratives and third-party accounts can produce meaningful change.

IMAGE REPAIR IN RESPONSE TO BLAME NARRATIVES

William Benoit (1995, 2015) has developed a pragmatic typology for individuals and organizations seeking to repair their reputations in response to
accusations of wrongdoing. Burke's concepts of victimage, mortification,
and transcendence, as well as the concept of apologia, are the foundation
of this typology (Ware & Linkugel, 1973). *Apologia* refers to speeches
delivered in defense of individuals or organizations when they are accused of violating "commonly held public values" (Hearit, 2005, p. 39).

To repair an image, individuals and organizations facing blame narratives answer two questions: "What accusation(s) or suspicion(s) threaten the image and who is or are the most important audiences?" (Benoit, 1995, p. 407). Sensitivity to the audience is essential to image repair. Although image repair strategies can be used to manipulate the audience's view of the crisis narrative, "effective image repair suggests those who are truly at fault should admit it immediately and take appropriate corrective action" (Benoit, 2005, p. 409).

Benoit described five general strategies: denial, evading responsibility, reducing offensiveness, corrective action, and mortification. The typology also includes secondary strategies for denial, evading responsibility, and reducing offensiveness of the event (see table 5.2). The image repair strategies serve as topoi, or places for speakers defending themselves in response to blame narratives to find arguments for defending themselves. We explicate each of these image repair strategies next.

Denial

Simple denial and shifting blame are distinct. Simple denial occurs when individuals or organizations explicitly deny all accusations presented in the blame narrative. An alternate denial strategy is shifting blame: the accused denies responsibility for the accusations by redirecting blame to someone (or something) else. In so doing, the accused accepts that an offense has occurred but places the blame on another party. As such, shifting the blame provides a replacement target for the offense and answers the pressing question, "Well, if you didn't do it, who did?" (Benoit & Hanzcor, 1994, p. 419).

Evading Responsibility

Speakers seeking to evade responsibility may accept some involvement in the crisis but insist they or their organizations should not be held accountable. There are four possible routes to evading responsibility (see table 5.2). The accused can claim "a lack of responsibility because the misdeed was a result of someone else's actions (provocation), a lack of information (defeasibility), an accident, or committed with good intentions" (Benoit & Brinson, 1994, p. 77).

TABLE 5.2 *Image Repair Strategies Based on Benoit*

Denial	Evading Responsibility	Reducing Offensiveness	Corrective Action	Mortification
Simple denial	Provocation	Bolstering		
Shifting blame	Defeasibility	Differentiation		
	Accident	Transcendence		
	Good intentions	Minimization		
		Attacking accuser		
		Compensation		

SOURCE: Benoit, W. L. (1995). *Accounts, excuses, and apologies: A theory of image restoration strategies*. Albany: State University of New York Press.

Reducing Offensiveness

If the accused cannot deny or evade responsibility for the accusations in the blame narrative, reducing offensiveness for the harm created by the crisis is a possibility. Benoit (1995) poses six alternatives for reducing the offensiveness of accusations (see table 5.2). Bolstering occurs when the accused counters the failures emphasized in the blame narrative with an emphasis on the far more extensive record of service and contributions made by the accused. Differentiation involves distinguishing the regrettable for which the accused is blamed from more egregious offenses implied by the accuser. Transcendence, one of Burke's response strategies, is another means for reducing offensiveness. Minimization is an effort by the accused to diminish the perceived impact of the accusations on the audience and surrounding environment. Attacking the accuser is an attempt by the accused to challenge the credibility of the accusers and thereby question the merit of the accusations. Finally, by offering to compensate those harmed by the crisis, the accused seeks to advance the blame narrative from the accusation to resolution.

Corrective Action

Corrective actions surpass compensation or other efforts to reduce offensiveness, attempting to reestablish "the state of affairs existing before the offensive act, and/or promising to prevent the recurrence of the offensive act" (Benoit, 1995, p. 77). Corrective action calls forth a narrative of compensation that also includes the termination of harmful behavior and, in its place, the creation of innovative strategies for preventing similar failures in the future.

Mortification

As the final strategy listed in Benoit's typology (1995), mortification demands the level of acceptance and redemption advocated by Burke (1961). Unlike any of the other strategies in the image repair typology, mortification requires the accused to "admit the wrongful act and ask for forgiveness" (Benoit & Brinson, 1994, p. 77). By contrast, accused parties can, and often do, provide corrective action without ever advancing the blame narrative to the point of accepting responsibility or asking for the audience's forgiveness.

MACROLEVEL BLAME NARRATIVES

Long-standing dominant narratives exist at the macrolevel in most societies. From a critical cultural perspective, a primary question is whether local narratives emerging from a single crisis have the potential to "bring about any liberation and emancipation from dominant master narratives" (Bamberg, 2005, p. 288). For example, strings of shootings in the United States, particularly those involving schools, have resulted in competing blame narratives. Groups that argue for greater gun control maintain that the shootings are symptoms of a national problem: easy access to guns by individuals with mental health issues. Pro-gun groups, such as the National Rifle Association, seek to transcend these accusations by creating stories that argue the larger problem is inadequate mental health care in the United States.

In some cases, blame narratives that transcend individual crises can create narrative space for positive change. For example, the melamine contamination of pet food and milk products made with ingredients imported from China in 2007 and 2008 inspired a discussion about policies in the United States to ensure the quality and safety of imported foods; it resulted in revised federal testing procedures and import policies. Similarly, the tragic loss of lives and unprecedented destruction of property caused by Hurricane Katrina and Superstorm Sandy inspired policy discussions. The hurricane warning system and the means for evacuating large populations from threatened areas were reviewed based on lessons learned from these tragedies. These storms also inspired conversations and policy discussions based on the destruction of wetlands and even more broadly about climate change and its impact on weather-related disasters.

Edward Snowden's leaking of classified documents in 2013 and thereby exposing the National Security Agency's (NSA) digital surveillance program is another example of how a crisis can energize or influence the larger narrative. Following the terrorist attacks on September 11, 2001, many legislators and citizens supported an expansion of surveillance efforts, data collection seen as essential to thwarting future terrorist activities. As we noted in Chapter 3, narratives often become homogenized and persistent over time. Such was the case for U.S. surveillance in the decade after 9/11 as more surveillance was accepted as necessary without an understanding of the details. The Snowden case, however, revealed just how extensive and, depending on one's point of view, offensive the NSA's surveillance had become. The blame narrative began with questions of Snowden's patriotism and the need to protect U.S. national security, but quickly transcended beyond Snowden to assign blame to the NSA and President Obama. The larger story became one of an insatiable desire to collect and store data from countless digital sources.

The blame narrative critiquing the NSA and President Obama outraged international figures such as Chancellor Angela Merkel of Germany and had an unanticipated impact on national and international business. From an information technology perspective, the Snowden case convinced organizations to review "how effectively they encrypt their most sensitive data" and reconsider cloud computing because data are more "accessible to surveillance agencies" (Hiner, 2013, para. 5). In addition, according to Hiner, organizations from countries outside the United States "are looking at ways to do less business with U.S. companies because the NSA has direct backdoors into many of them" (para. 5). The Snowden case created a blame narrative that quickly transcended from Snowden to the macronarrative balancing national security with the questionable ethics of spying.

CONCLUSION

One of the primary functions of postcrisis narratives is to establish blame and responsibility. Stories about who is at fault play into larger accounts, narratives about victimage, and stories of renewal. In many cases, competing blame narratives become divisive public arguments that detract from larger efforts to repair the damage, help the victims, learn from the crisis, and ensure it does not happen again. (We address the process of sorting out competing narratives in Chapter 10.) Debates about blame can last years as investigations work their way through the courts, and in some cases, these debates are never resolved. In such cases, crisis resolution is usually delayed and the harm may be extended. In other cases, however, blame narratives can help generate consensus and, ultimately, resolution of larger social issues that contributed to the crisis.

Too often these blame narratives are seen as strategic, self-serving, and deceptive, designed to avoid responsibility for the harm created. As a consequence, these narratives are sometimes dismissed as public relations spin or deception and as unethical ways to shift blame and avoid the costs associated with accepting blame. As the various ways of interpreting and framing blame illustrate, however, some approaches involve accepting responsibility and seeking forgiveness from those harmed. Moreover, the process of offering competing stories may help create consensus regarding blame and, ultimately, assist in learning and recovery. Stories of blame must be shared, discussed, and debated as individuals, groups, organizations, communities, and societies seek to move beyond the crisis.

CASES TO CONSIDER

Blame is usually a defining characteristic of crisis narratives. In some cases, the outrage inspired by a crisis makes blame the dominant feature, thereby occupying a significant part of the postcrisis narrative. Blame narratives are usually characterized by persuasive attacks that focus on assigning responsibility and emphasizing the offensiveness of the acts and the harm created by the crisis. In responding to blame narratives, organizations and individuals typically engage in image repair. Predictable image repair strategies include denying or shifting blame, evading responsibility, reducing offensiveness, corrective action, and mortification. Although blame narratives primarily identify individuals who are to blame, they can reach a macrolevel where narrative space for public discussion and policy change can occur. The following two cases are excerpts from blame narratives. The first case demonstrates the persuasive power of attack narratives. The second one illustrates the perils of attempting to shift blame, particularly when a crisis is aligned with a macrolevel blame narrative.

Blame as Persuasive Attack in Union Carbide Corporation's Bhopal Disaster

The Union Carbide Corporation (UCC) plant in Bhopal, India, synthesized the chemical compound carbyl, an agricultural pesticide. One of the compounds used as an intermediate in the synthesis of carbyl was methyl isocyanate (MIC). On December 2, 1984, and lasting until December 3, a series of events resulted in thousands of gallons of MIC being vented directly into the surrounding community. The Bhopal gas leak is believed to be the largest chemical industrial accident ever (Eckerman, 2005). Within the first week of the gas leak alone, 2,000 people died and another 100,000 were permanently injured, and in the years following the spill, many birth defects were attributed to the chemical exposure. As the blame narrative developed, Union Carbide suggested that unknown terrorist groups might have deliberately sabotaged the plant.

The following narrative is an excerpt from a 1985 report produced jointly by the International Confederation of Free Trade Unions and the International Federation of Chemical, Energy, and General Workers Unions (International Confederation, 1985). As you read the excerpt, note how the persuasive attack strategies summarized in table 5.1 are evident. The report increases the perceived responsibility by implying that UCC knew a catastrophic failure was likely and that the consequences would be deadly. For example the report notes that previous inspections had identified safety concerns to which UCC did not respond. Worse, smaller leaks had already occurred at the plant, causing death and injury. The report increases the perceived offensiveness of the act by emphasizing a pervasive disregard for worker and community safety. Specifically, the

report identifies dangerous insufficiencies in safety, maintenance, training, crew sizes, and supervision. The likely conclusion to these accusations is that the inadequacies were knowingly permitted or encouraged
to benefit UCC through enhanced profits.

THE REPORT OF THE ICFTU-ICEF MISSION TO STUDY THE CAUSES AND
EFFECTS OF THE METHYL ISOCYANATE GAS LEAK AT THE UNION CARBIDE
PESTICIDE PLANT IN BHOPAL, INDIA, ON DECEMBER 2ND/3RD 1984

In compiling this report, the commission relied on several sources of information. Including news accounts from Indian, European and American publications; articles from technical journals; Union Carbide technical manuals and
reports; documents compiled by the U.S. Congress; materials Published by
Indian Community and scientific organization; and Correspondence between
the unions representing Bhopal workers, The Company, and the government.
In addition, the delegation interviewed more than thirty Union Carbide Worker, including several who were on duty on the night of the release, as well
as leader of the local and national Union's. Victims of the disaster, medical
personnel, present and former government officials and community activists
working on behalf of are sometimes contradictory

Based on the information available to us, the mission has reached the
following conclusion about the causes of the Bhopal tragedy;

1. The disaster was caused by insufficient attention to safety in the process
design, dangerous operating procedures, lack of proper maintenance, faulty
equipment, and deep cuts in manning levels, crew sizes, worker training and
skilled supervision, smaller releases of toxic chemicals, and unskilled supervision. Smaller releases of toxic chemicals had occurred in the past, leading
to one death and numerous injuries. Little was done to correct these problems
despite vigorous protests by the Union representing Bhopal Workers.

2. The accident was probably triggered by a runaway reaction occurring
when water entered methyl Isocyanate (MIC) storage tank. A likely source of
the water was a faulty maintenance procedure on the evening of December 2,
1984.

3. The operating and maintenance errors which led to the MIC release
were made by management of the Bhopal plant and Union Carbide India limited (UCIL). However, responsibility for the disaster also rests with UCIL's

parent multinational, the U.S-based Union Carbide Corporation (UCC). UCC insisted on a process design requiring large MIC storage tanks, over the objections of UCIL engineers. In addition, a 1982 corporate inspection report demonstrates that UCC knew the Bhopal plant had major safety problems. But the company did not take sufficient action to correct them.

4. The government of India and the state of Madhya Pradesh did not cause, and are not directly responsible for the gas release. However, stronger worker safety and environment regulations, and stricter enforcement could have prevented it.

International Confederation of Free Trade Unions & International Federation of Chemical, Energy, and General Workers Unions. (1985). *The report of the ICFTU-ICEF Mission to study the causes and effects of the methyl isocyanate gas leak at the Union Carbide pesticide plant in Bhopal, India, on December 2nd/3rd 1984.* Retrieved from http://www.bhopal.net/oldsite/documentlibrary/unionreport1985.html

Shifting the Blame in the ConAgra Chicken Pot Pies Crisis

In October 2007, ConAgra Foods, a multinational packaged food company, voluntarily recalled its Banquet brand of frozen, single-serve pot pies, as well other store brands produced at its Marshall, Missouri, plant (Centers for Disease Control and Prevention, n.d.). The recall was in response to an investigation by the Centers for Disease Control and Prevention (CDC) into what was discovered to be salmonella poisoning of 272 individuals across thirty-five states. The CDC determined that the consumption of Banquet-brand potpies was the common factor in the outbreak. While ConAgra Foods took steps to ensure its facilities were clean, the company ultimately took the stance that it was impossible to control pathogens at the point of production considering the number of ingredients and their sources. The responsibility was placed with consumers for ensuring that the product is cooked thoroughly, thus ensuring pathogens are killed.

The following excerpts are from a case study written by Dr. Elizabeth Petrun as part of a research project for the National Center for Food Protection and Defense (cited in Sellnow, Ulmer, Seeger, & Littlefield, 2009). As you read the case study excerpts, take note of how ConAgra is described as shifting the blame for the salmonella outbreak to consumers for not properly preparing the product. Also observe how Petrun addresses the larger narrative of reputation as a possible motive for ConAgra's decision to shift blame for the crisis. Perhaps most important, take note of the ultimate lesson the ConAgra case teaches about attempting to shift blame in a crisis narrative.

> On October 9, 2007, the day after it was informed by health officials that a number of consumers had been diagnosed with *Salmonella* poisoning and that the infection was believed to be linked to its frozen pot pies, ConAgra Foods decided to make an advisory to the public, specifically pertaining to its Banquet turkey and chicken pot pies (ConAgra Foods, n.d.). In its first press release, ConAgra stated that it believed the issue to be related to improper cooking by *consumers* (ConAgra Foods, n.d.). Working with the U.S. Department of Agriculture, ConAgra Foods decided to revise the cooking instruction located on the food packages. . . . ConAgra immediately shifted the blame to the customer, asserting that customers were not cooking the pot pies properly. . . . The first news release even assured consumers that it was working with the "USDA to identify any additional steps that may be appropriate, including potential changes that may further clarify cooking instructions for consumers" (ConAgra, n.d.).

> ConAgra shifted blame for the *Salmonella* outbreak to consumers who, it alleged, were not cooking the product sufficiently. This is an inappropriate strategy and one that suggests that ConAgra was defensive in its postcrisis communication, focused on protecting its image rather than protecting its customers' welfare. Organizations should avoid shifting blame until they have substantive evidence that in fact someone else is indeed fully responsible.

> Sellnow, T. L., Ulmer, R. R., Seeger, M. W., & Littlefield, R. S. (2009). *Effective risk communication: A message-centered approach.* New York: Springer.

CHAPTER 6

Renewal Narratives

POSTCRISIS NARRATIVES of accountability, responsibility, and blame typically dominate public communication following a crisis. Blame narratives are generally retrospective, looking back on what happened, and they are often highly contentious. The individuals and groups associated with a crisis often try to place the blame on someone else, but alternative narratives of growth, learning, rebirth, resurrection, restoration, and renewal can also occur during the postcrisis stage. Sometimes these narratives exist in a complementary relationship to blame narratives, and sometimes they compete. These forward-looking, or prospective, narratives have been described as the discourse of renewal (Seeger & Griffin-Padgett, 2010; Seeger, Ulmer, Novak, & Sellnow, 2005; Sellnow & Seeger, 2013; Ulmer, Seeger, & Sellnow, 2007).

The renewal narrative develops after a crisis has created severe disruption to a region, community, or organization. Often basic elements of the establishment have been swept away and components of order and organization, including people, processes, and structures, are gone or no longer function as they have in the past. A crisis then can foster an immediate need to change and create both a literal and symbolic space for change. This space can be filled with stories focusing on rebuilding, recovery, and renewal. In some cases, renewal narratives focus on the meaning of the crisis for the future and opportunities to learn, grow, and improve. This form of renewal narrative may fundamentally reorder the community or organization down to its core purpose and values (Seeger et al., 2005).

This chapter describes the renewal narrative, including the factors associated with the development of this alternative form of postcrisis communication. Renewal is based on the inherent ability of a community or organization to self-organize in response to a severe disruption. These narratives are typically constructed through the public communication of established and credible public or community leaders. They are grounded in shared community and organizational values and a compelling vision of the future. Because renewal offers an alternative to what can become divisive narratives about blame and responsibility, these narratives can be particularly compelling and constructive forms.

POSTCRISIS RENEWAL

Renewal narratives are about rebuilding bigger, better, and more resilient than before. They are based on "connecting with core values, establishing the importance of the past in the present, and spurring efforts and energy toward process and the future" (Reierson, Sellnow, & Ulmer, 2009, p. 116). They feature calls to pull together to rebuild and recover better and stronger. Following the 2012 shooting massacre in a movie theater in Aurora, Colorado, for example, President Obama said, "Out of this darkness a brighter day will come" (Obama, 2012). The crisis is positioned as the impetus for a positive outcome. Through a process of learning and communicating the lessons of the crisis, renewal narratives can identify faulty assumptions or unforeseen vulnerabilities while reestablishing core values and facilitating consensus, cooperation, and support (Toelken, Seeger, & Batteau 2005).

Renewal narratives are typically offered by three sources: those who experienced the crisis, recognized community or organizational leaders, and emergency management professionals. For those who have experienced a significant loss, the renewal narrative is an effort to find hope for the future and learn lessons from loss. Themes of "we will rebuild/recover stronger and better," "we will not let this crisis defeat us," and "we will remember the lessons of this crisis" are common when members of a community have experienced severe loss of property or life. The Triangle Shirtwaist Factory fire of 1911 described in Chapter 3 spurred the development of a wide range of worker safety reforms, as well as the formation of the International Ladies' Garment Worker Union. Narratives of renewal by leaders often represent a call to action and reference core values of community, family, or help for victims. For example, two organizations, Malden Mills and Cole Hardwoods, constructed renewal narratives following fires. The facilities of both organizations were decimated in destructive fires, and in both cases, the organizations had strong, entrepreneurial leaders who immediately committed themselves to rebuilding. In both cases, the leaders announced that considerable resources would immediately be dedicated to rebuilding the facilities, and they did so even before the flames were extinguished (Seeger & Ulmer, 2002). Finally, emergency managers often engage in technical narratives of renewal based on available resources from state or federal funds for remediation efforts and rebuilding.

Floods, hurricanes, and terrorist attacks may be of sufficient scope and scale to create widespread collapse and disruption to established services, operations, and structures. In these cases, many basic assumptions, established procedures, and critical systems no longer operate. Structures and systems such as the electrical grid or transportation systems are necessary to maintain normal operations. Superstorm Sandy devastated parts of the U.S. East Coast, including Atlantic City, New Jersey. Many sections of the iconic boardwalk were destroyed, and parts of the electrical infrastructure were inundated with saltwater, causing widespread power outages for weeks. The Colorado floods of September 2013 saw major sections of Boulder County affected. Many houses were destroyed, and over eleven thousand people were evacuated. Some neighborhoods and even towns were cut off from access as the bridges and roads were washed away and not repaired for months.

According to the principles of chaos theory, these kinds of crises are called bifurcations, where an established path or structure of a system is disrupted or altered in a significant way. River systems, for example, often alter their path following a flood such that the river channel shifts within the larger floodplain. This shifting follows a predictable pattern, and new structures, including channels, islands, sandbars, and wetlands, are created at the same time that other structures are destroyed. During a flood, a new habitat is created, and fertile silt and sediment are deposited. The deposited silt may spur new growth of vegetation and may renew an ecosystem. In this way, river systems can be said to self-organize in response to a flood in a way that leads to a new form of stability or equilibrium. Systems disrupted by a crisis or bifurcation often experience this kind of self-organization, where an old order is destroyed and a new order takes its place. Self-organization involves the spontaneous emergence of order in systems that have been fundamentally disrupted (Comfort, 1994). This self-organization can help a system not just return to its previous state of operations but reach a higher level of operation and order.

Chaos theory also suggests that the process of self-organization occurs because of some natural underlying order or principle of order. These are called attractors or strange attractors because they attract elements in ways that encourage some new order or structure to emerge out of the chaos of the crisis. In social contexts, an attractor may take the form of a social force, shared value system, set of relationships, or economic motivation. Following the 9/11 attack on the World Trade Center, teams of volunteers spontaneously organized to help the injured and disabled evacuate, assisting people down emergency stairways because the elevators were not functioning. Many of the evacuees who left New Orleans after Katrina indicated a strong attraction to the community and an intense desire to "go home." This attraction occurred despite the fact that houses had been destroyed, jobs were gone, and many city services disrupted. The New Orleans population dropped by more than half after Katrina, but many of the evacuees eventually returned, attracted by culture, family, and community.

The process of self-organization occurs through communicative acts. Some verbal, written, or electronic form of communication allows stakeholders to orient themselves to the events and other stakeholders (Comfort, 1994). Communicative acts and the exchange of messages and information are the basic building blocks of the self-organizing process. Question such as, "What is happening?" "Is everyone okay?" and "What do you think we should do?" allow stakeholders to begin to impose some order on a chaotic situation (Comfort, 1994, p. 396). Mass communication systems, primarily contemporaneous systems such as new media, radio, and television, promote self-organization even further by disseminating information, instructions, and procedures even more broadly. In this way, these systems promote a common understanding and more generalized meaning for the event.

Among the most important sets of social attractors are shared systems of meaning and the need to create meaning. Crisis, as we noted, creates a meaning vacuum that is filled by various meaning-making crisis narratives. The meanings that are laid over and arise from a crisis may also become strange attractors (Dimitrov & Woog, 2000), that is, attractors whose lines of attraction function in unpredictable patterns. For example, during a crisis, a system of meaning such as faith or patriotism may become part of the narrative. In this way, the 9/11 attack became an event defined by strong values of national identity, patriotism, and devotion to country. Existing symbols were appropriated, such as the American flag. One very powerful image of 9/11 showed firefighters raising an American flag over the rubble of the World Trade Center (figure 6.1). This image, distributed throughout the world, evoked the larger grand narrative of American resilience and ability to overcome adversity. The image was also reminiscent of the iconic photograph of U.S. Marines raising a flag over Iwo Jima in World War II (figure 6.2). The values of patriotism and American resilience became attractors for the post-9/11 organization.

A comparative analysis of these two images helped demonstrate the significance of creating systems of meaning in postcrisis narratives (Hariman & Lucaites 2007). The emergence of a symbol that reaches iconic status (such as the images in figures 6.1 and 6.2) is associated with a convergence of a set of similar meanings. They also evoke a single or finite set of complementary values that then function as strange attractors in the postcrisis narrative. Symbols and strange attractors of meaning have what are called spatial and temporal characteristics (Dimitrov & Woog, 2000). The spatial characteristics refer to a static association that is always attached to a certain core context or scene. For example, the symbol of the flag raising over Iwo Jima reveals its meaning within the context of the specific struggle: it symbolizes the nation's sacrifice and victory in World War II (Hariman & Lucaites, 2007). What makes this image iconic are the codes of American public culture that are beautifully coordinated in it (Hariman & Lucaites, 2007). In essence, these complementary values function together as strange attractors attached to certain values about ideal national and civic identity.

The importance and power of the image of firefighters raising the flag in the aftermath of the 9/11 attacks, as well as photojournalistic contributions, are particularly powerful. "This visual representation of the event soon developed a narrative logic for reconstituting the public audience as a

FIGURE 6.1 Firefighters raising the U.S. flag at Ground Zero in New York.
SOURCE: "Firefighters Raising Flag," Thomas E. Franklin. © 2001 North Jersey Media
Group / The Record.

unified nation whose civic virtue guaranteed triumph over the disaster....
Fear and anger had not disappeared, but rather than accentuate resigna-
tion and despair, they were transformed into repeated performances of
civic pride" (Hariman & Lucaites, 2007, p. 128). The temporal characteristics become clearer when comparing the firefighters raising the flag
to the Iwo Jima image. The media, reinforcing core values and activating
them as attractors, made that comparison quickly and repeatedly.

The temporal characteristics of a strange attractor of meaning are associated with the ability of meanings to evolve, transform, and initiate
new meanings over time (Dimitrov & Woog, 2000). The association of
one symbol to another, like the 9/11 image to the Iwo Jima image, demonstrates this type of temporal characteristic within the symbols themselves. More important, the juxtaposition of the similarities that accessed
the comparison changes the meaning of both: "These are not pictures

FIGURE 6.2 U.S. Marines of the 28th Regiment, 5th Division, raising the American flag atop Mt. Suribachi, Iwo Jima.
SOURCE: AP Photo/Joe Rosenthal.

of 'war' . . . but of the reconstitution of civic virtues" (Hariman & Lucaites, 2007, p. 133). In a matter of days, this image was "transformed from a single representation of a news event into a historic marker for the disaster and an interpretive frame for national response" (p. 129). This symbol, functioning as a strange attractor, similar to the Iwo Jima image, provided an almost immediate basis for a narrative surrounding national and civic identity.

Systems of meaning also help motivate action or, in some cases, inaction. A narrative of victimage, for example, may impose a kind of paralysis on those who have experienced crisis. In other cases, systems of meaning may facilitate action and create coordinated and unified action. This outcome is sometimes called the rally-around-the-flag effect. As described earlier, a surge of patriotism created a spirit of national unity following 9/11, leading to high levels of support for political institutions. In many cases of renewal narratives, a rally-around-the-flag effect motivated unified action to help offset harm and rebuild a community following a crisis. The near bankruptcy of the Chrysler Corporation in 1979 resulted in high levels of support for the company from a wide variety of institutions, including local and state governments, competitors, suppliers, unions, and political and social organizations. The charismatic CEO, Lee Iacocca, framed the crisis as a threat to American manufacturing dominance, middle-class values, and a way of life. If Chrysler failed, he predicted the loss of 300,000 manufacturing jobs and the decline of communities and families that depended on them. An American way of life was threatened. These groups created a network of support that helped lobby the U.S. Congress for the passage of the Chrysler Corporation Loan Guarantee Act of 1979. This support also translated directly into the sale of Chrysler products (Seeger, 1986).

Resilience is an additional component of many renewal narratives. Community resilience is usually described as an attribute that allows communities to function efficiently and adapt successfully following the surprise and severe disruption created by a crisis (Norris, Stevens, Pfefferbaum, Wyche, & Pfefferbaum, 2008). In general, the term refers to some coping ability—the capacity to bounce back and work through and together to mitigate the disruption of a crisis (Sellnow & Seeger, 2013). Narratives of renewal describe resilience as both an attribute that allows communities to recover and as a desired outcome from a crisis. Margaret Chan, director general of the World Health Organization, for example, spoke about the need to build resilience into the public health system in response to the 2014 Ebola outbreak. Her suggestions include creating new public health capacity in developing countries while building on local knowledge, traditions, values, and cultures.

Renewal narratives are also built on the inherent need to change created by a crisis, which demonstrates the inadequacy of current systems and structures. The dramatic failure of the electrical grid in the northeast United States in 2003 resulted in many calls for investment in new equipment and infrastructure. At the same time, crisis can create an intense drive to rebuild. This need to build or rebuild is driven in part by the desire simply to replace what has been lost. In addition, those experiencing a crisis often report they don't want the crisis to break them. In some cases, the drive represents a kind of entrepreneurial spirit of optimism and inherent need to build or rebuild. Often a crisis presents significant opportunities to recreate systems and structures in more logical, resilient, and effective ways. When the lumber company Cole Hardwood experienced a devastating fire that destroyed all buildings and equipment, its CEO saw an opportunity to rebuild a much more efficient state-of-the-art-facility where work flow was integrated and logical and new machines increased productivity. Learning is part of the postcrisis narrative space because crises typically reveal important weaknesses or vulnerabilities. The postcrisis context is a space to openly discuss these failures and make a commitment to resolve them. In essence, the learning stage in the discourse of renewal expresses a desire to change and improve as a result of the crisis (Ulmer, Sellnow, & Seeger, 2010).

A final factor in the renewal narrative is some level of goodwill within the larger community or society. This goodwill may be a function of strong community networks or positive relationships that developed before the crisis. For example, a history of ethical conduct and fair treatment of customers, suppliers, and communities can translate to support following a crisis. A community that is well integrated and connected through social organizations or community values may be more resilient. Sometimes this goodwill develops as a consequence of the crisis and the rally-around-the-flag effect. Even where relationships before a crisis have not been positive, there may be an outpouring of sympathy and support. In any case, goodwill can facilitate and bolster the renewal narratives. It can be a kind of intangible asset during a crisis facilitating the allocation of resources to help offset the harm.

One way in which goodwill is manifest is in volunteerism. During disasters, many people and groups converge on the scene. These individuals and groups are not usually part of the established emergency management structure but are concerned volunteers who wish to help out of a sense of altruism and identification with the victims (Fernandez, Barbera, & van Drop, 2006). Disaster volunteerism is a pervasive behavior. By one estimate, 94 percent of Americans took some supportive action following the 9/11 attacks, including donating blood or money, flying the American flag, or attending an event or service. Some fifteen thousand disaster volunteers converged on the site of the World Trade Center (Demuth, 2002).

The drive to volunteer is a consequence of many factors. Media coverage of a disaster calls broad public attention to the event and often creates strong emotional responses among the larger public. Volunteers may be motivated by a need to act, particularly where they perceive some tangible issue that must be addressed and where they believe they can make a difference. A group of telecommunication professionals and companies that organized themselves following the World Trade Center attack as the Wireless Emergency Response Team created and deployed a new system to track victims based on their cell phones (Fernandez et al., 2006). While this volunteerism is most visible in the immediate aftermath of a disaster, it can be extended over a significant period of time. Volunteer groups, including nongovernmental organizations and faith-based organizations, continued to work in Haiti seeking to rebuild the country long after the earthquake of 2010.

FEATURES OF RENEWAL NARRATIVES

Narratives of renewal have several common features. First, they tend to be more provisional and natural than staged and strategic. Community leaders often react to crisis events spontaneously, reflecting core values and immediate impressions. Because emergent values and attractors such as patriotism or community typically drive these narratives, they are typically more organic than many other forms of postcrisis narrative. Crisis creates a meaning vacuum, and the renewal narrative can emerge as an immediate response to an event in the absence of planning and strategy. In the case of the devastating fire at Cole Hardwood, the CEO spoke of rebuilding bigger and better and continuing to pay his workers even as the fire burned. This was a spontaneous and natural response to the loss from a man who had spent his whole life building the company he was watching burn.

Crises serve to reveal or activate existing values, and narratives activate values in ways that generate support for rebuilding or reconstituting an organization or community. Values such as openness, honesty, responsibility, accountability, and trustworthiness play an important role in establishing the credibility of leaders and organizations before an event occurs (Ulmer et al., 2011). Following a crisis, values such as community, family, and altruistic support of those affected are often woven into narratives of renewal. Leaders draw on these values in creating meaning narratives for the loss.

A second attribute of renewal narratives is they tend to be forward looking, or prospective, rather than backward looking, or retrospective. Renewal is concerned with what will happen and how organizations and communities will move forward. These are stories of hope, possibility, and optimism. The prospective future-oriented focus is in contrast to more typical retrospective blame narratives. Following a crisis, these narratives concentrate on rebuilding rather than on issues of blame or fault (Ulmer et al., 2011). While seeking to rebuild and honor the past as part of a learning process, they typically feature descriptions of a future based on these lessons. Often these are general and generic descriptions that become more specific as the narrative matures.

The third characteristic of renewal focuses on the natural capacity of a system, community, or organization to recreate itself by capitalizing on the opportunities embedded within the crisis. These opportunities include the outpouring of goodwill, the leveraging of resources, and what is often an obvious need to change so that the same loss does not reoccur. A crisis may create many unique opportunities. The bankruptcy of General Motors in 2010 allowed the company to reorganize operations and shed significant debt and legacy costs. The company restructured relationships with dealers, merged several brands, and closed some unproductive plants. These changes could have happened only within the context of a severe crisis.

Finally, a leader or someone in a position of authority typically initiates this form of narrative. The CEO, mayor, or community leader who offers a forward-looking narrative early in the development of a crisis can often set in place a system of meaning around which activities, energy, and resources can coalesce (Seeger et al., 2005). These leaders' narratives sometimes take the form of a compelling vision of the future that energizes and motivates followers. Renewal discourse requires an effective leader or other spokesperson who is able to "structur[e] a particular reality for organizational stakeholders and publics," with the objective of persuading others to rebuild it better than it was before (Ulmer et al., 2011, p. 219). Such speakers must have the capacity to inspire, empower, and motivate. While the calls to action in renewal narratives are by definition persuasive, they also tend to be sincere expressions of the drive to renew and rebuild and are grounded in value positions. As such, renewal narratives are capable of engendering cooperation, commitment, and support through an emphasis on core values (Seeger et al., 2005).

A leader is often the focal point of a crisis and may emerge as a hero of the crisis (a topic we turn to in Chapter 8). The uncertainty, chaos, and confusion associated with a crisis create a need for the kind of direction and coherence that leadership can provide. The leader often becomes a personification of the crisis response and is usually visible in the response and often called on to provide public updates about what is being done, what progress is being made, and what might be expected in the future (Littlefield & Quenette, 2007). Crisis leaders and leadership processes may become attractors around which efforts to rebuild and renew are organized and coalesce.

CONCLUSION

The renewal narrative is a less common form of crisis response. Most often calls to work together to rebuild are overshadowed by divisive arguments about who will be blamed and who will pay for the crisis. But as a value-based and optimistic approach to creating a way forward, renewal narratives are compelling. They may spur more rapid and comprehensive recoveries and help organizations and communities create and take advantage of the inherent opportunities embedded in crises. Moreover, a renewal narratives can help facilitate self-organization and the development of stronger, more effective, and more resilient organizations, communities, and systems.

CASES TO CONSIDER

Narratives of renewal describe a kind of recovery that goes beyond simple resilience and rebuilding. They inspire shared visions of how the organization or community can be rebuilt to a level better than existed before the crisis. The human relationships and values central to the renewal process inspire creativity and commitment through self-organization that was likely unimaginable prior to crisis. Narratives of renewal have four primary features. First, they reaffirm the values that are central to the organization or community's heritage and identity and to its recovery. Second, they require a forward-looking focus, avoiding retrospective perspective and arguments over issues of blame. Third, they identify and exemplify the opportunities created by a crisis. Finally, they need strong voices of leadership. The following two cases capture the essence of renewal narratives. In the first case, the uniting force of values in renewal narratives is evident. The second case captures the importance of expressing the opportunities for improvement in narratives of renewal.

Values Revealed in the Renewal of Cantor Fitzgerald after 9/11

In the aftermath of the terrorist attacks on September 11, 2001, many businesses located in the World Trade Center were devastated by the loss of life. One company in particular felt the brunt of that loss. Cantor Fitzgerald, a stocks and bonds trading company, lost 658 of 960 employees that day. Cantor's offices were on the 101st to 105th floors of the North Tower, just above where one of the planes crashed. In the aftermath of this devastating loss, Howard Lutnick, Cantor Fitzgerald CEO, decided he would make sure Cantor would continue on and succeed so the company could help the grieving families of all those employees.

With so many employees lost and its offices destroyed, the company headquarters was essentially gone. Lutnick had lost many friends and coworkers, and his brother was killed. He noted that he too would have been at the World Trade Center except for the fact that he was dropping his son off for his first day of kindergarten.

In a tearful interview on ABC News on September 19, just days after the attack, Lutnick publicly committed to keep the company alive so that he could continue to support the families of those who were lost. The company was able to bring its trading markets back online within a week. Lutnick pledged to give 25 percent of the firm's profits for the next five years and committed to paying for ten years of health care for the families of its 658 former employees. According to CantorRelief.org, the firm donated a total of $180 million to support the victims of 9/11.

On *CNN Larry King Live,* in February 2009 Lutnick described his decision. As you read his comments, notice how he maintains a forward-looking focus as he consistently emphasizes the company's value of commitment to the families of the employees who were killed in the World Trade Center. In addition, he describes the efforts of the remaining employees as "Herculean" and praises their commitment.

So September 19th I came on to say that the company would give 25 percent—Cantor Fitzgerald, LP—25 percent of its profits would go to take care of these families for the long haul, because we were not just in this to try to take care of these families for a little while; but really to stay together with them for the very long time.

We cover not only the 658 families, but we had very young men and women who worked for us. So we had 30 fiancées and dozens of people who lived together. So we cover long-term domestic partners, as well, for 10 years. . . .

We lost 658 in New York, and we had about another 325 or 350 in New York. And then we had another 1,300 around the world. And it was really the rest of the world—our London office of 700 people—who worked around the clock to keep this company going. Our Dallas, our Chicago, Boston, Los Angeles, San Francisco, Darien, Connecticut, all of our regional offices all around the United States.

I mean these guys worked 24 hours a day, seven days a week, doing the work of all of their colleagues they lost in New York and our headquarters, to keep the company going. And they are the most impressive group of people you've ever met. I'm proud just to work with them. They are spectacular.

And employees that we have are Herculean. I mean I think they're doing the work of at least two, maybe even three people each.

So, you build your foundation. You make sure you know what you're doing. We have to take care of these families, so we have no room for waste.

Lutnick, H. (2002, February 22). *CNN Larry King live* [Television Broadcast]. New York, NY: Cable News Network. Retrieved from http://transcripts.cnn.com/TRAN SCRIPTS/0202/22/lkl.00.html. The full September 19 interview with ABC news can be viewed at https://www.youtube.com/watch?v=8rf35t4d214

Opportunities for Renewal in the GM Bankruptcy of 2009

On June 1, 2009, automotive giant General Motors filed for Chapter 11 reorganization in federal bankruptcy court. The company had been hit particularly hard by the financial collapse of 2008–2009 and in fiscal year 2005 lost over $10 billion. While the bankruptcy was precipitated by the financial collapse, the company had larger problems with flexibility, bureaucracy, and legacy costs. As you read GM CEO Fritz Henderson's comments, observe how he emphasizes opportunities made possible only by the crisis. The bankruptcy created an opportunity to rethink many fundamental assumptions and renew the company. Notice also his forward-looking perspective and how he expresses the values of loyalty and gratitude to investors, the governments of Canada and United States, customers, and others. He delivered these comments at the start of a press conference in Washington, D.C., on June 1, 2009:

> Good afternoon everyone. Thanks for joining us on a difficult but very important day for General Motors Corporation. You've all heard President Obama's comments, received copies of GM's press release, so let me offer a few observations before opening it up for your questions.
>
> Today marks a defining moment in the history of the General Motors Corporation. Our agreement with the U.S. Treasury and the governments of Canada and Ontario provide a fast-track plan to form a leaner, quicker, more customer-, completely product-focused company. One that's more cost competitive, and has a competitive balance sheet. The plan incorporates the terms of our recent agreements with the UAW and the CAW, as well as has received the support of a substantial portion of GM's unsecured bond holders. This new GM will be built with the strongest parts of our business, including our very finest products. We will have far less debt, fully competitive labor costs, and the ability to generate sustained and positive bottom line performance. The new GM will have a significantly stronger and healthier balance sheet, which will allow us to better support our brands and products through investment, increase our investment in new technology and be able to weather difficult times. Initially, the new GM will be owned primarily by the U.S. Department of the Treasury, the governments of Canada and Ontario, the

UAW's post-retirement healthcare VEBA trust, and the unsecured creditors, largely the bondholders of the old General Motors.

. . .

The actions we need to take to launch the new General Motors also include a number of extraordinarily difficult steps. Especially tough are the actions to close additional plants, and further reduce our U.S. hourly and salary deployment. I want to express my sincere and heartfelt appreciation and thanks to all who have sacrificed so much in this regard, who have sacrificed in the past, and will sacrifice in the future, including our dealers, suppliers, retirees, plant communities, as well as those who will continue to invest and in fact share the sacrifice in the future and in the days ahead. This includes very serious sacrifices on the part of other unsecured creditors of General Motors Corporation, whose recovery will come in the form of stock and warrants and reminds us of the importance of delivering in the future so that they get a recovery on their investment, and they are able to reduce the amount of damage that they sustained. It's the job of management to maximize the return of stock by producing results, including generating cash as soon as possible, to invest in our business, to grow, be product focused, and in fact to reward confidence of the taxpayer, taxpayers, of the U.S. and Canada, but of the very parties that we're asking to sacrifice so that there can be a new General Motors.

In the meantime, GM remains open for business. In addition to marketing and selling our cars and trucks, we will continue to honor our warranties, service our products, and support our customers. Importantly, our product launches and technology programs remain on track. In fact, a key part of our new agreement with UAW, for example, is our intention for the new General Motors to build a new small car here in the United States, and to do so profitably.

. . .

To our customers: We appreciate the confidence that many of you have placed in us over the years. Going forward, we intend to offer you nothing less than best in class cars and trucks, and even better service than before. And, to those of you who have never tried a GM vehicle, or have tried one and given up on us, we look forward to the chance to win your business and earn back your trust. Give us another chance. The GM that many of you knew, the GM that, in fact, let too many of you down, is history. Today marks the beginning of what will be a new company—a new GM dedicated to building the very best cars and trucks, highly fuel efficient, world class quality, green technology development, and with truly outstanding design. And above all, the new GM will be rededicated in our entirety as a leadership team to our customers.

A number of our cars and trucks, from the Chevy Volt, the Buick La Crosse, the Chevrolet Camaro and Equinox, the GMC Terrain, and the Cadillac SRX, amongst others, are already world class, or in the case of advanced technology, are breaking new ground. We need to make sure that all of our products are world class, and that will be our focus going forward. The days when General Motors would have fifteen launches, of which we would count on five or six of them being hits and the rest of them being okay, are history. We need to make sure that every one of our new vehicle launches is an outstanding car or truck.

Finally, on behalf of the entire GM team, some sincere thanks are in order, starting with President Obama and his automotive task force of the U.S. Department of the Treasury, and especially the U.S. and Canadian taxpayers, for the opportunity being provided to us to reinvent General Motors. We know we need to prove ourselves, and to do it every day, and we will. And we will do it right, and we will do it once. From here on, we move up. This is not the end of General Motors, but the start of a new and better chapter, one that needed to happen, and one that begins today. As we move forward, I want to make sure that we put a high priority on making sure that we are open and transparent. One way we will do that is through increased use of web chats and other information sources, and you'll be seeing and hearing a lot of me.

Henderson, F. (2009, June 1). *General Motors press conference.* Washington, DC: C-SPAN. Retrieved from http://www.c-span.org/video/?286752-1/general-motors -press-conference. Copyright by C-SPAN.

CHAPTER 7

Victim Narratives

VICTIM NARRATIVES ARE among the most common postcrisis stories. They focus primarily on the harm done by crises and personify both the physical and emotional damage that crises create. Although most victim narratives describe the suffering and recovery of individuals, they also have the potential to exploit victims and thereby manipulate public opinion. Compelling victim narratives are sometimes used to generate support for donations or for social change. By contrast, if organizations fail to show adequate compassion for those victimized by product or service failures, the resulting narratives can cause severe damage to their reputations (Coombs, 1999).

In crises caused by aggression such as terrorism or other forms of attack, victim narratives establish the innocence and vulnerability of those whose lives are affected by crises. In doing so, victim narratives often express the "absolute moral innocence" of those affected by the crisis in an effort to symbolize their struggles as a virtuous representation of the "moral community" to which they belong (King & deYoung, 2008, p. 125). For example, President Bush characterized those who died in the 9/11 attacks as innocent victims by declaring Americans were targeted for being "the brightest beacon for freedom and opportunity in the world" (King & deYoung, 2008, p. 124). By contrast, victim narratives focused on natural disasters typically depict victims as helpless to defend themselves against the powerful forces of nature. Bourk (2011), for example, analyzed the narratives emerging in media coverage following the 2004 Sri Lanka tsunami. A predominant theme characterized the tsunami as a monstrous force that grotesquely disfigured the many corpses it left behind. Portraying victims of natural disasters with such a high level of helplessness "can reduce political consciousness around the need to prepare for such happenings" (Bourk, 2011, p. 56).

Victim narratives can also serve as devices to influence and manipulate public opinion. For example, an organization recovering from a crisis can create a narrative portraying itself as victimized by a few malevolent or irresponsible employees. Kenneth Burke describes this as a process of victimage. In these cases, a scapegoat is offered as a vessel of some unwanted evils or transgression—"the sacrificial animal upon whose back the burden of these evils is ritualistically loaded" (Burke, 1973, pp. 39–40). In some cases, this narrative may be true, but in many cases, those singled out for blame in an organization are only a part of a much larger problem. These victimage narratives, however, may allow the rest of the organization to escape blame.

Conveying visual aspects of the victim narrative can also be problematic. According to Newton (2005), portraying crisis victims "begins and ends with power" (p. 434). Photojournalists, for example, have the power to portray subjects, particularly those victimized by crises, in a variety of contexts. The photographer may humanize or dehumanize victims. The crisis narrative is often influenced by the visual representation of its victims. Newton advises photojournalists to ask themselves questions such as, "Do we believe what we, the photojournalists, see is true to the exclusion of other ways of seeing the same situation—or perhaps a little 'more true' than the way someone else sees?" (p. 461). At a minimum, Newton (2005) argues that visual ethics invite practices that avoid causing harm. In short, the visual representation in victim narratives is both highly communicative and vulnerable to manipulation. In some cases, graphic images of victims have been described as disaster pornography for their explicit and dehumanizing portrayals. Others counter that such images are powerful illustrations of the harm.

In this chapter, we explore each of these features prevalent in victim narratives. We begin with definitions of victim and describe the characteristics of victimage. We then examine victim narratives from both extremes: the innocence and helplessness of victims and potential exploitation and manipulation. This distinction is based on the characterization and point of view that appears in the narrative plot. We also discuss the means by which victims, are often initially overlooked, find their voice and participate in the crisis victim narrative. We conclude with a discussion of how both organizations as a whole and individual employees can be victimized by crisis.

VICTIM DEFINED

A victim is a person or group harmed, damaged, or made to suffer from an act, circumstance, agency, or condition that is generally not of his or her own making and is of an illegitimate or unfair nature. Victims generally suffer as a consequence of conditions largely or entirely beyond their control. They are the subjects of sympathy and compassion and as such often generate economic, social, and spiritual support. "Pray for the victims" is a common request following a crisis. As with other social labels, victim is a conferred state. In some cases, however, individuals may claim the label for themselves. Victimage is the consequence of a wide range of conditions and acts, including crimes of various sorts, manipulation, abduction, rape, abuses, disorders, addictions, dependencies, exploitations, and syndromes. Individuals may be victimized by family, friends, strangers, organizations, systems, governments, society, or circumstances (Best, 1997).

Who are the victims of crisis? The most obvious are those directly and immediately harmed. Individuals who have died or been injured or had property damaged by a natural disaster or manufacturing facility explosion, for example, are typically described as victims. In other cases, victims are less visible or the consequences are less immediate. Individuals with underlying or chronic health conditions or at risk of exposure to chemical contamination, radiation, or adulterated food may be victims. Even less direct are the businesses and property owners who suffer longer-term harm as a consequence of a crisis or the family and friends of those harmed. In addition, first responders (police, fire, emergency managers) may become victims of a crisis. In some cases, the backgrounds and nationalities of victims can become an important part of the narrative. People from more than ninety countries died in the 9/11 World Trade Center attack, creating a point of international convergence around the crisis.

Victims have varying levels of immediacy to the crisis. Primary victims are those who actually experience the event. They are harmed by an explosion, infected by a tainted product, swindled out of money, or their homes and livelihood are devastated by natural disasters. Their losses and declining health are immediately visible and their needs clear. Primary victims, who are innocent and powerless, such as children or the disabled, engender particularly high levels of compassion and empathy. Secondary victims may suffer hardships extending from the crisis that are equally detrimental. Family members of a victim killed or disabled in a crisis may suffer extreme financial and emotional distress. Employees of organizations forced into bankruptcy by crises may face extended periods of unemployment and may be stigmatized by the organization's ethical wrongdoing. In some cases, primary victims may be revictimized during the recovery phase of a crisis. For example, government bureaucracy may be slow in providing the care and resources a victim needs. Insurance companies can deny coverage the victim assumed was in place. Media coverage can become invasive and exploitative as victims seek to recover. Sadly, crises sometimes attract unscrupulous individuals and organizations that take advantage of the situation through fraud and deception. In short, the number of victims and duration of suffering caused by crises extend well beyond the obvious.

Power inequities and moral positions are central components to the concept of victim. Victims have had something done to them or had something taken away and have been placed in powerless positions as a consequence. This loss was not a consequence of their actions. Thus, they are innocent and their loss is unfair. These losses, such as loss of money or property in a crime or loss of a home during a flood, may also create a state of dependency. Moreover, the psychological impact may create an additional level of powerlessness as the victims believe they have no control over what is happening to them. In addition, the moral dimensions of victimage deprive individuals of the right to pursue self-determination. Victimage is also inconsistent with the obligation to treat others in humanistic and dignified ways. A victim is usually described as someone who is treated unfairly, does not deserve what is happening, and is innocent. When people are victimized, they are often treated as objects or as means to an end. Their humanity, dignity, and rights have been violated. The victim of a crime or a crisis therefore is worthy of larger social support and assistance.

Because victims have been wrongly harmed in some way, they may be due a just response. Victims of crime, for example, may seek justice from the criminal courts. Victims of crisis, as we noted earlier, may turn to the courts for restitution or damages. Restorative justice has emerged as a popular approach to addressing the needs of crime victims. Enacting restorative justice, however, can create new forms of conflict. For example, some argue that in a crisis such as the 2012 Aurora, Colorado, shooting, the death penalty can bring "closure to families of homicide victims" (Berns, 2009, p. 383). By contrast, many families of murder victims argue there is "no such thing as closure" (p. 383). Others observe that the death penalty is enforced inconsistently in the United States with bias against the poor and minorities. Simply put, reaching resolution in a crisis narrative focusing on victims is complex and often intersected with questions of blame and responsibility.

VICTIMS AND RESPONSIBILITY

Victim narratives often focus on the issue of responsibility. Specifically, such narratives address the degree to which victims contributed to their own circumstances. At one extreme are victims who are blameless for the crises they face. Natural disasters and profound organizational failures are two types of crisis where victims bear no responsibility for the onset of their suffering. In natural disasters, crises are seen as acts of God not caused by human activity. In these cases, there is a strong imperative to help. Naturally, those who fail to heed evacuation warnings in low-lying or coastal areas during floods or hurricanes knowingly put themselves at risk. In these cases, victims are responsible for what happened to them. In most cases, however, natural disasters are seen as random forces of nature, leaving victims largely blameless. The blameless context of natural disasters often enables communities to shift their attention to prospective efforts to recover and enhance the community's resilience. For example, residents of western Kentucky endured a massive ice storm that left residents without electrical power in the frigid temperatures of January 2009. Inspired by positive interpersonal communication, residents created a narrative of camaraderie and collaboration that left them with community pride and positive recollections of the experience (Smith, Coffelt, Rives, & Sollitto, 2012).

Community leaders may respond to natural disasters by assuring victims that improvements will be made in the community's infrastructure. For example, in 2014, many Brunswick, Ohio, residents had no warning when an EF1 tornado touched down, traveling almost two miles through their community. The sirens had been silent for several years after computer hackers repeatedly turned on the sirens as a hoax, costing the community nearly $25,000 and causing local leaders to discontinue use of the sirens, opting instead for a telephone warning system. After the 2014 tornado, many residents complained they had not received the phone alert and had no warning that a massive tornado was descending. As a result, community leaders chose to reinstate the siren warning system (Brunswick to reactivate outdoor sirens, 2014).

Organizational failures can also occur suddenly, intensely endangering, disrupting, and victimizing the lives of consumers and residents. For example, the 300,000 residents of Charleston, West Virginia, were blameless victims when a Freedom Industries storage tank leaked 7,500 gallons of the chemical 4-methylcyclohexylmethanol into the Elk River. The leak contaminated the city's drinking water supply, leaving residents unable to drink or bathe in the water supplied to their homes for several weeks. Even after city officials declared the water safe, residents detected a foul odor in the water and many opted to avoid the water for several more weeks. By contrast, victims of diseases caused by tobacco products are seen as bearing some responsibility for their illnesses. The tobacco industries faced a crisis amid accusations of marketing dangerous products to children and having concealed information or misled customers about the addictive nature of nicotine. The resulting legal settlement involved billions of dollars. Despite this deception, those who use tobacco products did so by choice and therefore are typically seen as bearing some degree of responsibility for their own harm (Shanahan, Hopkins, Carlson, & Raymond, 2013).

In some cases, crisis narratives explicitly or implicitly assign blame to victims unfairly. Such blame is often assigned disproportionately to victims in large systemwide or organizational failures. For example, one of the narratives associated with the outbreak of foodborne illness in frozen pot pies produced by ConAgra (described in Chapter 5) blamed consumers for failure to cook the product to a sufficient temperature. Some auto companies have blamed victims for accidents involving sudden acceleration of vehicles. Smokers are seen as bearing some responsibility for their disease because they choose to smoke. Similarly, cases of hurricane damage blame victims for continuing to build and rebuild in vulnerable areas. The question of culpability is often featured in media accounts, as described in Chapter 4.

In other cases, victims are ignored by narratives that essentially render them invisible. For example, residents of the Mississippi Delta area that was decimated by Hurricane Katrina expressed outrage at the fact that attention from the national media and agencies such as the Federal Emergency Management Administration focused almost entirely on New Orleans (Anthony & Sellnow, 2011). Many residents insisted the media's exclusive focus on Louisiana put Mississippi residents at a considerable disadvantage in the recovery process. In other natural disasters, such as floods, narratives celebrating the recovery of communities often fail to account for victims whose low-cost housing in low-lying areas of the community was lost and not replaced. The only option for some residents in the aftermath of such flood devastation is to leave the community in search of affordable housing.

Victims may also be intentionally ignored. For example, in 2008, researchers argued that coverage in China's *People's Daily* treats AIDS "as a relatively innocuous social problem for the country" and presents victims in general and vague terms rather than as "specific individuals with clear faces and real-life backgrounds" (Dong, Chang, & Chen, 2008, p. 370). Whether isolated victims are ignored intentionally or unintentionally, this lack of concern or attention results in a troubling failure to address their needs following a crisis. The wide range of variance in victim narratives is in part due to the way power or powerlessness is framed. Victims are often placed in powerless positions and struggle to make their stories heard. The level of visibility is important in generating attention and ultimately in securing resources for those victimized by a crisis.

OVERLOOKED VICTIMS FINDING THEIR VOICE

Advocacy for victims may take many forms. The Sandy Hook parents' group we discussed earlier is an effort to reclaim power and provide voice to the children victimized by the tragic shooting. The told their stories to a number of audiences including politicians in an effort to change gun laws. Popular culture can also give voice to forgotten victims through radio, television, movies, and music. Television and radio talk shows often bring attention to victims otherwise overlooked or misunderstood by dominant crisis narratives. Oprah Winfrey's long-running television program, for example, afforded victims "a public forum for speaking out, for naming the unnamable" (Marshall & Pienaar, 2008, p. 536). Winfrey frequently exposed an international audience to problems endured by victims of the pharmaceutical industry and food processing industry, as well as incidents of environmental pollution and other social risks. Her program thus provided a podium for otherwise overlooked victims. The *Oprah Winfrey Show*, as with other television talk shows, provided "a space for 'breaking the silence' and beginning a path to recovery" for victims of many crises (Marshall & Pienaar, 2008, p. 536).

Popular narrative and documentary films such as *The China Syndrome* (1979), *The Insider* (1999), *Outbreak* (1995), *Erin Brockovich* (2000), *Bowling for Columbine* (2002), and *The Smartest Guys in the Room* (2005) often focus on the unseen victims of corporate incompetence and corruption. These narratives frequently take a victim's point of view to illustrate the harm and provide moral lessons. Movies of this magnitude may influence public policymaking by popularizing victim narratives and bringing issues to national audiences. *Erin Brockovich*, for example, called attention to the impact of industrial contamination of public drinking water and increased public awareness of the ensuing public health crises. Such popular narratives can stimulate policy change that both recognizes existing victims and protects citizens against future risks.

A victim's story is also a common part of the journalistic account, as described in Chapter 3. Background news stories about victims, their histories, and families are human interest stories that help humanize and personify a crisis. These stories are often structured around memories of those who died and the struggles of those who survived. Sometimes the victim/survivor account is framed around the anniversary of an event. In these cases, there may be a reading of the names of victims who died in a crisis, or victims who are survivors may be asked to speak. Victims are often the focus of memorializing narratives as we describe in Chapter 9. In some cases, these news stories have been critiqued as inappropriately exploiting victims, as creating a second level of harm, for invasion of privacy, for intrusion at a moment of trauma and grief, and for dehumanizing victims. Some wish to reclaim their privacy and simply be left alone. Professional associations such as DART Center for Journalism and Trauma (2003) have provided ethical guidelines for covering victims of crises. These include, "Always treat victims with dignity and respect . . . with sensitivity, including knowing when and how to back off" (p. 3).

ORGANIZATIONS AS VICTIMS

An organization as a whole can also be victimized by a crisis. Victimage on an organizational level can be fostered by internal forces, such as unavoidable failures or employee sabotage, or by external forces, such as product tampering, terrorism, natural disasters, or guilt by association. Malaysia Airlines suffered two major crises in 2014 that so devastated the company it was on the brink of bankruptcy. In the first event, Malaysia Airlines flight 370 simply disappeared. In the second, Malaysia Airlines flight 17 was shot down over Ukraine as the country faced a civil war. Malaysia Airlines, with heavy losses, was nationalized by the Malaysian government as a way to keep the company intact (Tan, 2014).

Stakeholders at every level of an organization can suffer from catastrophic failures. Stakeholders may include employees, members of the community, suppliers, customers, shareholders, and others. During crises, the expectations of distinct stakeholder may conflict. Marcus and Goodman (1991) observe that victims of organizational accidents demand corrective action and compensation that can be costly to the organization and its shareholders. Thus, organizations face a dilemma: meeting the needs and demands of victims can create conflict with a separate set of stakeholders—those who have a financial stake in the organization. Simply put, "if managers are accommodating to victims, shareholders are likely to suffer" (Marcus & Goodman, 1991, p. 281). For example, wide-ranging recalls such as those involving Toyota for acceleration issues or General Motors for ignition failures can be costly to future productivity, sales, and employee wages.

Dissatisfaction among employees can also cultivate crises for organizations. Communicating dissatisfaction upward is essential for organizations to effectively monitor and respond to problems that employees identify (Kassing & Armstrong, 2002). Failure to account for such dissent allows employee dissatisfaction to smolder, leading to workplace resistance. This resistance manifests in activities ranging from production slowdowns to outright sabotage (Prasad & Prasad, 2001). The term *sabotage*, by some accounts, originated when disgruntled workers, during the industrial revolution, threw their wooden shoes, *sabots*, into the gears of the machines they were operating to stop production. This potential for saboteurs to disrupt production, to the point of creating an organizational crisis, remains a threat to organizations today.

External adversaries engaging in product tampering or terrorism also victimize organizations. Perhaps the best-known case of product tampering occurred in 1982 when four people in the Chicago area died after consuming Extra-Strength Tylenol capsules containing potassium cyanide. Evidence indicated that the capsules were tampered with at the retail level rather than within the production facility, thereby ruling out employee sabotage. No motive for the crime was ever revealed and no one was ever arrested in the case. Johnson & Johnson, the parent company, lost an estimated $100 million in a massive recall of their product. The company was able to rapidly recover, however, in part because the narrative of victimage assigned blame to others. The Tylenol case led to extensive reforms in packaging of over-the-counter medications.

Terrorism is an increasing threat for organizations. Although defining terrorism is a difficult and often controversial process, we consider terrorism an attack on some facet of an organization in an effort to dissuade that organization from pursuing its goals. For example, the labs of organizations engaged in animal research have been destroyed by members of groups such as People for the Ethical Treatment of Animals. Controversies over landownership and use have inspired attacks on employees who work at organizations such as Dole in Latin America. While one can debate the justification of those who engage in such attacks, these violent acts create a form of victimage for organizations.

Natural disasters can also victimize organizations. The devastating tsunami in Japan turned Tokyo Electric Power Company's (TEPCO) Fukushima nuclear power plant into a global crisis. Rising water and loss of power crippled the capacity of some hospitals in Louisiana to serve immobile patients during Hurricane Katrina. Droughts can leave both large-scale food producers and small farmers bankrupt as crops fail and providing animals with food and water becomes overwhelming. Worse, these drastic drops in food production can lead to food insecurity for entire regions and nations. The possibilities for natural disasters to incapacitate organizations are profuse.

Through a form of guilt by association, the failures of one or a few organizations can also victimize an entire industry. Narratives of public disdain arose for the entire oil industry as the world watched daily coverage of oil spill disasters caused by Exxon in Alaska and again by British Petroleum on the American Gulf Coast. When the failures of a few organizations victimize an entire industry, spokespersons for others not directly involved in the crisis often speak up in defense of themselves and their industry (Millner, Veil, & Sellnow, 2011). Millner et al. label this process proxy communication and recommend organizations include, as part of their precrisis planning, strategies for defending themselves if another organization's crisis creates a narrative that victimizes an entire industry with guilt by association. For example, nuclear power producers worldwide were asked to explain their strategies for protecting their plants against earthquakes and tsunamis after TEPCO's disaster.

ORGANIZATIONAL EMPLOYEES AS VICTIMS

Organizations can seek to purge themselves of responsibility for a crisis by creating narratives featuring an employee, employees, or other affiliate of the organization as a scapegoat. Expunging this individual or entity from the organization completes the narrative with the organization being absolved of any guilt. In essence, a part of the organization is sacrificed to preserve the reputation of the whole. For example, *Exxon*

Valdez captain Joseph Hazelwood was accused of intoxication and negligence when grounding the tanker that caused the 1989 oil spill in Prince William Sound, Alaska. He was fired by Exxon and vilified publicly but was acquitted of the most serious charges filed against him. The incident ended his career. To some extent, the focus on Hazelton removed or distracted some of the public's attention away from Exxon.

In some cases, crises are completely the fault of a few individual employees or an affiliate organization. For example, gross negligence by an individual in the transportation industry can cause horrific accidents. External suppliers can sell an unsafe food ingredient, leading to product contamination and illness or death for hundreds or thousands of consumers. In many cases, however, creating a narrative of victimage is overly simplistic. In these examples, questions are likely to arise about how closely individuals are supervised or how much scrutiny goes into the selection of suppliers.

CONCLUSION

Victim narratives are among the most common and compelling postcrisis stories. They focus on the physical and emotional harm done by crises usually to innocent people who bear little or no responsibility for what happened. Whether in news accounts, on blogs, or in popular films, these narratives can be powerful and compelling. Victim narratives produce positive outcomes such as increasing visibility of those suffering, generating support, emphasizing the need for policy changes, and building alliances to accelerate recovery. Victims often seek opportunities to tell their stories so that others may learn from their loss. As we described in Chapter 3, this is a way meaning may be created for the loss.

Victim narratives can also foster negative outcomes such as manipulating, ignoring, punishing, and exploiting victims and placing them in voiceless and powerless positions. Victims who perceive themselves as ignored or silenced by victim narratives may have the capacity to speak out through alternative mediums such as radio, television, movies, music, or social media. In addition, memorials, such as those described in Chapter 9, communicate the experience of the victims. Memorials, for example, often include the names of victims.

The victim narrative is particularly powerful because it is the most direct expression of personal loss. A crisis by definition creates some victims who bear physical and psychological harm. The level of harm they experience is directly related to the ultimate social, political, and economic costs of the crisis. Victims are always featured in the larger crisis narrative and play a central role in accounts, memorial narratives, and blame narratives. Victims and their stories are also essential to the ultimate outcome and resolution of the crisis.

CASES TO CONSIDER

Many victim narratives express some degree of meaning or resolution for the suffering of innocent victims of crises. Victims themselves often contribute to the victim narrative, conveying the significance of the crisis in their life and the resulting self-discovery. The discovery of meaning also results in lessons learned and corrective actions, including policy changes that must occur to avoid similar crises in the future. The following two cases illustrate the capacity for victim narratives to assign meaning and resolution to crises. The YouTube series on the Station Nightclub fire creates an avenue for victims to tell their stories of remembrance, healing, and lessons learned. Dr. Kent Brantly's statement after receiving treatment for Ebola at Emory University exemplifies how individuals find meaning in their suffering and contribute this meaning to the greater victim narrative.

Remembering Victims of the Station Nightclub Fire

The devastating Station Nightclub fire occurred in West Warwick, Rhode Island, on February 20, 2003. At the time, the fire was the fourth worst nightclub fire in U.S. history, with 100 dead and 250 injured. The band Great White was performing at the nightclub, and the show included pyrotechnics, which ignited flammable sound insulation. The ensuing fire engulfed the club in five and a half minutes. To commemorate the tenth anniversary of the disaster, filmmaker David Bettencourt produced a YouTube video series remembering the event and sharing the experiences of the victims: *The Station: Learn. Remember. Heal* (available at youtube. com/TheStationWebseries). The series includes interviews with relatives of those killed, survivors who escaped, and officials who responded to the event and helped manage the aftermath. In these videos, the victims of this horrific fire share their experiences, feelings, emotions, and their efforts to recover and rebuild their lives. The documentary captures the voices and experiences of the victims. In the seventh video, the speaker shares the key lesson learned from the fire: sprinkler systems in public places such as the Station Nightclub can and must be equipped with life-saving sprinkler systems (Davis, 2013).

Finding Meaning in the 2014 Ebola Outbreak

Dr. Kent Brantly was an American physician working for the Christian relief organization Samaritan's Purse in Liberia, Africa, where he had moved with his wife and children in 2013 to serve as medical director of a clinic. He contracted Ebola from the patients he was treating and soon after was evacuated to Emory University Hospital to receive treatment. He released the following statement soon after his condition stabilized. As you read the statement, observe how Dr. Brantly finds meaning for his suffering. Consider how the selfless commitment he shows toward the people of Liberia and toward treating those with Ebola fits with the larger victim narrative focused on the Ebola outbreak of 2014.

> I am writing this update from my isolation room at Emory University Hospital, where the doctors and nurses are providing the very best care possible. I am growing stronger every day, and I thank God for His mercy as I have wrestled with this terrible disease. I also want to extend my deep and sincere thanks to all of you who have been praying for my recovery as well as for Nancy [Nancy Writebol, an American nursing assistant who also contracted Ebola] and for the people of Liberia and West Africa. My wife Amber and I, along with our two children, did not move to Liberia for the specific purpose of fighting Ebola. We went to Liberia because we believe God called us to serve Him at ELWA Hospital.
>
> One thing I have learned is that following God often leads us to unexpected places. When Ebola spread into Liberia, my usual hospital work turned more and more toward treating the increasing number of Ebola patients. I held the hands of countless individuals as this terrible disease took their lives

away from them. I witnessed the horror first-hand, and I can still remember every face and name.

When I started feeling ill on that Wednesday morning, I immediately isolated myself until the test confirmed my diagnosis three days later. When the result was positive, I remember a deep sense of peace that was beyond all understanding. God was reminding me of what He had taught me years ago, that He will give me everything I need to be faithful to Him.

Now it is two weeks later, and I am in a totally different setting. My focus, however, remains the same—to follow God. As you continue to pray for Nancy and me, yes, please pray for our recovery. More importantly, pray that we would be faithful to God's call on our lives in these new circumstances."

"First statement from Ebola patient: 'I am growing stronger.'" (2014, August 8). *NBC News*. Retrieved from http://www.nbcnews.com/storyline/ebola-virus-outbreak/first -statement-ebola-patient-i-am-growing-stronger-n176271. Courtesy of Religion News Service.

CHAPTER 8

Hero Narratives

NARRATIVES OF VARIOUS TYPES are structured around plot, setting, characterization, atmosphere, point of view, theme, and conflict. Plot often involves tensions and conflict between key characters, usually an antagonist and a protagonist. Characterization creates a point of view and usually drives tension and conflict in the narrative. The hero or heroine is a character and plot element typical of many narratives and is characteristic of the postcrisis communication narrative environment. In fact, the hero narrative, built around a central protagonist, is probably one of the oldest archetypes and can be traced to ancient Greek epic stories. In these stories, the hero is almost always male and usually a warrior overcoming disproportional odds in achieving some just victory.

This chapter examines the hero narrative and its function of personifying a positive, proactive response to crisis conditions. The hero narrative may serve as a counter to the loss of control and destruction associated with a crisis and also to highlight and model desired prosocial behaviors. Hero narratives are the consequence of the drama, chaos, and uncertainty created by the crisis and take several forms. Processes for developing hero status are described, including exhibiting self-sacrifice, resoluteness, altruistic behavior, rising to the requirements of the situation, and conferring hero status. We also describe some of the consequences of the crisis hero narrative.

THE HERO

The hero is an idealized cultural trope that can be traced back to the earliest narrative traditions. In the myth of Hercules, the hero was part human, part god and able to perform miraculous feats of strength in the service of good and the defeat of evil. As both human and divine, Hercules illustrated that heroes are often common people who accomplish uncommon feats. The Nordic hero Beowulf proved his strength and courage by defeating the monster Grendel. In so doing, he protected the larger community and was eventually rewarded by becoming king. In both cases, the hero as a protagonist is the primary force overcoming some evil or threatening antagonist. The mythological hero often takes on a journey, quest, or struggle that exceeds the capacity of the normal person (Campbell, 1973).

The hero story is closely associated with the great man/woman myth whereby a person through charisma, intelligence, strength, skill, or wisdom may have a disproportional impact on history. In great man myths, attributions of broad social and historical outcomes are made to the influence of an individual/leader/hero. The nineteenth-century writer Thomas Carlyle argued that history is a function of the decisions and actions of a few great men who propel the masses of humanity by virtue of their leadership. Alexander the Great, William the Conqueror, Napoleon Bonaparte, and George Washington, among others, are sometimes seen as great men who changed history. In the most common hero narratives, the great man possesses some unique attribute of skill or may bring some skill acquired in another context to the crisis. The great person, however, may also rise to the occasion and discover inner strength or skill during the intensity of a crisis.

A variety of distinctive behaviors may qualify as heroic, including risk taking, strength, altruism, moral courage, bravery, intelligence, wit, or specific skills. Heroes manifest leadership behaviors and take responsibility for the well-being of others at the risk of their own well-being. The attributes of the hero, however, are, by definition, extraordinary in the sense they go beyond what might be expected by the average person (Schulman, 1996). Heroic acts are distinctive because both the conditions of the crisis and the behaviors of the hero are extraordinary.

Following a 1904 coal mine disaster that claimed 181 lives, including 2 employees who died trying to rescue others, industrialist Andrew J. Carnegie established the Carnegie Hero Fund Commission to celebrate and support the everyday heroes of civilization. Carnegie Medals for Heroism are generally awarded to average persons who rescue others from life-threatening situations, such as fires, drowning, automotive accidents, or assaults. The commission publicly recognizes heroic acts with the Carnegie Medal and provides financial assistance when individuals are injured or killed while performing these acts. Since its inception, the commission has recognized 9,675 civilian heroes (Carnegie Hero Fund Commission, 2014) and holds up these heroes as models for others and as exemplars of desirable social attributes.

Other heroic subtypes include military figures, religious figures, political figures, martyrs, adventurers, underdogs, bureaucratic heroes, and whistleblowers. Two of these types, the Good Samaritan and the civic hero, are individuals who "attempt to save others from harm . . . while putting themselves at risk" or a person "who steps up to help others in need" (Franco, Blau, & Zimbardo, p. 102). Helping others overcome potential harm while putting one's own well-being at risk or taking extraordinary action in the service of some larger goal or value is the defining plot structure of the hero narrative.

The hero phenomenon is also a social ideal in its manifestation in leadership and in the civic virtue and self-sacrifice it manifests (Franco et al., 2011). Sociological investigations describe heroism as prosocial activity with five defining characteristics. Heroism is undertaken (1) in service to others in need—be it a person, group, or community—or in defense of socially sanctioned ideas or a new social standard; (2) voluntarily; (3) with recognition of possible risks or costs; (4) when an individual anticipates and is willing to accept sacrifice; and (5) without external gain anticipated at the time of the act (Franco et al., p. 101). Prosocial behaviors are directed toward helping others and are grounded in concern for their well-being, rights, needs, and values. As Philip Zimbardo notes, "Simply put . . . the key to heroism is a concern for other people in need—a concern to defend a moral cause, knowing there is a personal risk, done without expectation of reward" (Zimbardo, 2011). Heroism may also be learned, modeled, or serve as a form of instructed behavior, and, in fact, heroes are often venerated as with the Carnegie Medal social ideals and models for others. The hero narrative is designed to instruct and promote larger civic virtues in response to crises. In a way, the hero narrative functions as a social lesson in the implicit appropriate duty that is not required of every citizen but is encouraged in times of need.

A hero narrative may also be understood as a collective social response to a shared sense of helplessness and the threat of loss (Bennett,

2004). In this way, a group or community can be heroic in its response to a threat. Communities that face natural disasters such as floods often manifest extreme prosocial behavior in the form of volunteerism. Members of the community may donate equipment and supplies and work long hours sandbagging in heroic efforts to fight rising waters. In some cases, the established political system may function as a hero. Elisabeth Anker (2005) argued that following 9/11, the media portrayed American political systems as manifesting a compelling national identity of heroic redeemer. America was given a mandate for taking heroic action in response to villains of who had attacked the country.

CRISIS AND THE CREATION OF HEROES

The hero as a character and plot device emerges from the crisis situation. The crisis creates a conflict situation that can be resolved through the intervention of a heroic person or act and therefore can be understood as a situation creating a need for heroic acts to achieve some resolution. A crisis not only creates a narrative space appropriate for heroes to emerge but also provides the necessary dramaturgical conditions for hero development, including a high-risk situation where individuals are facing the potential of serious harm. The structural ambiguity and uncertainty of a crisis create the opportunity for symbolic leaders to emerge as heroes and reach a high level of public notoriety and recognition. Monahan and Gregory (2001) employ the status appropriation model to explore hero development in the 9/11 crises. This model "conceptualizes status as the product of dramaturgical processes of interaction; processes influenced by, and reflected in, the social, cultural, and structural factors that comprise the context of the event" (p. 2).

The context of 9/11 was a dramatic social event that positioned first responders as hero figures as they engaged in self-sacrificial behaviors consistent with altruism. The terrorist attacks on the World Trade Center resulted in the deaths of over four hundred first responders: New York City firefighters, police officers, port authority police officers, and emergency medical technicians. Many died as they sought to help others, including New York City Fire Department chaplain Father Mychal Judge, who was comforting the injured when the second tower collapsed. Another two thousand first responders were injured, and many face ongoing medical issues. These heroic acts stood in opposition to the 9/11 terrorists who set out to intentionally harm others. In this way, a hero emerges from the dramatic events of the crisis and is usually instrumental in helping resolve the crisis by containing or limiting harm. In the hero narrative, the protagonist is necessary to overcome or offset the harm.

Hero is a conferred status—a social attribution made by others rather than by the person who engaged in the act (Franco et al., 2011). Those helped during the crisis may publicly designate a person a hero. More often, the hero is designated as such by the larger community, and in most cases, the media framing propagates the hero status. In other cases, political or community leaders may designate a particular action as heroic and may publicly acknowledge the behavior with honors, citations, and tributes. The process whereby a person is called a hero is often a public ritual where the heroic actions are recognized, recounted, and praised. In 2013, President Barack Obama honored the six school staff members who died protecting students at the Sandy Hook Elementary School in Newtown, Connecticut. They were posthumously awarded the Presidential Citizens Medal, given to U.S. citizens "who [have] performed exemplary deeds or services for his or her country or fellow citizens" and "who have helped their country or their fellow citizens through one or more extraordinary acts" (White House, 2014). In calling the Sandy Hook staff heroes, he noted, "They gave their lives to protect the precious children in their care. They gave all they had for the most innocent and helpless among us" (Friedman, 2013).

These designations fit into larger media frames. Fraher (2011) notes, for example, that Captain Chesley (Sully) Sullenberger, the pilot of flight 1549, was almost immediately labeled a hero after successfully landing an Airbus A320 on the Hudson Rive after it had hit a flock of birds on takeoff, ruining the engines. The media immediately began referring to Captain Sullenberger as "the hero pilot," a status subsequently reified by appearances with New York City Mayor Michael Bloomberg and President Obama. We discuss Captain Sullenberger further in a case study at the end of this chapter.

Hero narratives are particularly important following a crisis because they interject a positive element into what is otherwise usually a negative story. The hero, standing in opposition to the harm caused by the crisis, helps create order out of the crisis and reduces or contains the harm suffered by virtue of skills, determination, and self-sacrifice. The hero narrative is a point where values of community, altruism, and selflessness are inserted into a crisis. These values create collective social understanding that it is possible to overcome some of the harm associated with a crisis through personal actions, courage, strength, and tenacity. Through heroism, it is possible to fight back and institute some human control over a chaotic crisis. Moreover, modeling of self-sacrificial behaviors promotes concern for others and community. A hero points the way for others. A fundamental function of the crisis hero narrative is empowerment.

HERO TYPES

Three primary hero types are evident in the postcrisis environment: the citizen/everyman hero, the first responder as hero, and the leader as hero. In each of these narratives, the hero character emerges from a different place or role in the postcrisis scene and carries a unique standpoint and motivation. Each narrative subtype therefore creates a different ethos.

In the citizen/everyman as hero, a common person, usually at the scene of the event, takes some action, often risking his or her own well-being to limit harm or provide help to victims. The citizen is usually poorly equipped to serve as a hero in terms of training or background but nonetheless steps up to help. Because the average citizen has no inherent obligation to act, this hero type is especially noteworthy. Research, however, generally supports the contention that a significant proportion of crisis victims are helped first by friends, family, or neighbors, usually because they are at the scene of the event. The citizen/everyman as hero narrative usually includes themes of acting without thinking—helping a friend, doing what was needed, and simply following instincts. The citizen/everyman as hero is also associated with a spirit of volunteerism. The volunteer rises to the occasion to meet a need.

Crises have a transformative quality. In the case of the crisis hero, an ordinary person placed in an extraordinary circumstance can be transformed into a hero. This "everyman as a hero" or the "unlikely hero" narrative suggests that strength, wisdom, and bravery are widely distributed in the population and people rise to the occasion when they confront threatening circumstances. Most large-scale crises include a variety of everyman hero stories of risking harm to help others, making self-sacrifices, or engaging in some form of altruistic behavior. This is a situational notion of heroism grounded in a larger view sometimes described as the banality of heroism. The capacity to act in heroic and altruistic ways is, according to some, quite common (Franco et al., 2011). Altruism, a selfless concern for the welfare of others, often in extreme conditions like crisis, is manifest in acts motivated by a sincere desire to help others in need. Volunteerism is a natural crisis response as individuals seek to help others by providing help and is closely associated with altruistic values. This larger value of selflessness activated during a crisis may also help explain other phenomena such as the reduction of crime that typically occurs after a major crisis (Szalavitz, 2012). Much of the symbolic power of a layperson acting out of instinct or altruism is precisely because that person is not an emergency response professional.

In contrast, the first responder—firefighter, police officer, emergency response professional—is trained to provide assistance in emergency situations, has the appropriate equipment, and is experienced. First responders' job is to routinely engage in behavior others would call heroic. As part of their professional obligations, they are expected to help those in need and regularly place themselves in harm's way. In cases where first responders are seen as going beyond what might be required for their normal professional obligations, such as obviously risking their life to help others, they may be conferred heroic status. Probably the most powerful archetype of the first responder as hero is the firefighter. As quintessential first responders, firefighters are trained to rush into burning buildings at the very moment others are fleeing. Helping others, saving property, and risking their lives to save others is their job. Images of firefighters emerging from burning buildings, rescuing victims, and braving conditions most others would find paralyzing are standard media frames for disasters. Political figures touring disaster sites often pose with firefighters, and International Firefighters' Day is celebrated every year on May 4 as a way for the larger public to acknowledge the social value of the profession.

One variant is the reporter as first responder and hero. Journalists are often among the first on the scene of a crisis and, aided by digital technologies, can provide near real-time reports on the status of a crisis. They may even take extraordinary risks to report on a story because they believe telling the story is important. The group Reporters without Borders maintains a list of so-called information heroes who have sacrificed their safety in war zones, conflict regions, and disaster areas to tell important stories. Reporters played a particularly instrumental role in the aftermath of Hurricane Katrina by reporting on those left behind in New Orleans. The reports created public pressure on the government response and bolstered those efforts, thereby leading to more effective rescue efforts and probably saving lives.

The leader as hero narrative is common in crises. It is most likely to emerge when a designated leader in a situation takes some decisive action that limits or contains the harm. In these cases, the visibility of leaders as symbols and models of stability, calm, and resoluteness helps them emerge as heroes. Because leaders already occupy positions of authority and responsibility in a system, they are visible and can exert some level of control by allocating resources and making decisions. The leader usually emerges as the official spokesperson for the crisis and is thus in the media spotlight. One exception is the emergent crisis leader—someone other than the designated leader who steps up and takes command of the situation. The emergent leader may be part of the more general emergent self-organization process.

In addition, the designated leader in a community or organization may reduce confusion, anxiety, and harm by exerting authority and control during a crisis. The confusion and uncertainty associated with a crisis usually create conditions for the emergence of more authoritarian leadership than might be manifest in normal conditions. Crisis leaders are expected to take charge and demonstrate a command of the situation. By imposing order on chaos, often through demonstrating and modeling personal calm and strength, the leader may become a hero.

New York City Mayor Rudy Giuliani has been called one of the heroes of 9/11. Prior to the disaster, he was known as a law-and-order mayor, and many observers criticized his leadership as too authoritarian. Some even suggested he did not respect civil liberties. However, following the disaster, he was widely praised for taking charge of the situation and projecting resolve, strength, and resilience in managing the event. Another example comes from Fargo, North Dakota, which has experienced several devastating floods. The 1997 flood of the Red River was among the most severe, causing an estimated $3.5 billion in damage. Dennis Walaker helped coordinate the flood response as Fargo's public works operations manager. Following his heroic efforts, Walaker was elected mayor in 2006 and has focused his leadership on increasing Fargo's resilience to an ongoing risk of annual flooding.

COMPETING HERO NARRATIVES

While the hero narrative generally celebrates success in responding to a crisis, in some cases, the narrative is more controversial and complex. Competing narratives reflect divergent notions of idealized behavior and serve to enrich the story. For example, a person is identified as a hero and rejects that designation as stigmatizing and unwarranted. This phenomenon is common for first responders who have faced a highly traumatic crisis. Many of the first responders who survived the collapse of the World Trade Center reject the hero title, noting that the real heroes are those who died trying to help others. First responders may also note that they were simply doing their jobs and the title "hero" is inappropriate.

In other cases, there is a debate as to whether the label is appropriate. The media are often quick to attribute heroic status to particular forms of behavior that fit the existing media frame. Richard Phillips, captain of the MV *Maersk Alabama* during its 2009 hijacking by Somali pirates, was initially lauded as a hero by the media. Subsequently members of his crew charged that his behavior was reckless, arrogant, and not heroic. Franco and Zimbardo (2006) note that it is not uncommon for behavior that might be judged as heroic in one case to be seen as reckless in another.

There are also cases where an individual may step up to take a leadership role during a crisis and violate expectations for what is appropriate. A leader may be seen as too eager to exercise authoritarian control, for example. Following the attempted assassination of President Ronald Reagan in 1981, Secretary of State Alexander Haig tried to reduce the public's level of uncertainty and in a hastily assembled press conference at the White House famously said, "As of now, I am in control here, in the White House, pending return of the Vice President and in close touch with him. If something came up, I would check with him, of course." (CBS News.com Staff, 2001). While some suggested Secretary Haig was showing appropriate crisis leadership, others noted his statement was not consistent with the line of succession outlined in the U.S. Constitution.

Finally, the hero narrative may be complicated by an individual's larger character flaw or shortcoming, sometimes described as "feet of clay." For example, some first responders have had substance abuse problems or psychological difficulties as a consequence of their stressful jobs, and individuals with criminal records have been known to help others during disasters. These flaws may humanize heroes within a larger narrative, making them more accessible.

CONCLUSION

A hero is the ideal and, during the destruction and despair of a crisis, provides a point of positive reference within the larger narrative. The hero narrative provides a social comfort and vicarious relief from what can be an overwhelming sense of loss and loss of control (Goren, 2007). The hero or heroine is a central figure in many crisis narratives. As the protagonist, he or she is the solution to the antagonistic crisis conditions. It is not surprising, therefore, that almost all crises give rise to some heroes.

The hero is also held up as a model of crisis behavior for others. Heroes help us understand what we stand for and value and how we would like to behave during the extreme conditions imposed by a crisis. As mayor, first responder, or common citizen, the hero manifests the prosocial behaviors and self-sacrifice that allow social order and community to continue within the chaos and disruption of the crisis.

CASES TO CONSIDER

In this chapter we have noted how crises create tragic circumstances that can be resolved through the actions of heroic people. Their actions institute some level of human control over the seemingly hopeless and chaotic circumstances of crises. Hero or heroine narratives publicly designate people as heroes. Thus, hero status is conferred by others such as those having been rescued, media reporters, and community or national leaders. An ordinary person placed in an extraordinary circumstance can be transformed into a hero. First responders who persevere in their rescue efforts with exceptional skill despite overwhelming danger can be proclaimed heroes. Similarly, community and national leaders who reduce confusion, anxiety, and harm by exerting authority and control during a crisis are also often featured in hero narratives. The following two cases exemplify how hero status is conferred on ordinary people in the Aurora, Colorado, shooting and Captain Sullenberger, the pilot who landed a jetliner in the Hudson River.

Heroic Actions in the Aurora, Colorado, Shooting

On July 20, 2012, James Eagan Holmes entered an opening night screening of the movie *The Dark Knight Rises* in Aurora, Colorado. After setting off tear gas grenades, he proceeded to shoot at the audience with different types of firearms. Seventy people were injured and twelve people lost their lives in the incident. Three of those who died were ordinary people declared heroes because they were killed protecting their loved ones while using their own bodies as human shields. This news article tells the story of their heroic acts and the character of the heroes. As you read the article, note how the three men who are proclaimed heroes exerted some level of control with their spontaneous and selfless actions in the chaotic instant of the gunman's attack.

In final acts of valor, Jon Blunk, Matt McQuinn, and Alex Teves used their bodies to shield their girlfriends as convicted madman James Holmes turned the Aurora complex into a shooting gallery:

> Three survivors of the Colorado movie-theater massacre escaped with minor wounds, but were left with broken hearts because their heroic boyfriends died saving them.
>
> Blunk's girlfriend, Jansen Young; McQuinn's girlfriend, Samantha Yowler; and Teves' gal pal Amanda Lindgren made it out of the bloodbath—but they would have been killed had it not been for the loves of their lives.
>
> "He's a hero, and he'll never be forgotten," a tearful Jansen Young told the *Daily News* of Blunk. "Jon took a bullet for me."
>
> She was too distraught to speak more, but her mother called Blunk, 25, who had two young children from a previous relationship, "a gentleman."

"He was loving, the kind of guy you want your daughter to be with, and ultimately, she's alive because of this, because he protected her," Shellie Young said.

She said Blunk, a security guard, had served in the Navy and had recently filled out papers to reenlist with a goal of becoming a Navy SEAL. "To her, he was a hero anyway because he wanted to serve his country," she said of her daughter, who was left with shrapnel wounds to her side. "He said that all the time: 'I was born to serve my country.'"

Jansen Young, 21, said Blunk took her to see Friday's midnight premiere of "The Dark Knight Rises" to celebrate her graduation from veterinarian school. As the black-clad killer burst into the theater and unleashed tear gas and a torrent of indiscriminate gunfire, Blunk selflessly protected his girlfriend. . . .

Equally heroic was the 24-year-old Teves, who hurled his girlfriend to the floor as bullets whizzed through the theater.

"He pushed her to the floor to save her and he ended up getting a bullet," said his aunt, Barbara Slivinske, 57. "He was gonna hit the floor himself, but he never made it."

Samantha Yowler had a similar story of horror and heroism about her boyfriend, Matt McQuinn, whose last living act was to shield her from death. Yowler, 26, survived with a gunshot wound to the knee and is in fair condition after undergoing surgery.

McQuinn's family credited his quick actions for saving Samantha's life. Witnesses said he dove on top of his girlfriend as the shooting started and that Samantha's brother, Nick, who was also in the theater, helped get her out of harm's way. Nick Yowler was unharmed in the shooting.

"Both the Yowler and McQuinn families thank everyone for their concerns, thoughts and prayers during this difficult time," the McQuinns' lawyer, Robert Scott, said in a statement. "Unfortunately, Matt perished from the injuries he sustained during the tragic events that unfolded . . . and went home to be with his maker."

Crosson, J., Wills, K., & Hutchinson, B. (2012, July 21). "Dark Knight Rises" shooting: Three heroes died in Aurora taking bullets for their girlfriends. *New York Daily News*. Retrieved from http://www.nydailynews.com/news/national/aurora-shooting -died-bullets-sweeties-article-1.1119395. © Daily News, L.P. (New York). Used with permission.

US Airways Flight 1549 Captain Sully Sullenberger

Captain Chesley B. "Sully" Sullenberger landed a US Airways jetliner on the Hudson River after the plane he was piloting struck a flock of birds immediately after takeoff. New York Mayor Bloomberg and President Obama immediately lauded him as a hero, as did many media reports. As the passenger jet lost power, Sullenberger guided the plane safely and smoothly through the landing process. As a pilot, Sullenberger can be considered a first responder: he was expected to respond quickly and appropriately in an aircraft emergency. Captain Sullenberger had an excellent background and training in emergency response. He has worked with National Transportation Safety Board (NTSB) officials in other crash investigations and had helped develop methods for emergency evacuations. He was a distinguished graduate of the Air Force Academy and had flown military jets.

While his actions might be considered typical for pilots, his extreme circumstances, unprecedented and innovated response, exceptional skill, and unwavering commitment to seeing every passenger safely off the plane before departing himself elevated Captain Sullenberger to hero status. In the subsequent narrative, he was seen as acting fast, as decisive, and as a leader.

As you read these excerpts from the NTSB and from media reports, note how the passengers and others justify conferring hero status on Captain Sullenberger despite his unwillingness to accept the accolade.

Capt. Chesley B. Sullenberger III, age 57, was hired by Pacific Southwest Airlines on February 25, 1980. Before this, he flew McDonnell Douglas F-4 airplanes in the U.S Air Force. At the time of the accident, he held a single and multi engine airline transport pilot (ATP certificate issues August 7, 2002). . . .

The professionalism of the flight crewmembers and their excellent crew resource management during the accident sequence contributed to their ability to maintain control of the aircraft, configure it to the extent possible under the circumstances, and fly an approach that increased the survivability of the impact. (NTSB Accident Report, 2010, p. 6)

While the world clamored Friday for his story, and government leaders applauded his professionalism, and fan pages sprang up on the Internet, Captain

Sullenberger retained his focus, avoiding the limelight as he awaited an interview Saturday with federal investigators studying what went wrong with US Airways Flight 1549.

Heroes are often born in an instant, the split second it takes to recognize a pending disaster and react, the blink of an eye it takes a Wesley Autrey to throw himself under a subway train to save a man fallen on the tracks. (Rivera, 2009)

The report adopted by the [National Transportation] Safety Board validated the Captain's decision to ditch into the Hudson River saying that it "provided the highest probability that the accident would be survivable." Contributing to the survivability of the accident was the crew resource management between the captain and first officer, which allowed them to maintain control of the airplane, increasing the survivability of the impact with the water (NTSB Public Affairs, 2010).

Contributing to the survivability of the accident was (1) the decision-making of the flight crewmembers and their crew resource management during the accident sequence; (2) the fortuitous use of an airplane that was equipped for an extended overwater flight, including the availability of the forward slide/rafts, even though it was not required to be so equipped; (3) the performance of the cabin crewmembers while expediting the evacuation of the airplane; and (4) the proximity of the emergency responders to the accident site and their immediate and appropriate response to the accident. (NTSB Public Affairs, 2010)

"If it wasn't for him, I wouldn't be here today," said Mary Berkwits, a passenger from Stallings, N.C. "He was just wonderful."

Captain Sullenberger fielded congratulatory phone calls from President Bush and President-elect Barack Obama on Friday, but mostly stayed secluded somewhere in the city. He did not attend a ceremony at City Hall, where Mayor Michael R. Bloomberg said his actions "inspired people around the city, and millions more around the world." (Rivera, 2009)

National Transportation Safety Board. (2010, May 4). *Loss of thrust in both engines after encountering a flock of birds and subsequent ditching on the Hudson River US Airways Flight 1549 Airbus A320-214, N106 US, Weehawken, New Jersey, Janu-*

ary 15, 2009. Retrieved from http://www.ntsb.gov/investigations/AccidentReports/Reports/AAR1003.pdf

National Transportation Safety Board. Office of Public Affairs. (2010, May 4). *CREW actions and safety equipment credited with saving lives in US Airways 1549 Hudson River ditching, NTSB says.* Retrieved from http://www.ntsb.gov/news/press-releases/Pages/CREW_Actions_and_Safety_Equipment_Credited_with_Saving_Lives_in_US_Airways_1549_Hudson_River_Ditching_NTSB_Says.asp

Rivera, R. (2009, January 16). A pilot becomes a hero years in the making. *New York Times.* Retrieved from http://www.nytimes.com/2009/01/17/nyregion/17pilot.html?_r=1&ref=nyregion&pagewanted=all&

CHAPTER 9

Memorial Narratives

MEMORIAL NARRATIVES are one of the most important forms associated with a crisis. They are often very public, have longevity, are repeated frequently, and frame the core meaning of the crisis. The tragedy of crises often inspires feelings of loss, meaninglessness, and confusion. The narrative space calls for an expression of unity through shared values and a search for meaning. To fill this narrative void, Stob (2012) explains that memorials and memorial narratives assign meaning to crises in three ways. First, they instill meaning in a way that unites a community devastated by the chaos of crisis. Second, memorials place the crisis in context with the past. They position moments of crisis into a larger story about "a nation's purpose, importance, and ideals" (p. 254). Third, memorial narratives teach "civic virtues" (p. 254).

Memorials and the corresponding memorial narratives established in response to crises celebrate the resilience of the human spirit and the drive to create and document larger meaning. They sort through competing interpretations of tragedy to preserve the memories and lessons judged worthy of commemorating. In doing so, memorials serve as "places where memories converge, condense, conflict and define relationships between past, present and future" (Marschall, 2006, p. 146). From a narrative perspective, memorializing includes the development of stories that inspire public memory (Mayo, 1988). Moreover, memorials contribute to the healing process for individuals, groups, cities, regions, nations, and, in extreme cases, an alliance of multiple nations. This healing process invites narratives that contribute to crisis explanations by contrasting what should be remembered and repeated with what is best forgotten and avoided (Seeger, Sellnow, & Ulmer, 2003). Making such choices in the grieving and healing process requires considerable cultural sensitivity. Memorials cannot contribute to the emotional resolution of a crisis unless larger cultural values and traditions are honored (Littlefield, Reierson, Cowden, Stowman, & Long Feather, 2009).

In this chapter we describe the memorial narrative and its primary features and functions. We examine how a memorial functions to create ceremonial and instructional outcomes. Memorial narratives that are structured in specific ways have a greater probability of promoting appropriate learning and helping a community move beyond a crisis. They are, however, often the subject of intense conflict as members of a community offer various competing stories of what happened and what a crisis means. In addition, as the meaning of a crisis shifts over time, memorials may fall out of favor or in some cases become more relevant as the stories are rediscovered.

MEMORIALS

Crises often produce victims and heroes whose toils are remembered and honored in memorial narratives. A memorial is a structure, event, or activity designed to promote and preserve a memory, meaning, or interpretation of a person, event, or accomplishment (Eyre, 2007). Physical monuments, such as the Oklahoma City Bombing Memorial and the TWA Flight 800 Memorial, are usually built to commemorate the location of the disaster. Speeches, ceremonies, and services—such as the Mariners' Church in Detroit ringing its bell twenty-nine times in November 1975 to commemorate the sinking of the freighter SS *Edmund Fitzgerald* in a Lake Superior storm—often occur when memorials are dedicated and may be repeated annually as remembrances. To forget the hardship endured by the victims demeans their struggle. Those who suffer or die in a crisis are typically remembered positively, and through memorials they are held up as models. In contrast, the violence and destruction of crises are often judged as best forgotten. Those who have experienced a crisis can have difficulty moving on if they remain fearful that appropriate measures have not been taken to avoid similar crises in the future (Seeger et al., 2003). If a community's vulnerability and loss are belabored, memorial narratives have the potential to lose their effectiveness in helping people move on from a crisis.

If memorial narratives provide an appropriate balance of remembering and forgetting, they establish more opportunities for renewal, as we discussed in chapter 6. The stories promoted in memorials establish frames of reference through which a crisis is interpreted for others, including future generations. Veil, Sellnow, and Heald (2011) explain, "The creation of a memorial illustrates the significance of a tragedy and establishes guidelines for how future generations should remember the event" (p. 168). Memorial narratives explain what should be remembered and honored as a community learns to look beyond the crisis and begin anew. The memorial synthesizes the crisis to a set of core messages. In essence, then, memorial narratives serve ceremonial or epideictic, persuasive, and instructional purposes.

MEMORIAL NARRATIVES AS EPIDEICTIC

When memorializing in the wake of a crisis, people create and participate in official symbolic rituals. These rituals are often public and seek to create a sense of order and purpose for what otherwise would be a seemingly meaningless misfortune (Vivian, 2006). Epideictic or ceremonial narratives in response to tragedies allow for an "unfolding of central commemorative traditions and thereby assign coherent meaning and purpose to events that seem to defy explanation" (Bradford, 2010, p. 82). In doing so, memorial narratives provide the means for expressing "collective grief" (Hasian, 2004, p. 66). They function at least in part as ceremonial or epideictic representations of crises. In an epidictic context, a speaker creates a sense of connection around collective values and seeks to amplify and enhance those values (Perelman & Olbrechts-Tyteca, 1969). Ultimately, epideictic narratives focus on bringing people together through "shared interpretations and celebrations" (Sullivan, 1994, p. 286). Interpretations and celebrations cannot be truly shared, however, unless the memorial narrative accounts for the audience's diversity. To address this diversity, Liu and Pompper urge crisis communicators to avoid personal biases by embracing "worldviews beyond their own comfort zone" (p. 143). Doing so promotes inclusivity needed for healing after a crisis.

Memorials and the accompanying epideictic rhetoric are practically indispensable in crises involving catastrophic death. When a community has been disrupted by death, especially when the death is unexpected or widespread, epideictic messages of restoration are needed. Death of children or death on a large scale generates intense feelings of grief, loss, and a profound sense of unfairness. Both action and symbolic efforts are essential for addressing this grief and reuniting the community (Smith & Trimbur, 2003). President Obama faced the challenge of proclaiming unity on December 16, 2012, at the Sandy Hook Interfaith Prayer Vigil days after the tragic school shooting. He sought to unite the survivors and mourning families with a grieving nation:

> Here in Newtown, I come to offer the love and prayers of a nation. I am very mindful that mere words cannot match the depths of your sorrow, nor can they heal your wounded hearts. I can only hope it helps for you to know that you're not alone in your grief; that our world too has been torn apart; that all across this land of ours, we have wept with you, we've pulled our children tight. And you must know that whatever measure of comfort we can provide, we will provide; whatever portion of sadness that we can share with you to ease this heavy load, we will gladly bear it. Newtown—you are not alone. (White House, 2012, para. 3)

Ultimately epideictic communicators responding to the crisis situations, such as President Obama faced in Sandy Hook, frame a collective and unifying memory of the tragic event (Hasian, 2004). President Abraham Lincoln with the Gettysburg Address and President Ronald Reagan with his remarks about the *Challenger* space shuttle disaster engaged in similar epideictic narratives about crises.

From an epideictic perspective, those who engage in creating a crisis memorial narrative frame how the victims are remembered by selecting which stories to accentuate (Hasian, 2004). The range of emotions generated by crises complicates these decisions. For example, those tasked with creating the United States Holocaust Memorial Museum "had to walk a fine line between popular voyeurism and reverence for the dead and visceral education and gratuitous violence" (Hasian, 2004, p. 75). In every sense, the Holocaust was a horrific crisis requiring memorializing. Doing so in a way that respected the human dignity of the victims required considerable sensitivity.

Epideictic narratives can give moral significance to crises (Sullivan, 1994, p. 286). The memorial narrative identifies and solidifies widely accepted values and aligns them with the crisis. Although such presentations are not typically contested, they sometimes include persuasive dimensions as particular meanings are presented (Perelman & Olbrechts-Tyteca, 1969).

MEMORIAL NARRATIVES AS PERSUASION

Memorial narratives take on a persuasive dimension for many reasons. In some instances, the narrative may align with larger political issues and questions. As time passes, the central values of the narrative may shift due to changes in social consciousness or discovery of previously unknown or intentionally concealed aspects of the crisis. In other cases, memorialized events are threatened by the indifference or disinterest of new generations. As values and agendas change over time, what was an appropriate and desirable memorial may change. The Soviet Union embalmed and has kept the body of Nikolai Lenin on public display since his death in 1924. Following the collapse of the Soviet Union, some argued that such a display is inappropriate and that the body should be buried. Adapting or preserving collective memory in these cases requires persuasion. As with the case of Lenin, "societies change politically, culturally, and technologically," and, as they change, so do the memorial narratives (Autry, 2012, p. 147).

When these narrative transformations arise, the likelihood of disagreement grows. In these cases, memorial speeches may become the occasion for "differing, divided, and uncertain claims about how the public is constituted and who has grounds to memorialize the dead" (Smith & Trimbur, 2003, p. 11). Whereas an epideictic presentation typically treats audience members passively as observers, the persuasive memorial narrative requires an audience's active participation as they are asked to change attitudes or take some action. Memorials may function to help audience members "persuade themselves" as they recognize the need for change based on the stories and texts emphasized in the memorial narrative (p. 8). In doing so, active audiences make a conscious decision about acknowledging and applying the "first-person plural" to the commemoration efforts (Kitch, 2002, p. 300). When audiences see tragic crises such as the AIDS epidemic as a national rather than personal issue, they typically use the inclusive term *we* in asking the important question: "What can we do to about this crisis?"

The AIDS Memorial Quilt comprises individual panels, each of which commemorates the life of one of the thousands of victims who have died of AIDS. By inviting those mourning the loss of a loved one or loved ones to AIDS to submit a panel, the quilt provides an opportunity for audiences to actively participate in and contribute to the memorial process. Many individuals and groups participate in the memorial process by sewing quilts for loved ones lost to the illness. Others participate purely out of sympathy or empathy for those who suffered from both the pain of disease and social rejection. For example, one quilt maker acknowledged in her story, "I'm just a housewife. . . . I thought there would be no recognition from his family. I felt bad about that. I feel bad about all the people who die of AIDS that nobody knows" (Jones, 2007, p. 591). Cleve Jones, one of the founders of the AIDS Memorial Quilt, was forthright in expressing his intent for the quilt to serve a persuasive purpose: "The Quilt was and is an activist symbol—comforting, yes, but mortally troubling. If it raised a single question, it was, What are you going to do about it? That was the challenge we laid at the national doorstep" (Jones, 2007, p. 591).

Audiences also actively participate in memorializing by projecting the qualities they admire and desire onto the characters in the crisis narrative. Audiences expect and even demand that daily journalism reflects mythic themes. In doing so, Kitch (2002) argues, "Journalists are not lying; their comforting narratives are constructed not out of whole cloth but out of cultural beliefs with real meaning" (p. 305). For example, media coverage of John F. Kennedy Jr.'s death in a private plane crash emphasized the characteristics the public wanted to see in him, whether or not those characteristics were fully present (Kitch, 2002). At times, the expectations of audiences require journalists to engage in "narrative repair to have a happy ending" (Kitch, 2007, p. 37). Stories of celebrities, for example, are often woven into the pattern of guilt and redemption. The twists and turns in the long lives of celebrities such as Johnny Cash, Ray Charles, Marlon Brando, and Richard Prior were reported using "the long-instructive story of 'the sinner redeemed,'" revealing that this narrative pattern "is now repeatedly told not just in church but also in entertainment magazines" (p. 54).

The untimely deaths of celebrities such as Paul Walker in a car crash or Philip Seymour Hoffman of a drug overdose evolve or devolve into celebrations of characteristics in their lives that audiences hope to emulate. These relationships that audiences generate for such fallen celebrities usually represent their own personal value structure. As such, "these stories are not merely entertainment; they are, for many people, the central tales of an ideal American life" (Kitch, 2007, p. 54). The celebrity often is moralized as a hero, as we discussed in chapter 8.

The shifting tenor of public sentiment, whether from changes in perspective or a disconnection with the past, also heightens the persuasive element of memorial narratives. This narrative evolution occurs because "the process of shaping collective memory is ongoing and involves political, cultural, and sociological dimensions, as different interpretations compete for their place in history" (Zandberg, Meyers, & Neiger, 2012, p. 66). Memorial narratives are preserved when they are passed down from generation to generation with stories of courage and resilience (Azarian-Ceccato, 2010). As a form of collective memory, however, they are subject to the same form of homogenizing and distortion as individual memories. In some cases, memorial narratives can facilitate denial, forgetting, and "cultural amnesia" as some issues and details are foregrounded and others ignored (Hasian, 2004, p. 67). Crises, both in the past and more recent ones, are often particularly prominent within a community, nation, or culture's memory. They inspire a commitment to preserve memorial narratives from generation to generation. Subsequent crises can also create a shift in longstanding memorial narratives.

Preserving a crisis narrative requires the memory to progress through time, carried by people who did not experience the trauma directly but experienced the event through the accounts and stories of others. Azarian-Ceccato (2010) provides a compelling case study of how the Armenian population preserves the memory of the Armenian genocide their ancestors endured around the time of World War I, when approximately 1 million Armenians were massacred (Bloxham, 2005). Thousands of Armenians eventually immigrated to Fresno, California, after being deported from

Turkey. Now these genocide survivors seek to preserve the memory of their ancestors' struggles through their great-grandchildren. In interviews with these great-grandchildren, Azarian-Ceccato (2010) observed that the Armenian genocide is memorialized for subsequent generations in a collective memory composed of the collected personal stories about the crisis.

In the case of the Armenian genocide, the challenge is persuading future generations to remember and honor the struggles their ancestors endured. In contrast, some monuments and memorial narratives fall out of favor as political sentiments shift, such as with the Voortrekker Monument in South Africa. Constructed in 1949 in Pretoria, the memorial commemorated the "Great Trek" into the interior of the country by Afrikaner pioneers, known as Voortrekkers, as they sought to escape British rule (Autry, 2012). These pioneers battled native tribes in the inner region of South Africa as they established farms and ranches. In 1949, the Voortrekker Monument stood as the "embodiment of Afrikaner nationalism and mythology" (p. 146), but fifty years after its construction, it would be the setting for a confrontation between opposing sides of a politically divided Afrikaner society (Autry, 2012). South Africa's "National Party was split between those advocating reform and power-sharing and those demanding the tightening of apartheid codes" (p. 152). At one point in 1988, both sides organized competing commemoration events at the monument. The Voortrekker Monument remains, but it has been refurbished with a new narrative intended to "refute the myths and memories of Afrikanerdom" (p. 162). Whether these changes are sufficient to accurately reflect current political sentiment is debatable, but Autry contends that maintaining and refurbishing the monument may have been the best choice. Removal and "wholesale disavowal by national leaders" of monuments whose celebrated values are questioned can "provoke backlash, sometimes violent, from citizens whose identities are linked to a specific version of the past" (p. 161). Similar reframing of memorials and monuments and the meaning of the events they commemorate occur frequently when politics shift. Monuments may be vandalized and defaced, and statues of well-known figures may be pulled down as happened in Iraq after the fall of Saddam Hussein.

Clearly, memorial narratives can advocate for one particular view of an individual or event. They can position individuals or events in relation to one another as when names of victims are inscribed on a memorial wall. They can also prioritize events in the history of a culture. As time passes, memorials can evolve or even fade in popular appeal and, in some cases, may be vandalized or destroyed. In other cases, memorials may be rediscovered as a crisis reemerges in popular cultural. Memorial narratives that survive and stay in favor often project life lessons.

MEMORIAL NARRATIVES AS INSTRUCTIVE

In addition to celebrating the memories of those fallen by crises and persuading people to adopt selected value structures, memorial narratives provide explanations by instructing or teaching observers, both immediate and remote, about the crisis. The instructive element of memorial narratives helps both current and future generations derive meaningful lessons from crisis events. Thus, memorial narratives create context where the commemorative speaker "turns educator" (Perelman & Olbrechts-Tyteca, 1969, p. 51). In so doing, "commemorative monuments 'instruct' their visitors about what is to be valued in the future as well as in the past" (Blair, Jeppeson, & Pucci, 1991, p. 263).

As individuals visit memorial sites, they are invited to relive and learn from the past. A memorial narrative "imports into the present—the time of the visitor—the tactical rhetoric that draws attention, announces resolve, and enjoins the moral agency of the individual" (Blair & Michel, 2000, p. 47). Through such explanation, memorial narratives offer lessons learned from the crisis and demonstrate model qualities worth emulating. These enduring lessons remind visitors that those who suffered or perished did not do so in vain and the narratives emphasize the qualities in human endurance that should be taught to all generations. The lessons provided in memorial narratives define a culture's "criteria of competence" (Sullivan, 1994, p. 286) and discern the responsibilities of future generations (Stob, 2012).

The instructive element of memorial narratives involves both remembering and forgetting. Those who commemorate crises must distill the valuable lessons that communities seek to retain from the elements of fear and defeat that are best forgotten. In essence, those charged with the instructional aspects of memorial narratives must decide which histories to repeat and preserve (Hasian, 2004). Through these processes of "remembering and forgetting, individuals learn how to act in accord with the values and ideals of a nation's or a community's past" (Stob, 2012, p. 254).

Instruction presented in memorial narratives often occurs through a cyclical form of repetition that future generations can comprehend. This repetition is vital to commemoration as "participants enact verbal and symbolic rituals that sustain collective memories from one generation to the next in familiar ways, at conventional times, in common places" (Vivian, 2006, p. 6). For example, the United States celebrates Memorial Day each year through annual parades, picnics, banquets, and other festivities, recognizing the heroic and selfless sacrifices made by those who served in all wars involving the United States. Israel's Holocaust and Heroism Remembrance Day serves a similar function. Commercial television in Israel forgoes commercials during the holiday to make space for messages commemorating the bravery and resilience of those citizens who suffered and died during the holocaust. These events commemorate the difficulties in the nation's history and emphasize recent successes and achievements (Zandberg et al., 2012). Lessons of heroism, dignity, national or cultural pride, and the greater good are all taught annually during such recurring holidays. These acts of commemoration play a major role in passing down interpretations of historical events to new generations (Azarian-Ceccato, 2010).

Longstanding, carefully and laboriously constructed memorials are not the only means of narrative instruction, however. Ad hoc or spontaneously erected memorials at places of death also serve to commemorate and instruct (Suter, 2010). Perhaps the most common spontaneous memorials appear at the sites of fatal traffic accidents. For example, artist Phillip March Jones (2011) published a nearly three-hundred-page book containing nothing but his Polaroid photos of spontaneous roadside memorials. Most often, these spontaneous memorials take the form of crosses with the names of the deceased. When such memorials are constructed, they immediately transform an otherwise common location into a point of both ritual and danger. From a ritualistic perspective, these memorials become a symbolic tribute signifying the place of an often tragic event

(Baptist, 2013). Such memorials are an expression of loss and serve to preserve the memory of those who died. The instructive element of roadside memorials is derived from the warnings they express. Drivers who know nothing of the specific accident or its victims see such memorials and are reminded of the potential danger of traffic accidents.

The instructive feature of roadside memorials is well documented. For example, the presence of a roadside memorial at an intersection in the Canadian city of Calgary reduced the number of red light violations over a six-week period by nearly 17 percent (Tay, 2009). Similar results inspired the Georgia Department of Transportation (DOT) to create a program enabling friends or family to sponsor a DOT sign posted at the site of a deadly accident for $100. The signs read "Drive Safely; In Memory of . . ." (Nielson, 2011, para. 1), and the sponsor inserts the name or names of the victim or victims being remembered. The signs stay posted for one year. Impromptu memorials of stuffed animals, flowers, notes, wreaths, and similar artifacts often emerge around shootings or the death of celebrities. Spontaneous memorials like these can serve an important role by providing an outlet for community emotion, anger, and grief and as a visible sign of support. In some cases, such memorials become the basis of more permanent installations.

Whether spontaneous or carefully designed, memorial narratives serve an important instructive function that can be quite formal. For example, the Oklahoma City and 9/11 memorials invite students to visit. The memorials include classroom-style facilities where visitors can learn about the perils of hatred, terrorism, and world conflict. The United States Holocaust Memorial Museum emphasizes educating future generations as one of its central purposes so such a tragedy is never repeated. In his remarks at the opening of the museum, President Clinton focused on balancing the "darkest lessons in history" to the "hopeful soul of America" as he encouraged every American visiting Washington, D.C., to visit the museum (Hasian, 2004, p. 83). The need for such instruction in the commemoration is obvious: if we do not retain the lessons from the past, we are likely to recreate the very circumstances that precipitated the crisis.

CONCLUSION

Memorial narratives are central to the grieving, healing, remembering, and learning associated with crises. Deciding what is best remembered and what is best forgotten are challenges that are complicated by diverse and sometimes evolving cultural values. Consideration and reconsideration of these values continue throughout the life span of a memorial narrative. When done effectively, memorial narratives reflect widespread sentiment and provide timeless life lessons. There is a strong emotional need to tell the story of crises through memorials. Memorials are also used to designate disaster sites, which can become destinations of pilgrimages and locations for annual ceremonies of remembrance as the meaning of the crisis is passed down from generation to generation. Most important, memorial narratives contribute to the essential grieving and healing that must take place after crises.

CASES TO CONSIDER

Memorial narratives help to provide resolution for the diverse audiences that experience crises. Selected stories of anguish and triumph are framed prospectively and shared for generations. Memorial narratives are composed of epideictic, persuasive, and instructing elements. Epideictic components appeal to diverse cultural values and unify communities. Persuasive segments advocate for what should be remembered and how it should be memorialized. Instructing dimensions provide lessons learned and share them with current and future generations. All of these elements intertwine in an appeal to broadly shared cultural values. The following cases accentuate the instructive and persuasive elements of memorial narratives. The first case reveals how the overwhelming loss of life in Banda Aceh caused by the 2004 tsunami is memorialized with lessons learned. The persuasive actions of families and friends to memorialize the passengers and crew killed in the crash of Northwest Airlines flight 255 are described in the second case.

Instructive Elements of the Aceh Tsunami Museum

On December 26, 2004, a 9.1 earthquake occurred on the floor of the Indian Ocean off the western coast of the island of Sumatra. Banda Aceh, a city of 200,000, was the closest major city to the earthquake and shortly after the earthquake was struck by a devastating tsunami. Banda Aceh was the most severely hit of the locations affected by the tsunami. Sadly, 167,000 people died and many more were injured in and around the city. The tsunami ultimately left its mark on fourteen countries, killing 230,000 people primarily in coastal communities. The Aceh Tsunami Museum was designed as a symbolic reminder of the disaster and as a resource to educate the public about the devastation of tsunamis. The museum is also designed as an emergency disaster shelter for the public in the case of another tsunami. This description of the museum provided by international journalist Ivan Sigal speaks to the instructing nature of crisis memorial:

"The Aceh Tsunami Museum in particular embodies this goal of civic instruction. Photos of death and destruction, taken after the tsunami, loop endlessly; video monitors play images of traumatic moments, now pixelated and bordered by benign blue-bubble backgrounds. Colorful dioramas restage scenes of terror and death: clay figures hang from model boats or flee massive blue *papier-mâché* waves. A miniature of the city's famed Baiturrahman Grand Mosque, one of the few buildings not destroyed by the waves, stands alone in front of a painted screen of rough sea and sky. Rusted motorcycles and seismographs, encased in glass, have been repurposed into objects of reverence and sentiment. Interactive maps depicting the changes in coastline are cast in rough gray fiberglass. A model house built on a hydraulic jack simulates the experience of shaking earth. These objects allow us both to look directly at horror and to distance ourselves from it, through facsimiles reduced in scale, rendered in clay and captured and framed in glass. They keep the experience at a safe remove while providing instruction in the value of creating and preserving order—implicitly supporting the post-conflict state.

Sigal, I. (2013, 27 December). Projections of the future: Tsunami memorials and disaster response. *Oximity*. Retrieved from https://www.oximity.com/article/Projections-of-the-Future-Tsunami-Memo-1

Remembering and Forgetting in Memorializing
the Crash of Northwest Flight 255

On August 16, 1987, Northwest Airlines flight 255 crashed shortly after takeoff next to the highway leading to Detroit Metropolitan Airport. Six crew members and 148 passengers died. The only survivor was a four-year-old girl, Cecelia Cichan. Subsequently a memorial was built at the site of the crash at the entrance of the airport, and a website is also maintained (http://www.flight255memorial.com) that includes the names of those who died, resources regarding airline safety, and documents and recordings related to the crash. The website also has a description of the persuasive efforts required for the memorial to be built and erected. Construction of the memorial was controversial, with some suggesting that both the airport authority and the airlines were opposed to building a physical reminder of the disaster in such a prominent location. Landscaping now shields the monument from the direct view of travelers coming to the airport. On August 16, 2012, family and friends gathered at the memorial site to mark the twenty-fifth anniversary of the crash. Among the speakers was the now twenty-six-year-old Cecelia Cichan.

The excerpts that follow are taken from an article published in the *Detroit News* that was featured on the website established by the families and friends of those who died in the crash. As you read, notice how those interviewed for the story subtly reflect on the persuasive efforts that preceded the placement and dedication of the memorial.

"My God, We Finally Did This." After 7 years of heartache and anguish, a chapter is finally closed. The permanent memorial marker at the crash site honors Flight 255's dead. Families of the 156 dead people who died in the crash of Flight 255 have erected a permanent memorial for their loved ones at the site.

The 5-ton, four-piece marker containing the names of the dead was unveiled at 7:00 PM on August 16, the 7th Anniversary of the crash, on a hill at I-94 and Middle Belt Road. On the 7th Anniversary, Betty Polec of Clinton Township, whose pregnant daughter and son-in-law were killed in the crash at Detroit Metropolitan Airport [said], "It's been a very hard 7 years. This will bring a new meaning to the crash. We only wish it would have been sooner."

The 3-section 14-foot long black granite monument was erected the week before the 7th Anniversary by crews from Black Monument, The Grand Rapids based company, which also designed the memorial.

Flight 255 family members raised the money to pay for the monument. While they would not give an exact cost, a spokesman for Black Monument said it was "more than $10,000 and less than $20,000."

The 6-foot tall centerpiece is flanked by two 54-inch side sections and encircled with newly planted pine trees. The design is a compromise between the 10-foot tall marker the families wanted and the flat monument that the state suggested, Polec said. On the back of the monument is a poem written by Duane Adams of Royal Oak titled, "Final Flight".

"It is really beautiful" said Kay Gleason of Shelby Township, who lost her husband, Pat, in the crash. "It has been a long time coming." Some of the Flight 255 Family members, including Polec and Gleason, are convinced that it took so long to get the marker because the county, state and Romulus didn't want a memorial at the site.

We accomplished our goal, Polec said. "We wanted a marker on that crash site. It's really an end of an era. It's like, My God, we finally did this.

Reprinted with permission from the Detroit News. "My God, We Finally Did This." Retrieved from http://flight255memorial/marker.html

CHAPTER 10

How Narratives of Crisis
Compete and Converge

THE SUDDEN SHOCK created by a crisis often causes an abrupt loss of meaning, creating a space that is quickly filled with narratives from multiple sources. As this space is filled, the narrative explanations for the event differ based on many factors that can range from seeking to absolve oneself of guilt to assigning guilt and seeking retribution. Because those with different points of view often generate distinct narratives, crises frequently foster competition among multiple narratives, each of which seeks broad acceptance (Venette, Sellnow, & Lang, 2003). At an extreme level, "the narrative of one group can be a counterstatement and perhaps a corrective to the narrative of another group" (Heath, 2004, p. 173). An organization criticized as irresponsible prior to or during a crisis may promote a counternarrative that positions its actions more favorably.

Those experiencing a crisis from a different ideological, cultural, or even physical standpoint may offer very different narratives. A recent court case involving the National Football League (NFL) offers an example of competing narratives. The NFL faced a crisis when a group of former players sued the league for failure to address the frequency and severity of concussions, particularly multiple concussions, that players experienced. Former players created a narrative featuring themselves as unwittingly participating in games with brain injuries that were worsened by continued contact. As a result, some players faced early-onset dementia and other life-altering brain disorders. The NFL countered with a narrative that players were protected based on the best information available at the time and that injured players often insist on playing, even concealing injuries to their coaches. Ultimately the NFL and the players reached a financial settlement.

Although the debate between the NFL and its former players over concussions will likely continue, the case illustrates how crisis narratives can begin with seemingly polar opposite views of a crisis. These views compete for public acceptance, but over time, this competition often gives way to a form of convergence among narratives. By *convergence* we mean the development of a coherent, unifying story that subsumes many other stories, themes, perspectives, and pieces of information. While these converged narratives may not subsume all the stories, they are understood to capture the essential elements and are generally accepted as the primary story. In the NFL example, both the players and the NFL now acknowledge that many former players are afflicted with a debilitating syndrome caused by brain damage due to repeated concussions. Although the extent of the NFL's legal responsibility is still contested, the organization has taken important steps to reduce the frequency of concussions and protect the health of players who are concussed in practice or games. This response has also influenced policies at the college, high school, and youth levels regarding protective equipment, game rules, practice activity, and medical detection and treatment. Thus, the initial competition among narratives on this topic has in many ways given way to convergence that reflects a recognition and clear sense of urgency for addressing the problem and leads to important changes.

As this example illustrates, comprehending the beginning of a crisis is like a jigsaw puzzle poured from a box without first allowing the assemblers an opportunity see the puzzle's final picture. As the pieces are slowly connected, competing assumptions about the appearance of the puzzle, fully assembled, are inevitable. When the puzzle grows closer to its final assembly, however, these competing views are put aside as consensus emerges about the actual picture. Similarly, disputing the broad conceptualization of crises at their onset gives way to convergence as further details are revealed, collected, and assembled into a clear understanding of what took place and how.

In this chapter, we explore the form and consequences of crisis narrative competition and convergence. We begin with a review of how competing crisis narratives naturally emerge, expand, and contract cyclically. Next we describe the motives that various parties in a crisis situation have for accentuating competition among narratives. We then characterize the process by which competing narratives typically converge over time into one dominant narrative. We conclude with an explanation for how the convergence process creates lessons learned from the crisis and helps generate a unified response.

The dramatic nature of crises commands the attention of observers, pulling them from their daily routines to contemplate the shocking nature of the events. Thus, crisis perceptions are initially an individualized experience. Observers search for words and emotions to express their reactions to events they could not have fully anticipated. This individualized moment in perception is, as we discussed earlier, characterized as a cosmology episode where, for a moment, the observer cannot comprehend what is happening (Weick, 1993). As we described in chapter 3, crises can force victims to "question the viability of their world and self-views" (Park & Folkman, 1997, p. 123). When the initial distress begins to dissipate, observers are able to participate in a dialogue about what happened, why the crisis occurred, and what steps should be taken to resolve the situation. This dialogue is the manifestation of a crisis narrative.

Many people learned about the attacks on 9/11 from morning news reports on television or radio. Others learned from friends, family, or strangers. As the news spread, small groups of individuals congregated around television sets or radios, listened to news accounts, discussed the events, and tried to make sense of what was happening. People shared very personal stories of having visited the World Trade Center before the tragedy, of family and friends who were traveling, and of similar national tragedies that could provide some context for the shocking disaster. These individual stories helped begin the process of generating a national narrative.

In Chapter 3, we explained how crises create vivid, individualized memories that influence an individual's perceptions of a crisis. We discussed how those observing a crisis maintain deeply entrenched flashbulb memories of crisis events influenced by the stress and complex emotions of the event. These memories form filters through which all other dialogue about the crisis must pass. For example, a resident of Fargo, North Dakota, witnessed floodwaters overwhelm the dike behind her house during the 1997 flood. She stood by emotionally frozen as the water filled her basement and then the main floor of her home. From that moment on, any discussion of the 1997 flood caused that memory to resurface for her. For this resident, witnessing the loss of her home was the lens through which she viewed the flood event. Fargo residents whose homes were spared harbored very different memories. Many of them saw the 1997 flood as a battle in which the community was victorious. Their flashbulb memories were of holding back floodwaters and sparing the city during a flood that consumed entire communities along the river's path.

Expression of emotional turmoil present in the flashbulb memories of those physically and emotionally harmed by the crisis resonates with others who experienced similar pain or loss. Such stories of bereavement also foster empathy in the minds of observers who were not touched directly by the crisis. Through this process of expression, stories that were deeply personal initially combine with similar stories to create a consistent narrative of loss, remorse, and a resounding need for corrective action (Benoit, 1995).

Competing crisis narratives also evolve toward unity as more information about the crisis is revealed. Technical information can provide understanding of how or why the crisis happened. Firsthand accounts of the loss and discomfort contribute to the narrative by humanizing the impact of the crisis. Emotional expression helps to reconcile divisions in preliminary and competing crisis narratives. As we discussed in Chapter 2, questions of evidence, intent, and responsibility characteristically emerge in the crisis narrative. As time goes on and more is known, evidence is validated or invalidated, the intent of those involved in the crisis begins to crystalize, and blame or responsibility is assigned. Through this process, narratives that were initially divided or divergent begin to homogenize as they move toward a common understanding of the crisis.

At their best, competing narratives create space for broader consideration and more inclusive understanding. The ensuing dialogue allows the expression of remorse or grieving as well as a functional understanding of the crisis and what steps could, should, or must be taken to avoid similar events in the future. At their worst, competing crisis narratives create space for manipulation. Parties fearing punishment or unfavorable policy changes due to the crisis often contribute to the postcrisis dialogue by interjecting a narrative reflecting their bias. As we discuss next, contrived competition poses perceptual challenges for observers. The divergence of these interpretations is typically resolved through the observation of convergence in the distinct narratives.

MOTIVES FOR COMPETING NARRATIVES

The uncertainty inherent in all crisis events makes the emergence of multiple, competing narratives inevitable. Speculation, bias, experience, past reputation, opportunism, deceitfulness, and heroism are forces that fragment the initial discussion of crises. Those observing the public narratives, typically an expansive and diverse public audience, are tasked with reconciling these diverse narratives. Naturally there are parties that dedicate considerable effort to supporting their particular version of the crisis narrative. Specifically, organizations responding to crises often seek to project a narrative featuring their organizations in as favorable a light as possible. By contrast, those advocating for victims of crises often support a narrative assigning blame to the organization and seeking retribution and compensation. For instance, as crude oil steadily gushed into the waters of the Gulf Coast, British Petroleum was vilified for engaging in highly dangerous off-coast drilling without taking the precautions necessary to protect the environment. In response, BP argued that the company was the victim of an unforeseeable natural catastrophe. Moreover, it insisted that the company was engaging in the most technically advanced techniques to stop the continuous escape of oil.

In cases where blame is contested among multiple organizations, relevant organizations may create contrasting narratives where they assign blame to another organization while exonerating their own. Such was the case in a crisis pitting Ford and Firestone Tires against each other. As the 1980s gave way to the 1990s, a pattern of automobile accidents involving Ford vehicles outfitted with Firestone tires accumulated. Individually, the accidents were seen as isolated tragedies, but taken together, they claimed nearly 150 lives. Collectively, the accidents revealed a pattern of tire failure at high speeds that many argued should have been recognized and responded to by both Ford and Firestone far sooner than they did (Venette, Sellnow, & Lang, 2003). Ford claimed Firestone manufactured flawed tires, while Firestone insisted Ford was to blame because the company recommended the tires be inflated at inappropriate tire pressure levels. As the two companies publicly traded accusations of blame, public frustration intensified. Ford and Firestone ended their almost one-hundred-year customer–supplier relationship, and the debate moved to litigation involving the families of accident victims.

The Convergence Process

The splintered depiction of crises through multiple narratives is both natural and beneficial. As we discussed previously, the limited availability of information and the diverse perspectives from which a crisis is experienced or observed inspire diverse interpretations of the crisis. Perelman (1979) used the term *pluralism* to characterize such a diversity of perspectives. Pluralism can be empowering at the outset of a crisis because it "refrains from granting to any individual or group, no matter who they are, the exorbitant privilege of setting up a single criterion for what is valid and what is appropriate" (p. 71). As a result, the many narrative versions that occur at the outset of a crisis allow multiple perspectives to be heard. Diversity of perspectives and divergent narratives are most pronounced when there is a lack of information or inadequate communication from prominent sources. The case of Malaysia Airlines flight 370, for example, was characterized by high levels of uncertainty, with officials offering incomplete information about what was a highly unusual circumstance. The plane was a scheduled international passenger flight from Kuala Lumpur to Beijing. On March 8, 2014, it lost contact with air traffic controllers. The lack of information spawned a wide variety of narrative explanations including terrorism, hijacking, and catastrophic failure. Speculation regarding the location of the plane ranged from the bottom of the Indian Ocean to a desert air base in Central Asia.

Over time, multiple views are shared, and additional information about crises emerges. As a result, the narratives, which may be scattered in the earliest stages, begin to align or converge (Sellnow, Ulmer, Seeger, & Littlefield, 2009). Convergence begins when narratives told from competing perspectives share points of common ground. For example, four months after Malaysia Airlines flight 370 disappeared, Malaysia Airlines flight MH-17 was struck by a surface-to-air missile while flying over Ukraine, killing all 295 passengers. The missile was attributed to pro-Russian rebels, supported by Russian government officials, who assumed the passenger jet, flying at 33,000 feet, was a military aircraft. Prior to this crisis, opinions varied widely on how or whether the United States and the European Union should respond to Russia's support of the rebels in Ukraine. A similar variance of opinion existed on the need for, extent of, and potency of economic sanctions levied against Russia for contributing to the conflict in Ukraine. After flight MH-17 was obliterated by a missile provided to the rebels by Russia, however, the United States and the European Union were steadfast in their imposition of new sanctions.

Convergence allows for some degree of debate about the crisis to continue. As such, convergence is distinct from congruence, where all parties align in their thinking to form one consistent narrative. This level of agreement is highly unlikely with most crises. Even events in history that are thoroughly studied and well documented continue to be debated at some level after narratives have converged. For example, few would contest that the *Titanic* disaster involved poor design of the ship. However, historians differ in their views of the role Captain Edward Smith's decisions played. Thus, historians and naval experts have considerable convergence in their views of the disaster. However, debate about the subtleties of the cause continues.

Convergence is also unlike dominance, where one version of the story is established and no others are tolerated. Dominance of this nature occurred in response to the severe acute respiratory syndrome (SARS) epidemic in China. (SARS is a viral respiratory disease that developed in animals and moved into the human population.) Between November 2002 and July 2003, an outbreak of SARS in southern China led to 775 deaths reported in multiple countries. Initially the Chinese government failed to report the rising number of SARS cases in their country. The World Health Organization was highly critical of the Chinese government for this delay, claiming the spread of the disease could have been contained sooner if the Chinese had been forthright in their reporting. The delay is part of the government's larger effort to control the SARS narrative. However, once the Chinese government was criticized globally for understating the severity of SARS within its borders, the country shifted its narrative to focus on the heroic efforts of Chinese doctors and nurses to treat and contain the disease. The subsequent narrative acknowledged the toll the disease was taking on patients and health care workers and emphasized the heroic sacrifices doctors and nurses were making—many of whom contracted and succumbed to the disease (Liu, McIntyre, & Sellnow, 2008).

As the SARS narrative in China evolved, points of message convergence were apparent. Most important, the progressing Chinese narrative concurred with the global narrative depicting the sense of urgency surrounding the outbreak. The lethal and highly transmissible nature of the disease was also a point of agreement or convergence with the global narrative of SARS. While the emphasis on the tremendous sacrifices of health care workers to contain the disease was less central to the global narrative, this dimension of the story did resonate with the fact that SARS is frighteningly contagious.

Message convergence theory offers three tenets or propositions explaining the convergence process and its influence, all of them relevant to crisis narratives. The first proposition contends that "convergence in the claims made by distinct sources, be it partial or complete, increases the strength of those claims" (Anthony et al., 2013, p. 349). As observers hear multiple narratives, they can distill points where seemingly distinct accounts of a crisis overlap or agree. These points of convergence in narratives are particularly compelling. Their believability stems from the assumption that if multiple sources with dissimilar or even competing objectives and viewpoints are sharing the same components in their narratives, there is a high likelihood that this aspect of the story is true. Thus, points of agreement in a cluster of narratives have the greatest strength in an argument regarding how the crisis should be viewed (Perelman & Olbrechts-Tyteca, 1969).

The second proposition of message convergence observes that "the more significant the points of convergence are to the audience, the stronger the claims" (Anthony et al., 2013, p. 350). Audiences observing crises are complex and diverse. Some of them are the people directly harmed by the crisis physically or financially. Others are affected by the policies that change or emerge in response to the crisis. Still others are emotionally involved with the crisis through feelings of empathy, sympathy, or shame. This impact or emotional involvement makes various aspects of the crisis narrative more or less significant or captivating. For example, those whose community was destroyed in 2011 by a massive tornado in Joplin, Missouri, were most interested in narratives explaining the financial details about how the city would recover. Those who were not directly affected were likely more concerned about aspects of the crisis narrative describing the influence of climate change on events such as tornados and the ability of communities to warn residents and for those residents to find adequate shelter from storms.

The third proposition of message convergence theory addresses the evolving nature of crisis narratives. It explains that "the strength of convergence may be modified as a result of a reflection about this very convergence" (Anthony et al., 2013, p. 350). From the outset of this chapter, we have argued that the uncertainty and bias inherent in crises inspire a diverse set of narratives. As these narratives evolve, points of convergence replace these more splintered portrayals of the crisis. The convergence process, however, is fluid. Points of agreement can give way to new interpretations with the discovery of additional information. In addition, the longer a narrative exists, the more likely it is that convergence will expand into a lasting narrative.

An additional way to understand the convergence process involves Fisher's view of narrative we discussed in Chapter 2. His view suggests that humans evaluate stories using standards of coherence and fidelity. Narrative coherence simply asks if the story hangs together. The expected structure of a story (beginning, middle, end) and the characters (protagonist, antagonist) are expected to fall within the same general lines as other stories. For example, a crisis story that features a hero figure who chooses to help some victims and not others would not be coherent because it fails to meet the expectations for hero behavior. The test of narrative coherence is whether the characters act in a reliable manner.

A second test of narrative coherence concerns the agreement of a story with broader beliefs, expectations, and experiences. Fidelity assesses if the story fits into larger notions of how the world works. Both the Deepwater

Horizon BP spill and the *Exxon Valdez* spill fit into larger belief systems about the failure of large oil companies to respect the environment. In fact, "big oil" is often perceived as exploiting the environment for short-term economic gain, so stories that fit into this larger belief system are more likely to be accepted. In contrast, a story that portrayed big oil as forgoing profits in favor of environmental protection might be questioned on the grounds of fidelity and even rejected as corporate spin.

Fidelity and coherence help determine which stories and which parts of a story will be retained and connected with others through the process of convergence. As audiences assess fidelity and coherence, they begin to make the connections that lead to a converged narrative. Fidelity and coherence are both features that lead to narrative coherence and are the outcome of narrative coherence.

LOCATING CONVERGENCE

The convergence process is manifest in at least three ways: informal reports and proceedings, popular narratives, and community and family narratives passed down over time. Formal accounts, commission reports, court proceedings, and investigatory boards, as we described in chapter 4, seek to compile an accurate record of what happened. By so doing, they take a number of individual stories, pieces of information, and views from experts and witnesses and sort through them to create a coherent and correct story.

The Rogers Commission investigated the dramatic and shocking 1986 space shuttle *Challenger* (mission STS 51-L) explosion, which led to the deaths of all seven crew members. President Ronald Reagan appointed the commission with a mandate to "1. Review the circumstances surrounding the accident to establish the probable cause or causes of the accident; and 2. Develop recommendations for corrective or other action based upon the Commission's findings and determinations" (Presidential Commission on the Space Shuttle Challenger Accident, 1986). Satisfying these mandates required sorting through a wide variety of accounts, information sources, and testimony and identifying points of convergence.

An additional location for convergence is in popular narratives. A disaster in television, film, and other fictional accounts often becomes the dominant narrative for an event. The story of the *Titanic* has been the subject of several fictional accounts, including the 1997 Hollywood film. Such popular narratives typically do not claim to be accurate portrayals of the events. The reach and power of these narratives, however, influence larger understandings and often can perpetuate a converged understanding of the crisis. For many, the 1997 movie, *Titanic*, is *the* defining narrative of the disaster.

Finally, converged narratives often become family or community accounts of an event. These accounts, typically passed down by word of mouth, position a family or personal experience within the larger story of a disaster. In this way, the narratives converge and support one another. Returning to our example of the 1997 flood of the Red River, the disaster forever altered the North Dakota towns of Fargo and Grand Forks. Downtown Grand Forks was devastated by high water and fire, while Fargo residents spent weeks holding back the water with sandbag dikes built by thousands of volunteers. Smaller communities in the region faced similar struggles, and the flood eventually cost the region more than $3.5 billion in losses. While there were divergent stories of failure, inadequate preparation and response, and inaccurate forecasting, one larger narrative that emerged concerned the pioneering spirit of the community, its resilience, and its ability to pull together. One story from the Fargo floods tells of long hours spent volunteering with others in sandbagging efforts to build dikes to protect the city. This personal narrative plays into larger beliefs and values, is consistent with other narratives about pioneers working together to overcome adversity, and positions an individual story within a larger narrative context.

LESSONS LEARNED

A fundamental advantage of the convergence process in crisis narratives is the renewed understanding of risks. Crises reveal failures in existing protective strategies, warning systems, beliefs, norms, and regulating policies. These failures constitute a loss in meaning where familiar, trusted procedures and norms fail and create narrative space for reconsideration of risk and its avoidance. The convergence process allows the crystallization of the debate and, ultimately, the identification of points of agreement that constitute lessons learned and influence future crisis planning.

Identifying the lessons learned from crises is a narrative process. As we have noted, crises begin with surprise and uncertainty. Consequently, various groups offer distinct reactions and interpretations of the crisis that in the early stages can be frustrating for audiences demanding a clear explanation. This pluralism of interpretations, however, allows many voices to be heard in response to the crisis. The natural cycle of these competing narratives leads to increasing agreement as more information is revealed. As the competing interpretations of the crisis converge, lessons learned from the crisis are revealed. The most compelling lessons are those that share widespread agreement and are clearly relevant to preventing similar crises in the future (Anthony et al., 2013). Without convergence of the narratives surrounding a crisis, lessons learned are unlikely to emerge. If such lessons are proposed without narrative convergence, they are unlikely to be influential.

The crises that BP and the NFL faced offer examples of the narrative convergence process. BP's failures in the Gulf reveal a need for better strategies for oil containment before drilling continues at such depths and in such ecologically fragile areas. The belief that big oil does not respect the environment supports the conclusion that more regulation is needed. Similarly, the NFL concussion problem has expanded to include reconsideration of protective equipment, injury policies, and even techniques for participating in sports such as hockey, soccer, gymnastics, and lacrosse at all levels. In these cases, converging interpretations of a complex and unfortunate crisis narrative have manifested in widespread strategies for curtailing similar harm in the future.

CONCLUSION

The uncertainty inherent in crises creates a narrative space for multiple interpretations of crisis events that provide an opportunity for pluralism where all sides of a crisis can be heard. In some cases, the competing narratives are motivated by bias and an urge for self-protection. In others, the shock of the crisis inspires the human need to understand the crisis experience through dialogue, face-to-face interaction, and both traditional and new forms of media. Diverse and competing narratives tend to converge over time. The points where narratives converge are most compelling for observers. As more information is revealed, points of convergence can shift and change. Eventually the convergence process reveals lessons learned that may be implemented in the form of new policies, norms, and procedures. A converged narrative helps individuals, organizations, and communities take actions to protect themselves in the future.

CASES TO CONSIDER

By their nature, crises are surprising and create uncertainty. Due to the confusion and lack of information surrounding most of them, multiple narratives emerge to explain what has happened and why. As more information is established, these diverse narratives evolve through a natural cycle of discovery and convergence. In many cases, this convergence process reveals lessons learned or key strategies for improving the policies and procedures that were in place prior to the crisis. The two cases that follow characterize the movement of crisis narratives from a divided, pluralistic view at the outset to a more unified or convergent view as additional information is revealed. The Ford and Firestone recall case reflects the deep narrative divide that can emerge in crisis narratives, particularly in the early stages. The Red River Valley flood case depicts the process through which narrative divergence can give way to convergence.

Competing Narratives in the Ford and Firestone Recall

The Ford Motor Company and Firestone Tire Company had a long and close relationship going back to the time of the founding of the two companies. The relationship became contentious in 2000 when problems were reported with Firestone tires on Ford Explorer vehicles: tire separation problems may have been associated with close to 250 deaths and as many as 3,000 serious injuries. The two companies established competing narratives, with Firestone suggesting the problem was associated with the vehicles and Ford pointing to the tires. There was also little agreement on when the problem was identified and when Ford was notified.

Early in the crisis, the CEOs of both companies were asked to testify before Congress. As you read their testimony, observe the clear contrast in the interpretations that each CEO provided. Although Ford and Firestone never fully reconciled their stories, the natural cycle of competing narratives did eventually produce a form of convergence. Information related to accident reporting and trend analysis became central to the converging narrative. The U.S. Congress recognized that existing procedures for reporting and identifying trends in automobile accidents needed improvement. It therefore insisted that the National Highway Traffic Safety Administration (NHTSA), the agency charged with identifying and reporting such trends, be overhauled. NHTSA responded without hesitation, and Congress provided the resources needed to transform the agency. This example exemplifies how convergence can lead to actions related to major policies.

PREPARED STATEMENT OF JOHN LAMPE, EXECUTIVE VICE PRESIDENT, BRIDGESTONE/FIRESTONE, INC.

Chairman McCain, Senator Hollings, and Members of this Committee: We want to thank you for calling this hearing. It has been a new experience for us to be appearing before Congress, and probably for any company to be subject to such an intense Congressional investigation as has occurred over such a short period of time. But, we are greatly benefiting from this process to learn about our own mistakes, and to work with you, Members of the Committee, toward ensuring that our tires and all tires are as safe as possible.

Firestone has manufactured hundreds of millions of safe tires for over one hundred years. Americans have driven billions of safe miles on safe Firestone tires. That is why this situation, with deaths and serious injuries, must be addressed and should never happen again.

It is little more than a month ago, on August 8, that we met with the National Highway Traffic and Safety Administration and together reviewed the performance of tires that have been associated with tread separations. These accidents have primarily occurred on the Ford Explorer vehicle. We regret that almost 10% of those rollovers involved tire separations. In light of that fact, we announced a voluntary safety recall of 6.5 million tires.

We also are trying to work with Ford Motor Company to understand the cause. This has led us to understand a key point for the future. The government and others have tended to look at auto safety and tire safety separately.

We believe that it is important to look at both issues together. Correct tires must be matched with vehicles; the mutual duties of tire manufacturers and automobile manufacturers must be made absolutely clear. If only it were possible to find a simple cause, such as certain tires made at a certain time and a certain plant, we would have resolved the problem.

But, we cannot today provide you with a conclusive cause of our past problems. We will not rest until we determine the cause. . . .

Fifth, we will work with this committee to develop any necessary legislative remedies that will assure to the American public that their tires and vehicles are safe. The distinct roles of tire and vehicle manufacturers regarding safety need to be brought together, rather than looked at separately. We will work with you to bring this disconnect to an end.

The Chairman. Ford executives allege that they became suspicious of a potential problem with Bridgestone/Firestone tires in foreign markets and that Ford requested data that you may have then possessed confirming their suspicion. They say that in response you only provided warranty adjustment data which showed no sign of problems, and not claims data, which would have indicated a problem. Is that true?

Mr. Lampe. Senator McCain, we have supplied Ford over the years any technical data, engineering data, that they have requested. Ford never requested, to the best of my knowledge—and we have had this conversation within my company—Ford never requested claims data until the middle of this year, June or July. We had been requested by NHTSA to supply that claims data as well. We were putting it together for NHTSA. We supplied it to NHTSA in July. And within 2 to 3 weeks after that, we supplied it to Ford. I have absolutely no knowledge of any requests for claims data prior to that from Ford.

STATEMENT OF JAC NASSER, CHIEF EXECUTIVE OFFICER, FORD MOTOR COMPANY

Mr. Nasser. Thank you, very much. Good afternoon, Chairman McCain, Senator Hollings, and Members of the Committee. I appreciate this opportunity to update you and the American people on the Firestone tire recall. But before I discuss the Firestone tire recall, I would like to say a brief word about the Ford Motor Company if I may.

Ford Motor Company is a company that throughout its history has in its strength been its employees and its customers. I have been with the Ford Motor Company for over thirty years. I started as a trainee in Ford Australia. And I am honored to lead this company into the 21st Century as we look after our customers going forward.

We have had some good discussion this morning. And I think it did get to the heart of the issue. And that is when did people know there was a problem with the Firestone tires? What have we done about it so far? And where are we heading in the future? And I appreciate the comments from many of the Senators who really concentrated on what do we all do collectively going forward?

Let us start with when did Ford know that there was a problem with the Firestone tires. I think it is worth repeating that because tires are the only component of any vehicle that are separately warranted, Ford did not know that there was a defect with the tires until we virtually pried the claims data from Firestone's hands in late July, early August, and analyzed it ourselves.

It was only then—and that was only a few days before the recall was announced—that Ford engineers found conclusive evidence at that point that the tires were defective. We then demanded that Firestone pull the tires from the road.

I must say that as we look back, the first signs of this problem developed in Saudi Arabia when our dealers reported complaints about certain Firestone tires. (SIC) So we asked Firestone to conduct additional tests on the tires. And I must say that after each and every test, Firestone reported that there was no defect in the tires. This did not satisfy our Saudi customers. So we replaced the tires about a year ago.

I should add that at about the same time, we wanted to know if our U.S. customers were having similar tire problems. And earlier last year, we asked Firestone to review its U.S. data in general. And we were assured by Firestone that there was no problem in this country regarding Firestone tires.

When he went back, our data, the government safety data and you heard from Mr. Slater and Ms. Bailey this morning, did not show anything either. Despite this, we asked Firestone for one more test. And Firestone examined tires in a special study in Texas, Nevada and Arizona. And they reported back as before that there was no defect to be found.

As you know, contrary to those repeated assurances, we later learned a very different story from Firestone's confidential claims data. And when we did, at that point in August of this year, we insisted that Firestone recall the defective tires.

Although I take no personal or professional pleasure in saying it, Firestone failed to share critical claims data with Ford that might have prompted the recall of these bad tires sooner. And I should say that last week I listened in disbelief as senior Firestone executives not only acknowledged that Firestone had analyzed its claims data, but also identified significant pattern of tread separations as early as 1998.

Yet, Firestone said nothing to anyone, including the Ford Motor Company. This is not the candid and frank dialog that Ford expects in its business relationships.

Partial Transcript of Senate Hearing 106–114, before the Committee on Commerce, Science, and Transportation, U.S. Senate, 106th Congress. Retrieved from https://www.gpo.gov/fdsys/pkg/CHRG-106shrg85219/html/CHRG-106shrg85219.htm

Threat and Convergence in the Fargo, North Dakota, and Moorhead, Minnesota, Flood of 1997

April and May 1997 saw a historic flood of the Red River that flows through Fargo and Grand Forks, North Dakota, and Moorhead, Minnesota. The river flows north into Canada and the surrounding area is very flat. The region is prone to flooding, but the 1997 floods were the most severe in at least one hundred years. What follows is my (Tim Sellnow) personal account of narrative convergence in response to the flood. I lived and worked in Fargo during the flood, and my home, neighborhood, and university were threatened by the rising water. My family and I spent days filling and passing sandbags along human chains to build temporary dikes. As you read the account, pay close attention to how information alerting the communities to increasing levels of risk provided the motivation for narrative convergence.

A Personal Account of the 1997 Red River Valley Flood

Sidewalks became topless tunnels in the winter of 1997 for residents of Moorhead, Minnesota, and Fargo, North Dakota. The record snowfall signaled certain severe flooding for the cities divided by the north-flowing Red River. Before the snow began melting in earnest, the cities held meetings separately to form their flood management plans. The two cities were courteous to one another, but had competed on a number of levels for decades and the clear intent was for each city to form and manage its own flood plan. The individuality of flood planning was also evident in the neighborhoods throughout the two cities. For example, residents in the northern sections of the cities perceived different levels of threat than residents in newly formed neighborhoods in the southern portions of the cities.

An ice storm, a rapid rise in temperatures, and ice jams along the river quickly escalated the flood situation beyond the most pessimistic expectations. Other towns and cities, both south and north of Fargo and Moorhead, were overrun by floodwaters, destroying thousands of homes and flooding main street businesses. Residents of Fargo and Moorhead watched this devastation, but remained focused on their separate community and neighborhood plans. These individual narratives ended when predictions for an overwhelming surge in water levels were provided by the National Weather Service.

The new warnings depicted water levels as much as a foot over what the Fargo and Moorhead neighborhoods were prepared to resist. This moment created a single, convergent flood narrative that turned the flood fight from individualized interpretations of risk into a single narrative of community-wide survival. The two mayors joined together in news conferences at least twice per day. Employees from the two cities shared information, networked their sandbagging resources, and collaborated in making their flood plans.

Volunteers filled sandbags around the clock. The universities, high schools, and middle schools in the two cities released their students to join the human chains of sandbaggers along both sides of the river. Buses loaded with volunteers from cities throughout the region streamed into town. The two cities worked together to distribute these volunteers to needed areas. National Guard troops from both states were dispatched and worked together to build clay dikes down the middle of high-risk neighborhood streets. Residents from both cities listened to the largest AM radio station in the area as broadcasters worked, commercial free, to provide updates and to announce urgent appeals for sandbaggers.

As the floodwaters crested, Fargo and Moorhead, northern and southern neighborhoods, and residents of both cities whose homes were on high ground watched as one community, united by one narrative. In the end, the dikes held, the water slowly descended, and the community was spared. The collaborative spirit had resulted in millions of sandbags being filled and placed on the banks of both cities. A single narrative of collective and cooperative resilience, perseverance, and survival was shared throughout the two cities.

CHAPTER 11

The Consequences of Crisis Narratives

HUMANS BY THEIR VERY NATURE are storytellers. Disasters, tragedies, and crises are powerful and disruptive forces that change the course of lives, families, institutions, communities, and societies. As such, they become the stuff of stories. We use stories to make sense of what we have experienced, contextualize events within larger experiences and personal and public systems of meaning, and pass on lessons learned to others, including subsequent generations. Accounts help us make sense of the facts of crisis. Stories of blame and responsibility are necessary for sorting through fault and cause and help us move beyond these events. Sharing stories of renewal leads to paths of recovery and rebuilding. Heroes give us models of how to behave, and victim stories generate empathy, emotional connection, and support. Memorial narratives promote individual and collective healing and memory across time.

Crisis narratives come from a variety of sources, take many forms, and lead to various outcomes. They are the expressions of the diverse experiences, values, perspectives, and insights of many different crisis participants: victims, first responders, community members, journalists, survivors, observers, family members, and leaders. These narratives are expressed by word of mouth; in newspapers, film, songs, books, television, blogs, and web pages; and through monuments and memorials.

In summarizing narratives of crisis, we describe their power and importance. These are stories that need to be told, but they also need to be understood as stories with limitations, distortions, and inaccuracies. We describe the power of crisis narratives to induce widespread change, and the process of change involves a narrative sequence. A narrative is necessary to create cohesive responses, facilitate policy changes, and generate public support. Crisis narratives also serve different functions for individuals, agencies, and organizations, communities, and societies.

UNDERSTANDING THE POWER OF CRISIS STORIES

Because humans frame meaning and understanding through stories, the narrative form is particularly powerful in shaping action. When a blame narrative frames a crisis as an accident, a one-time and unintentional mistake, the subsequent action is different than when a crisis is framed as a sign of a systemic flaw. Mistakes may be forgiven, but systemic flaws require changes in the system. Crises or disasters framed as intentional acts are typically labeled terrorism or crimes and usually result in direct and sometimes extreme responses. The responses to the terrorist acts of 9/11 are examples of the sweeping policy, social, and economic changes that can occur when a crisis narrative is constructed as an intentional act of terrorism. Billions of dollars, widespread changes in transportation policy, and the largest reorganization of the U.S. federal government since World War II followed the 9/11 terrorist attacks.

Crisis narratives can sometimes take the form of cautionary tales or morality plays, particularly as they are used to instruct. When a crisis is of sufficient scope and scale, the narrative may reach wide audiences and become part of popular cultural, as happened with the sinking of the *Titanic*. The Great Chicago Fire of 1871, another iconic crisis, burned much of the central city and killed an estimated three hundred people. The fire spread quickly because of rapid growth, poor building practices, drought, and an inadequate first-response capacity. The cause was never fully determined, but the *Chicago Tribune* published what was at best a speculative account that the fire was caused when a cow kicked over a lantern while being milked by Catherine O'Leary, a poor Irish immigrant. The story became the explanation and formed the basis of a popular children's song (Bales, 2002):

Late one night, when we were all in bed,
Old Mother Leary left a lantern in the shed,
And when the cow kicked it over, she winked her eye and said,
"There'll be a HOT time on the old town tonight."
FIRE, FIRE, FIRE!

The story of Catherine O'Leary and her cow is known to generations of Americans and helps instruct children about the dangers of fire.

Whether in the form of a children's song, Hollywood movies, or journalistic accounts, crisis stories have the power to shape understanding and action. They tell us in vivid and memorable ways who is a victim and who is a hero. They tell us what happened, establish blame and legal liability, and indicate who must pay. They help society assess what is risky and dangerous and what actions need to be taken to avoid harm. Because many of our social institutions and processes are designed to manage risks, crisis stories have broad implications for how we structure our institutions and we live our lives.

PROMOTING THE STORIES OF CRISIS

Crises are news, and in an era of 24/7 news reporting, they can be expected to generate significant news coverage. Journalistic accounts of crises have become ubiquitous as the news industry has become increasingly global, information has become instantly accessible through the Internet, and the media space has expanded. Some observers have even suggested that the ongoing coverage of crisis, crime, and violence has promoted a view of the world as dangerous and risky (Gerbner, Gross, Morgan, & Signorielli, 1980). Risk factors are often amplified and sometimes distorted through the media. This social amplification of risk has profound implications for societies, communities, and economies as attention and funding are directed to the risks that have generated the most compelling stories (Kasperson et al., 1988). The debunked link between child vaccinations and autism, fueled by media and Internet reports based in rumor and speculation, is an example of the significant harm a crisis story can create. Some parents have elected to forgo lifesaving vaccinations for their children because of junk science. This has also contributed to the reemergence of diseases such as whooping cough and measles.

In others cases, the coverage of crises by the media promotes learning, understanding of risk, and support for recovery efforts (Wilkins, 1984). The Amber Alert system, for example, generates an immediate and unified call to the community to assist in the recovery of missing children. The twenty-four-hour reporting of the Weather Channel draws attention to climate change and the resulting shifts in weather patterns and increasing frequency of weather events such as tornadoes and hurricanes. Media reports on water contamination may encourage residents to stockpile bottled water and help reduce exposure to harmful contaminants. Constant media attention also persuades viewers to contribute to recovery efforts through agencies such as the Red Cross and UNICEF. The larger public may learn strategies for response through media accounts. In short, the ever-expanding access to crisis coverage has led to many positive outcomes.

In addition to media accounts, personal stories of crises are increasingly found on the Internet. Blogs, websites set up for specific events, open forums, Facebook, and Twitter have become domains for telling personal stories of crisis and posting pictures and videos. The Sandy Hook shooting was memorialized on several Facebook pages, which included pictures and stories about the victims. Mysandyhookfamily.org was established by the families of the victims as a place to share pictures, memories, and stories, as well provide contact information for each other. Web-based archives of the *Exxon Valdez* oil spill for accounts and documents were established by several groups, including the Regional Citizens Advisory Council, which maintains an oral history site of personal stories from the *Exxon* disaster. The National Oceanic and Atmospheric Administration also maintains accounts of its role in the disaster on its website. Such sites allow individuals and groups to tell their stories, often with the goal of supporting a specific postcrisis policy agenda. The resulting public attention can facilitate appropriate individual, community, and social change.

Creating places for stories and promoting the narratives of crisis enable the sharing of important lessons learned, facilitate personal and social healing, and assist in creating meaning. Websites and memorials that help preserve the memory of an event are increasingly common narrative forms designed to preserve a meaning of the event. While the lessons may not always be the collectively agreed-on ones and the meaning is often a distortion of the actual events, the telling of the crisis story serves important individual and collective functions.

UNDERSTANDING CRISIS NARRATIVES AS STORIES

Crisis narratives must be understood as stories with limitations inherent in the narrator and the storytelling form. Experiences are often molded and reframed to fit established narrative forms, expectations of the audience, larger belief systems, and the limitations of forum. When a crisis does not fit the established narrative structure, it is less likely to be accepted. When a narrative is familiar and recognizable—with heroes and villains and a logical plot progression—and coherent and consistent with other beliefs, it is more easily understood and believed. The tendency to see crisis through familiar frames influences how an event is perceived.

Myths of crisis have been well documented (Tierney, 2003; Quarantelli, 1994), and crisis sociologists consistently find that these widespread social beliefs are generally incorrect. The belief that crises are accompanied by widespread panic, looting, and a general breakdown in social organization is an example of such myths. The panic myth, or the belief that people will engage in irrational behavior during a crisis (such as running into a burning building after escaping or needlessly jumping to their deaths), has been largely debunked. Generally people experiencing a crisis behave in rational ways given the circumstances, and looting and high rates of crime are rare conditions of crisis. In fact, crime rates typically go down during a major crisis or disaster. Despite evidence to the contrary, these beliefs persist and are often widely reported in the media.

Following the chaos and disruption of Hurricane Katrina, media reports of crime, particularly in the New Orleans Superdome, were widely reported. Reports included roving gangs, widespread looting, rapes, murders, and a general breakdown in social order. One study, however, found that while crime did occur during the Katrina disaster, behavior described as looting might have actually been cases of scavenging for survival. In addition, overall crime rates for New Orleans declined during the disaster (Barsky, Trainor, & Torres, 2006). The *New York Times* noted that the widespread media reports of many crimes were unconfirmed rumors best described as urban legends (Carr, 2005).

The myths of panic, looting, and breakdown in social order during crisis are part of broader narrative scripts. The story of a society descending into chaos is widely represented throughout popular culture, books, and film. From a postwar dystopia to the outbreak of pandemic disease and even to the Zombie apocalypse, the story of a breakdown in social order is a narrative mainstay of the media. That modern life, particularly urban life, is one short step from catastrophic chaos appears to be a fundamental belief (Smith, 1995). Moreover, the basis and shape of such disorder are associated with other widespread beliefs about such things as technology, the role of government and large institutions, threats from unrestrained growth, and fears and prejudices regarding race and culture. Catherine O'Leary was likely blamed for the Chicago fire as a symbolic representative of the Irish Catholic immigrant community that was widely seen as bringing chaos and disorder to Chicago at the turn of the century. Anti-Irish sentiment was high in the United States at the time, and the O'Leary narrative played into those beliefs. New Orleans has a long history of racial tensions, and media reports of crime and disorder following Katina reflected this larger racial bias. African Americans attempting to leave a flooded New Orleans were often seen as threats. In one case, the Danziger Bridge shootings, two people were killed and four were wounded five days after Katrina. The unarmed group was trying to leave the city when officers from a suburban community confronted them. Cultural assumptions, beliefs, prejudices, and myths are reflected in the development and propagation of crisis narratives. Crisis narratives are often used as vehicles to reify existing beliefs and in this way may mask a more accurate account of what actually happened, when, and why.

CRISIS NARRATIVES OF CHANGE

Crises are change-inducing events. They create the need, perceived or real, for significant social, economic, physical, or political change. They induce change by altering the physical, social, political, and economic landscape. They demonstrate, often in dramatic ways, that established activities, beliefs, and systems are inadequate. The stories told about crisis frame and encode experiences, thereby creating and encompassing the meaning of the event. Crises create and perpetuate new ways to see and respond to risks, and the resulting stories stimulate new ways of thinking and acting.

Following Hurricane Sandy's devastation in New York and New Jersey, public discussions were initiated about how and where to rebuild, what building codes should be changed, the adequacy and resilience of the infrastructure, and the overall risks of such extreme weather events. The San Francisco earthquake of 1906 led to the development of many modern building practices. A little over a month after the earthquake and fire destroyed the city, the Structural Association of San Francisco was founded (it later became the Structural Engineers Association of California). The Galveston hurricane of 1900, which claimed over six thousand lives, helped spur the development of modern forecasting and warning techniques and the reform of the U.S. Weather Bureau. The 1918 influenza pandemic helped usher in modern public health practices and continues to serve as a cautionary tale for public health preparedness.

Crises are some of the most powerful forces of systematic social change. In many ways, the most significant elements of a crisis are its larger impact and its resulting consequences. By *consequences*, we mean the social, political, economic, demographic, physical, and technological changes that follow a crisis. Crises create the need for change and precipitate change due to the intersection of several factors: the extreme disruption of the status quo, the demonstrated inadequacy of the current system, and leveraging of resources for change. By removing the assumption of the status quo, many of the impediments to change are similarly removed. By demonstrating inadequacy in the current system, a crisis can create a sense of urgency for change. Resources are often made available for responding to a crisis given this sense of urgency. As we described in chapter 10, narratives are part of the process used to discuss, debate, and agree on what happened. Factors changed by a crisis include population shifts; changes in agencies, capacities, and technologies; new monitoring, warning, and response systems; realignment of relationships; new laws, procedures, and regulations; and modified beliefs and norms about risk and risk avoidance.

British sociologist Barry Turner (1976) has described the change process initiated by a crisis. A crisis begins through a failure in foresight where sets of accepted beliefs about hazards and risks, and precautionary norms, practices, and procedures are believed to be adequate. Failure in foresight is a breakdown or deficiency in this structure of beliefs and associated norms regarding some risk or a failure to perceive how those risks emerge. A failure of foresight is a collapse in a system of risk avoidance strategies that were considered adequate. These precautionary norms, practices, and procedures are often encoded in a dominant narrative of crisis, and when these collapse, a need is created for a new nar-

TABLE 11.1 *Narrative Sequence for the Consequences of a Crisis*

1. Narratives of risk: Dominant narratives of risk-encoding experiences, beliefs, values, precautionary norms, practices, and procedures regarding risks and their avoidance

2. Crisis-induced confusion, uncertainty, and disruption of meaning systems: Dramatic demonstration of inadequacy of existing narrative and disruption in channels of communication, including relationships and media

3. Need for sense making and reconstruction of meaning: Widespread community and social need to create or recreate meaning for the crisis event

4. Narrative processes/competing/converging narratives: Development of various narratives (accounts, blame, renewal, victim, hero, and memorial)

5. Social consensus and the emergence of new dominating narratives: Emergence of social consensus around a dominant narrative encoding meaning and lessons

6. Change: Modification of policies, procedures, agencies, structures, beliefs, and so on to reflect new meaning and understanding

7. Narrative of memory and memorializing: Reifying meaning and lessons in a form that preserves or promotes learning and remembering

rative. The process whereby a crisis results in a change in the dominant or consensual narrative is outlined in table 11.1.

A crisis occurs within the context of existing narratives reflecting established beliefs about risk and threats. The crisis demonstrates these are inadequate by creating confusion and uncertainty and providing the elements of a new narrative. Postcrisis narratives often compete with one another for dominance until a general convergence eventually arises around the larger meaning of the crises. This new narrative incorporates the larger lessons of risk and risk avoidance. When this happens, the political, social, and media agendas may change to reflect the new understanding and the lessons learned. Eventually this new narrative is incorporated into memorials and commemorations in ways that perpetuate this narrative of risk.

Thomas Birkland (1998) described crises using the concept of focusing event: "an event that is sudden; relatively uncommon; can be reasonably defined as harmful or revealing the possibility of potentially greater future harms; has harms that are concentrated in a particular geographical area or community of interest; and that is known to policy makers and the public simultaneously" (p. 54). Dynamic media agendas are directly influenced by dramatic crises by focusing the public's attention and activating dormant public issues such as gun control, climate change, or regulation of industry. Subsequent media coverage is most likely to follow the general frame established by the crisis. This often extends to coverage of public debates, policy changes, and anniversaries of the event or similar events.

Beyond influencing the media agenda, the political agenda is also influenced by a crisis. Birkland (1998) observed that policy agendas are often focused due to the disruption of the status quo, a sense of urgency, and the mobilization of resources associated with a crisis. Narratives of accountability tend to frame the specific nature of policy changes, particularly as they support the larger issue agendas of advocacy groups. In these cases, groups tend to incorporate the crises into their larger change narratives. While it is perhaps unfortunate that so many large public policy questions and issues of social change are driven by the crisis of the moment, it is clear that crises are a primary force of social, political, and economic change. A crisis is often required to disrupt the status quo and leverage the resources to induce change. The specific shape of the change is governed largely by the stories that are told.

CONSEQUENCES OF CRISIS NARRATIVES

In the most basic sense, a crisis narrative is just a story. However, we have shown at several points that these narratives have important and often far-reaching consequences. In most cases, the narrative becomes the crisis in the sense that it is the way most people experience and understand these events. A narrative that grounds a crisis as a technological failure, for example, may lead to greater regulation of technology. Narratives that describe a crisis as a natural disaster caused by natural forces suggest that nothing could be done to avoid the harm and therefore no human agent is responsible. Beyond this, however, a crisis narrative has important consequences for individuals, organizations, and communities.

For Individuals

For the individual, a crisis can be a significant life event that needs to be incorporated into larger personal systems of meaning and a sense of self. The individual's relative position within the story may influence the form and level of impact. For example, when individuals see themselves as heroes, the impact will be different than if they see themselves as victims. Hero, victim, survivor, or refugee can become central parts of identity following a major crisis.

One of us personally experienced a devastating house fire. In this case, members of the family described themselves as heroes who were able to defeat the threat of the fire. Although no loss of life or serious injury occurred, all of the family pets and possessions, including clothing and pictures, were lost. The family home was completely destroyed. Fire is a profoundly destructive force because valued possessions are quite literally turned to ash, and the possessions that are not burned are often so damaged by toxic smoke they usually cannot be used. In this case, three young children, their parents, and grandmother escaped on a chain ladder from a third-story window. These family members were described by others not as victims but rather as victors who had not been beaten by the fire. In fact, the grandmother of the family was characterized as a hero for first sounding the alarm in the middle of the night while others were sleeping. While the distinction may be subtle, it is an important characterization in this family narrative of a devastating personal event and lead to a more constructive and empowering meaning.

For Organizations and Agencies

By definition, crises are one of the primary factors in the failure of organizations. Excellent products, state-of-the-art facilities and technology, robust markets, innovative approaches, cooperative supplier relationships, and committed and skilled employees can all be seriously degraded or destroyed through a crisis. Large-scale natural disasters, such as Hurricane Katrina or Superstorm Sandy, can devastate small businesses by damaging and destroying facilities and markets. Industrial accidents, fires, and explosions can halt production or service operations, create long-term liability, and undermine employee confidence. Faulty and even dangerous products can destroy brand reputation and consumer confidence in products. Management misconduct can result in regulatory and legal problems and create long-term liability and uncertainty. These and similar other crises can call into question an organization's fundamental legitimacy or the degree to which an organization is perceived to be operating in a manner consistent with larger social norms (Dowling & Pfeffer, 1975). Organizations and agencies that lose legitimacy may no longer have the support and resources necessary to keep operating.

Enron, a giant in the global energy industry, was the sector leader in energy trading through the 1980s and 1990s but was caught up in major scandals regarding fraud, manipulation of markets, and unethical and illegal conduct. Before declaring bankruptcy in December 2001, Enron had more than twenty thousand employees. Its story was thus one of "corporate greed run amok, an illustration of political influence, and as a morality play about the relationship between accounting firms and their clients" (Seeger & Ulmer, 2003). Much of the company's business model was based on exploiting accounting loopholes and manipulating markets, and Enron exploited and exacerbated the California energy crisis in summer 2001. Other loopholes and schemes involved not just ethical misconduct but fraud. Investors lost billions of dollars, and Enron's accounting firm, Arthur Andersen, was also effectively destroyed by the scandal. The Enron crisis and the distrust of corporations it generated contributed to a sharp downturn in major stock markets. The demise of Enron, based in a crisis created by illegal and unethical conduct, harmed thousands of investors and retirees, effectively destroyed the reputations of suppliers, and caused hardship for many communities.

For the Community

As one of only two events ever rated a level 7 incident on the International Nuclear Event Scale, the Chernobyl disaster was among the worst nuclear disasters in history. The incident began on April 26, 1986, at reactor number four of the Chernobyl plant in Ukraine. A sudden power surge was followed by a reactor vessel rupture and fire, and a cloud of radioactive material spread over a large area of Ukraine and other parts of Europe. Thirty-one staff and emergency workers died in the incident, and another sixty died from radiation exposure. Radiation-induced cancers and disease among residents and workers may still claim many more lives. Given the tenacity of radiation, emergency management officials determined that residents would need to be permanently relocated. The

Chernobyl Nuclear Power Plant Zone of Alienation is a 30 kilometer radius area, covering approximately 1,000 square miles. Prior to the accident, some 120,000 people lived in the area. The zone, which is considered the most heavily contaminated radiological site in the world, is home to only a few hundred mostly elderly returnees who have refused to leave despite the risk. A similar relocation program followed the Fukushima Daiichi nuclear disaster. Some 80,000 people were evacuated from a 12 mile zone around the Fukushima nuclear plant, and former residents are allowed to briefly visit their homes only once a month.

In extreme cases such as these, a disaster may essentially destroy a community. In other cases—such as the 2013 fertilizer plant explosion in West Texas that killed 15 people and injured another 150 out of a population of fewer than 3,000 or the 2011 tornados in Joplin, Missouri, that killed 158 and destroyed 25 percent of the city—communities are altered in fundamental ways. Buildings, landmarks, and sometimes whole neighborhoods are destroyed; jobs are lost; and people die, are injured, or move away. Community values, beliefs, and norms are also affected by these events, and they become part of the stories communities tell about themselves. In some cases, communities emerge from these events much more resilient with a greater understanding of risk and greater capacity to respond. The stories community members tell help pass on the lessons and preserve the resilience. The may include the full narrative range of victim and hero, renewal and blame, and cautionary tales.

For Society

Disease pandemics are among the most devastating form of crisis, and no other modern pandemic has been as devastating as the 1918–1920 influenza outbreak. The so-called Spanish flu infected as many as 500 million people and may have killed as many as 50 million people worldwide. The virus was particularly virulent, with a mortality rate roughly three times the rate of typical seasonal flu, which is usually under 1 percent. Following on the heels of World War I, the pandemic spread rapidly through communities as soldiers were relocated from Europe. The crisis changed the way Americans lived: local flu ordinances limited public gatherings like sales, sporting events, and even funerals to slow the spread of the disease. Health care facilities were overwhelmed, as were burial services. In many cases, several members of a family died from the flu within a few days of one another.

The U.S. Centers for Disease Control and Prevention has archived many family accounts of the 1918 influenza pandemic. One story was told by Arthur Duery Davis (September 7, 1893–September 8, 1975), who worked as a grave digger during the pandemic.

> One morning, at 6:00 AM, I was set to work digging three graves for a family of six that lived down the road from my home. Around 9:00 AM, the doctor sent word to dig yet another grave. Then around lunchtime, I got word to dig yet another grave and by 4:00 PM, I was instructed to dig the final grave for that entire family. (Centers for Disease Control and Prevention, 2014)

This narrative helps generate a broader understanding of the personal toll of the crisis. The pandemic influenza was a global event of almost unprecedented proportion. Changes in public health practices developed as a consequence of the pandemic, and many of these are still used today. During the pandemic, in addition to using social distancing by limiting large gatherings of people, various levels and branches of government coordinated their efforts, health systems and hospitals developed surge capacity, and containment efforts involving isolation were employed. Evidence suggests that communities that instituted these kinds of measures fared better during the pandemic (Ott, Shaw, Danila, & Lynfield, 2007). In addition, the lessons of the 1918 pandemic influenza have been passed down in stories that the public health community still uses to help prepare society for the inevitability of another pandemic.

STORIES WE CHOOSE TO TELL

Storytelling is a deliberate and intentional process designed to achieve goals and accomplish specific outcomes. It may involve teaching, sharing, meaning creation, achieving psychological catharsis, and developing a larger understanding of what happened and why. Storytellers are strategic in their choices about how best to achieve their goals. Often some aspects of the story are emphasized over others. Characters and their motives are changed. Events may be reordered. In some cases, entirely new explanations may be invented, such as with Catherine O'Leary and her unruly cow. Stories may also be strategically framed to create alternative narratives that shift blame. No story can capture the entirety of an event and, as described earlier, how one perceives an event is a matter of perspective. Often, however, crisis narratives are intentionally incomplete. Leaving out details may position the narrator more favorably or may lead the audience to a particular view of the cause. In other cases, the narrative may be incomplete because all the details are not known or the crisis is unresolved. In addition, the narrator may choose to allow the audience to draw their own conclusion from an incomplete narrative.

Crisis events often play into existing or emerging political agendas, and narratives are often intentionally constructed as political responses. Highly visible cases of mass shootings, including Sandy Hook elementary school where twenty children and six adult staff were killed, have intersected with the larger issue of gun control and have led to reinvigorated efforts to promote restrictions on high-volume, rapid-fire weapons in the United States. Parents of the deceased students formed the group Sandy Hook Promise "to honor all victims of gun violence by turning our tragedy into a moment of transformation" (Sandy Hook Promise, 2014). Many Sandy Hook parents, such as Mark Barden, frame the story of their losses to support gun control. Barden authored a powerful call for gun control for *Time*. In it he recounted the story of his anguish of losing his son Daniel: "I can still feel the softness of his 7-year-old cheek when I kissed him and put him on the school bus to go to Sandy Hook Elementary School on December 14, 2012, never to see him alive again" (Barden, 2014, para. 1). Barden also asked that the lessons from the Sandy Hook tragedy be used to help change the laws so that future deaths can be avoided: "It's too late for my sweet little Daniel . . . but it's not too late to protect your children and the children that you love" (para. 7).

Sometimes such stories and their storytellers are criticized for using the narratives to achieve political goals. The individuals who choose to share their grief in these ways, however, are usually motivated by a sincere interest in ensuring that similar events do not occur again. For these storytellers, the meaning of the crisis is closely connected to the change that is ultimately created. Stories are repositories for experiences and emotions of those involved with a crisis and are the underlying source for the postcrisis lessons and future policy decisions.

CRISIS NARRATIVE AS MORAL

Crises almost always raise important ethical and moral questions. The ensuing crisis narrative, as we have pointed out, is sometimes framed as a cautionary tale. These stories often include lessons about right and wrong, good and bad, and desirable and undesirable actions. Many narratives include more explicit moral lessons tied to heroes, victims, and villains of the story. In fact, storytelling is generally regarded as one of the fundamental processes in moral education in part because stories allow audiences to identify with the characters (Tappan & Brown, 1989). Stories of crisis also create empathy for victims, instruct in the principles of responsibility and virtuous behaviors, and in general stimulate the moral imagination (Day, 1991). Stories of crises illustrate the virtues of character and help instruct in the processes of moral reasoning. They help us understand the deep emotional and human impact of loss, fear, and uncertainty. Many moral lessons typify crisis narratives, but dominant among them are human hubris and the power of nature, human greed, and the failure to heed warnings. In addition, more positive moral lessons about helping others, overcoming hardship, self-sacrifice, and pulling together as a community are common.

The story of human hubris, particularly in the face of natural forces, is common in many of the crises we have discussed in this book, including the *Titanic* disaster and Hurricane Katrina. In these stories, humans failed to respect the power of nature and as a consequence suffered catastrophic consequences. One variant of the hubris moral is technological hubris. The narratives about the Fukushima Daiichi and the Chernobyl radiological episodes included moral lessons about our ability to control these powerful forces of nature and what happens when atomic forces are unleashed. Hubris also carries over into the failure to heed warnings, ignoring the signs of impending harm, and the belief that larger risks will not become manifest. Human greed—particularly in the case of organizational crises, such as the Enron crisis, the Deepwater Horizons spill, or the contamination of food produces with melamine—is also a common moral lesson for crisis. In these narratives, an organization seeking to increase its profits creates a crisis. The profit motive and the drive for wealth, in stories of crisis as greed, led to unwarranted risk taking, a failure to invest in and take precautions, and inevitable catastrophe. In some cases, the lessons of morality and profit are carried over to a refusal of companies to assist victims and pay for the harm they have created.

In addition to pointing out moral failure, narratives also offer more positive moral lessons about helping others, human virtue, overcoming hardship, and pulling together as a community. The hero/heroine narrative, described in chapter 8, passes on models of desired behaviors for others, including moral lessons about helping others in need, and is grounded in ethics of humanism and care. Many of the accounts of 9/11, including the sacrifices of ordinary people and first responders, include moral lessons about the importance of helping others. The powerful documentary *9/11: Heroes of the 88th Floor* tells the story of personal sacrifice and the organized efforts of everyday citizens that ultimately saved the lives of more than seventy people. Stories also emphasize the morality of working together as a community to overcome hardships imposed by a crisis. The story of the Fargo, North Dakota, floods was one of community resilience, working together, and tenacity in resisting the forces of nature. These stories promote the ethics of resilience, cooperation, and, ultimately, renewal.

CONCLUSION

Fukushima and Chernobyl, Columbine and Katrina, 9/11 and the *Titanic*, the Oklahoma City and Boston Marathon Bombings, the Great Chicago Fire, and the tragedy of the Sandy Hook Elementary School murders will continue to live on in stories. The lessons from these and other crises and disasters will influence public policy and individual actions. The memorials that communities build will serve as physical reminders, and social media memorials will include powerful personal recollections, pictures, video footage, and calls to action. Hollywood filmmakers and independent documentarians will continue to tell and retell these stories in dramatic visual ways. Songwriters will set the story of sinking ships to music, and family histories will record memories of fires, floods, and hurricanes.

We live in an uncertain world where risks are evolving rapidly and interacting with increasingly complex technological, social, political, and economic systems. Climate change, technological complexity, geopolitical turmoil, emerging diseases, growing populations, terrorism, environmental degradation, and the interaction of these and other factors will create more disasters and crises. Uncertainty, lack of predictability, instability, and loss of meaning will accompany these events. This will result in secondary crises, higher levels of harm, and questioning of the ways in which risks are managed. Stories told about villains and heroes, risk and blame, and ruin and renewal will frame broader meaning and response. As more crises occur, the stories we choose to tell will play a central role in how these events are managed at individual, institutional, community, and societal levels.

References

CHAPTER I

Benoit, W. (1995). *Accounts, excuses, and apologies: A theory of image restoration strate-gies*. Albany: State University of New York Press.

Bruner, J. (1991). The narrative construction of reality. *Critical Inquiry, 18*(1), 1–21.

Burton, I., Kates, R. W., & White, G. F. (1978). *The environment as hazard*. New York: Oxford University Press.

Coombs, W. T. (2010). Parameters for crisis communication. In W. T. Coombs & S. J. Hol-laday (Eds.), *The handbook of crisis communication* (pp. 17–53).Hoboken, NJ: Wiley.

Covello, V. T. (2009). *Strategies for overcoming challenges to effective risk communication*. In R. L. Heath & D. H. O'Hair (Eds.), *Handbook of risk and crisis communication* (pp. 143–167). New York, NY: Routledge.

Fink, S. (1986). *Crises management: Planning for the inevitable*. New York: American Management Association.

Fritz, C. E. (1961). *Disaster*. Alexandria, VA: Institute for Defense Analyses, Weapons Systems Evaluation Division.

Heath, R. L. (1995). Environmental risk communication: Cases and practices along the Texas Gulf Coast. In B. R. Burelson (Ed.), *Communication yearbook 18* (pp. 225–277). Newbury Park, CA: Sage.

Heath, R. L. (2004). Telling a story: A narrative approach to communication during crisis. In D. Millar & R. L. Heath (Eds.), *Responding to crisis: A rhetorical approach to crisis communication* (pp. 167–188). Mahwah, NJ: Erlbaum.

Heath, R. L., & O'Hair, H. D. (Eds.). (2009). *Handbook of risk and crisis communication*. New York: Routledge.

Hermann, C. F. (1963). Some consequences of crisis which limit the viability of organiza-tions. *Administrative Science Quarterly, 8*(1), 61–82.

Jasinski, J. (2001). *Sourcebook on rhetoric: Key concepts in contemporary rhetorical stud-ies*. Thousand Oaks, CA: Sage.

Kaplan, S., & Garrick, B. J. (1981). On the quantitative definition of risk. *Risk Analysis, 1*(1), 11–27.

Kreps, G. A. (1984). Sociological inquiry and disaster research. *Annual Review of Sociol-ogy, 10*, 309–330.

Mair, V. H. (2010). *The Columbia history of Chinese literature*. New York, NY: Columbia University Press.

McClam, E. (2013, April 10). Teen daughters find strength to lift 3,000-pound tractor off father. *NBC News*. Retrieved from http://usnews.nbcnews.com/_news/2013/04/10/17689146-teen -daughters-find-strength-to-lift-3000-pound-tractor-off-father?lite

McFarlane, A. C., & Norris, F. H. (2006). Definitions and concepts in disaster research. In F. H. Norris, S. Galea, M. J. Friedman, & J. Watson (Eds.), *Methods for disaster mental health research* (pp. 3–19). New York, NY: Guilford Press.

Ngak, C. (2013, April 19). Boston manhunt complicated by Ustream, Twitter. *CBS News.* Retrieved from http://www.cbsnews.com/8301-205_162-57580551/boston-manhunt -complicated-by-ustream-twitter/

Perrow, C. (1984). *Normal accidents.* New York, NY: Basic Books.

Perry, R. W. (2007). What is a disaster? In H. Rodriguez, E. L. Quarantelli, & R. R. Dynes (Eds.), *Handbook of disaster research* (pp. 1–15). New York, NY: Springer.

Quarantelli, E. L. (1984). *Evacuation behavior and problems: Findings and implications from the research literature.* Newark: Disaster Research Center, University of Delaware.

Seeger, M. W, Sellnow, T. L., & Ulmer, R. R. (2003). *Organizational communication and crisis.* Westport, CT: Praeger .

Sellnow, T. L., & Seeger, M. W. (2013). *Theorizing crisis communication* (vol. 4). Hoboken, NJ: Wiley.

Safety of life at sea convention text. (1914). London: His Majesty's Stationery Office by Harrison and Sons. Retrieved from http://www.imo.org/KnowledgeCentre/Referenc- esAndArchives/HistoryofSOLAS/Pages/default.aspx

Smart, C., & Vertinsky, I. (1977). Designs for crisis decision units. *Administrative Science Quarterly, 22*(4), 640–657.

Weick, K. E. (1993). The collapse of sensemaking in organizations: The Mann Gulch disas- ter. *Administrative Science Quarterly, 38,* 628–652.

CHAPTER 2

Badger, K., Royse, D., & Moore, K. (2011). What's in a story? A text analysis of burn sur- vivors' Web-posted narratives. *Social Work in Health Care, 50,* 577–594.

Benoit, W. L. (1995). *Accounts, excuses, and apologies: A theory of image restoration strat- egies.* Albany: State University Press of New York.

Bormann, E. G. (1983). Symbolic convergence: Organizational communication and culture. In L. L. Putnam & M. E. Pacanowsky (Eds.), *Communication and organizations: An interpretive approach,* Thousand Oaks, CA: Sage.

Browning, L., & Morris, G. H. (2012). *Stories of life in the workplace: An open architecture for organizational narratology.* New York: Routledge.

Congress members criticize auto executives' corporate jet travel. (2008, November 19). *Wall Street Journal.* Retrieved from http://blogs.wsj.com/autoshow/2008/11/19/congress -members-criticize-auto-executives-corporate-jet-travel/

Coupland, D. (1996). *Polaroids from the dead.* London: Flamingo.

Dearin, R. D. (1969). The philosophical basis of Chaim Perelman's theory of rhetoric. *Quar- terly Journal of Speech, 55,* 213–224.

Dowling, J., & Pfeffer, J. (1975). Organizational legitimacy: Social values and organizational behavior. *Pacific Sociological Review, 18,* 122–136.

Fiderer, D. (2013, November 9). Rewriting history to blame Tim Geithner: An incomplete story of the AIG bailout. *Huffington Post.* Retrieved from http://www.huffingtonpost .com/david-fiderer/rewriting-history-to-blam_b_372127.html

Fisher, W. R. (1980). Rationality and the logic of good reasons. *Philosophy and Rhetoric, 13,* 121–130.

Fisher, W. R. (1984). *Human communication as narration: Toward a philosophy of reason, logic, and action.* Columbia: University of South Carolina Press.

Fisher, W. R. (1987). *Human communication as narration: Toward a philosophy of reason, value, and action.* Columbia: University of South Carolina Press.

Foss, S. K. (2009). *Rhetorical criticism: Exploration and practice* (4th ed.). Long Grove, IL: Waveland Press.

Frank, D. A. (2011). 1958 and the rhetorical turn in the 20th-century thought. *Review of Communication, 11,* 239–252. doi:10.1080/15358593.2011.60215

Ghorbani, M., Liao, Y., Caykoylu, S., & Chand, M. (2013). Guilt, shame, and reparative behavior: The effect of psychological proximity. *Journal of Business Ethics, 114,* 311–323. doi:10.1007/s10551-012-1350-2

Hearit, K. M. (2006). *Crisis management by apology: Corporate response to allegations of wrongdoing.* Mahwah, NJ: Erlbaum.

Heath, R. L. (2004). Telling a story: A narrative approach to communication during crisis. In D. Millar & R. L. Heath (Eds.), *Responding to crisis: A rhetorical approach to crisis communication* (pp. 167–188). Mahwah, NJ: Erlbaum.

Hermann, C. F. (1963). Some consequences of crisis which limit the viability of organizations. *Administrative Science Quarterly, 8*(1), 61–82.

Jasinski, J. (2001). *Sourcebook on rhetoric: Key concepts in contemporary rhetorical studies.* Thousand Oaks, CA: Sage.

Johnson, J. D., & Case, D. O. (2012). *Health information seeking.* New York, NY: Peter Lang.

Kahneman, D. (2011). *Thinking fast and slow.* New York, NY: Farrar, Straus and Giroux.

Langer, E. J. (2009). *Counter clockwise: Mindful health and the power of possibility.* New York: Random House.

Langer, S. (1953). *Feeling and form.* New York, NY: Scribner.

Luhmann, N. (2008). *Risk: A sociological theory.* New Brunswick, NJ: Aldine Transaction.

Martin, W. (1986). *Recent theories of narrative.* Ithaca, NY: Cornell University Press.

Mencl, J., & May, D. R. (2009). The effects of proximity and empathy on ethical decision-making: An exploratory investigation. *Journal of Business Ethics, 85,* 201–226. doi:10.1007/s10551-008-9765-5

Pennebaker, J. W. (1990). *Opening up: The healing power of confiding in others.* New York, NY: Morrow.

Perelman, C. (1979). *The new rhetoric and the humanities: Essays on rhetoric and its applications.* Dordrecht, Holland: D. Reidel.

Perelman, C., & Olbrechts-Tyteca, L. (1969). *The new rhetoric: A treatise on argumentation.* London: University of Notre Dame Press.

Richardson, B. (2008). Denarration. In D. Herman, M. Jahn, & M. Ryan (Eds.), *Routledge encyclopedia of narrative theory* (pp. 100–101). London: Routledge.

Rowland, R. (2009). The narrative perspective. In J. A. Kuypers (Ed.), *Rhetorical criticism* (pp. 117–142). Lanham, MD: Lexington Books.

Sellnow, D. D. (2014). *The rhetorical power of popular culture: Considering mediated texts.* Thousand Oaks, CA: Sage.

Sellnow, T. L., & Ulmer, R. R. (2004). Ambiguity as an inherent factor in crisis communication. In R. L. Heath & D. Millar (Eds.), *Crisis communication: A rhetorical approach* (pp. 251–262). Mahwah, NJ: Erlbaum.

Sharf, B. F., Harter, L. M., Yamasaki, J., & Haidet (2011). Narrative turns epic: Continuing developments in health narrative scholarship. In T. L. Thompson, R. Parrott, & J. F. Nussbaum (Eds.), *The Routledge handbook of health communication* (pp. 36–51). New York, NY: Routledge.

Ulmer, R. R., & Sellnow, T. L. (2000). Consistent questions of ambiguity in organizational crisis communication: Jack in the Box as a case study. *Journal of Business Ethics, 25,* 143–155.

Venette, S. J. (2008). Risk as an inherent element in the study of crisis communication. *Southern Communication Journal, 73,* 197–210. doi:10.1080/10417940802219686

Wallace, K. R. (1963). The substance of rhetoric: Good reasons. *Quarterly Journal of Speech,* 49(3), 239-249.

Weick, K. E. (1995). *Sensemaking in organizations.* Thousand Oaks, CA: Sage.

Youssef, N. A. (2013, November 9). CBS retracts "60 Minutes" story on Libya attack. *Lexington Herald Leader,* A6.

CHAPTER 3

Argenti, P. A. (2011, February 19). Crisis communication: Lessons from 9/11. *Harvard Business Review.* Retrieved from https://hbr.org/2002/12/crisis-communication-lessons-from-911

Centers for Disease Control and Prevention. (2012, February 23). Public health matters blog [Web log post]. Retrieved from . http://blogs.cdc.gov/publichealthmatters/2012/02/disaster-movies-lessons-learned/

Cosgrove, B. (2013, May 13). Lower Manhattan's lost anchors: Remembering the twin towers. *Time.* Retrieved from http://life.time.com/culture/world-trade-center-remembering-the-twin-towers/#end

Douglas, M., & Wildavsky, A. (1983). *Risk and culture: An essay on the selection of technological and environmental dangers.* Berkeley: University of California Press.

Erikson, K. T. (1976). Loss of communality at Buffalo Creek. *American Journal of Psychiatry, 133*(3), 302-305.

Frankl, V. E. (1985). *Man's search for meaning.* New York, NY: Simon and Schuster.

Hermann, C. F. (1963). Some consequence of crisis which limit the viability of organizations. *Administrative Science Quarterly,* 8(1), 61–82.

Kan, N. (2013, October 28). Encountering the Fukushima Daiichi accident. *Huffington Post.* Retrieved from http://www.huffingtonpost.com/naoto-kan/japan-nuclear-energy_b_4171073.html

Kammerer, N., & Mazelis, R. (2006, July). *Trauma and retraumatization.* Paper presented at the After the Crisis: Healing from Trauma after Disasters Expert Panel Meeting, Bethesda, MD. Retrieved from http://gainscenter.samhsa.gov/atc/text/papers/trauma_paper.htm

Law, B. M. (2011). Seared in our memories. *Monitor on Psychology,* 42(8), 60.

Norris, F. H., Friedman, M. J., Watson, J., Byrne, C. M., Diaz, E., & Kaniasty, K. (2002). 60,000 disaster victims speak: Part I. An empirical review of the empirical literature, 1981–2001. *Psychiatry,* 65(3), 207–239.

Norris, F. H., & Murrell, S. A. (1988). Prior experience as a moderator of disaster impact on anxiety symptoms in older adults. *American Journal of Community Psychology,* 16(5), 665–683.

Ogden, C. K., & Richards, I. A. (1927). *Meaning of meaning.* New York, NY: Harcourt, Brace.

Park, C. L., & Folkman, S. (1997). Meaning in the context of stress and coping. *Review of General Psychology, 1*(2), 115–144.

Rendall, M. S. (2006). *Breakup of New Orleans households after Hurricane Katrina* (WR-703). Santa Monica, CA: Rand Corporation. Retrieved from http://www.rand.org/content/dam/rand/pubs/working_papers/2009/RAND_WR703.pdf.

Reynolds, B., & Seeger, M. W. (2005). Crisis and emergency risk communication as an integrative model. *Journal of Health Communication, 10,* 43–55.

Saulny, S. (2006, June 21). A legacy of the storm: Depression and suicide. *New York Times.* Retrieved from http://www.nytimes.com/2006/06/21/us/21depress.html?pagewanted=all&_r=0

Seeger, M. W, Sellnow, T. L., & Ulmer, R. R. (2003). *Organizational communication and crisis*. Westport, CT: Praeger.

Sellnow, T. L., & Seeger, M. (2001). Exploring the boundaries of crisis communication: The case of the 1997 Red River Valley flood. *Communication Studies*, *52*(2), 153–167.

Veil, S. R., Sellnow, T. L., & Heald, M. (2011). Memorializing crisis: The Oklahoma City National Memorial as renewal discourse. *Journal of Applied Communication Research*, *39*(2), 164–183.

Weick, K. E. (1988). Enacted sensemaking in crisis situations. *Journal of Management Studies*, *25*(4), 305–317.

CHAPTER 4

Berkes, H. (2012, September 27). Coal mine company denies responsibility despite disaster settlement. NPR. Retrieved from http://www.npr.org/sections/thetwo-way/2012/09/27/161920764/coal-mine-company-denies-responsibility-despite-disaster-settlement

Boudes, T., & Laroche, H. (2009). Taking off the heat: Narrative sensemaking in post-crisis inquiry reports. *Organization Studies*, *30*(4), 377–396.

Buttny, R. (1993). *Social accountability in communication*. Newbury Park, CA: Sage.

Daily Mail Reporter. (2010). "There was an awful rumbling, then screams and cries": Harrowing firsthand account of Titanic disaster published for first time. Daily Mail.com. Retrieved from http://www.dailymail.co.uk/news/article-1316804/Firsthand-account-Titanic-disaster-published-time.htm

Dawes, C. (2012, October 30). *Hurricane Sandy in the Dumbo Section of Brooklyn*. Retrieved from https://www.youtube.com/watch?v=4sC4foWTjf4

Dershowitz, A. M. (1994). *The abuse excuse: And other cop-outs, sob stories, and evasions of responsibility*. Boston: Little, Brown.

Jackall, R. (1988). Moral mazes: The world of corporate managers. *International Journal of Politics, Culture, and Society*, *1*(4), 598–614.

Lerner, J. S., & Tetlock, E. (1999). Accounting for the effects of accountability. *Psychological Education*, *125*(2), 255–275.

Loftus, E. J. (1980). Impact of expert psychological testimony on the unreliability of eyewitness identification. *Journal of Applied Psychology*, *65*(1), 9–15.

Mulgan, R. (2000). "Accountability": An ever expanding concept? *Public Administration*, *78*(3), 555–573.

Murray Energy Corporation. (2013, October 12). Setting the record straight about what happened at Crandall Canyon Mine. Fox News Opinion. Retrieved from http://www.foxnews.com/opinion/2013/10/12/setting-record-straight-about-what-happened-at-crandall-canyon-mine.html

National Transportation Safety Board. (2013). *The investigative process at NTSB*. Retrieved from http://www.ntsb.gov/investigations/process.html

Nature's Beauty. (2010, April 5). *!!Father saves 2-year-old after she slipped and fell into New York's East River!!* Retrieved from https://www.youtube.com/watch?v=FeCLnXMzjr4

9/11 Commission. (2004). *The 9/11 Commission report*. Retrieved from http://www.9-11commission.gov/report/

Oskin, B. (2013, April 19). Mine disaster CSI: Earthquakes shed new light on Utah collapse. LiveScience. Retrieved from http://www.livescience.com/28864-earthquakes-explain-crandall-canyon-collapse.html

Perry, R. (2011). The Deepwater Horizon oil spill and the limits of civil liability. *Washington Law Review, 86*(1), 1–68.

Ray, S. J. (1999). *Strategic communication in crisis management: Lessons from the airline industry*. Westport, CT: Quorum Books.

RT. (2013, April 18). *Caught on camera: Moment of Texas fertilizer plant explosion*. Retrieved from https://www.youtube.com/watch?v=v-zI84TYnCI

Scott, M. B., & Lyman, S. M. (1968). Accounts. *American Sociological Review, 33*(1), 46–62.

Top five: Natural disaster stories. (2011, August 25). *CNN iReport*. Retrieved from http://ireport.cnn.com/blogs/ireport-blog/2011/08/25/top-five-natural-disaster-stories

Varela, F. J., & Shear, J. (1999). First-person methodologies: What, why, how? *Journal of Consciousness Studies, 6*(2–3), 1–14.

Weick, K. E. (1979). *The social psychology of organizing*. Reading MA: Addison-Wesley.

Weick, K. E. (1995). *Sensemaking in organizations* (vol. 3). London: Sage.

CHAPTER 5

Anthony, K. E., & Sellnow, T. L. (2011). Information acquisition, perception, preference, and convergence by Gulf Coast residents in the aftermath of the Hurricane Katrina crisis. *Argumentation and Advocacy, 48*, 81–96.

Bamberg, M. (2005). Master narrative. In D. Herman, M. Jahn, & M. L. Ryan (Eds.), *Routledge encyclopedia of narrative theory* (pp. 287–288). New York, NY: Routledge.

Benoit, W. L. (1995). *Accounts, excuses, and apologies: A theory of image restoration strategies*. Albany: State University of New York Press.

Benoit, W. L. (2015). *Accounts, excuses and apologies: Image repair theory and research* (2nd ed.). Albany: State University of New York Press.

Benoit, W. L., & Brinson, S. L. (1994). AT&T: "Apologies are not enough." *Communication Quarterly, 42*(1), 75–88.

Benoit, W. L., & Dorries, B. (1996). Dateline NBC's persuasive attack on Wal-Mart. *Communication Quarterly, 44*, 463–477.

Benoit, W. L., & Hanczor, R. S. (1994). The Tonya Harding controversy: An analysis of image restoration strategies. *Communication Quarterly, 42*, 416–433.

Burke, K. (1961). *The rhetoric of religion: Studies in logology*. Boston: Beacon Press.

Burke, K. (1984). *Attitudes toward history*. Berkeley: University of California Press.

Centers for Disease Control and Prevention. (n.d.). Investigation of outbreak of human infections caused by Salmonella I 4,[5],12:i:-. Retrieved from http://www.cdc.gov/salmonella/4512eyeminus.html

Dillon, R. L., & Tinsley, C. H., (2008). How near-misses influence decision making under risk: A missed opportunity. *Management Science, 54*(8), 1425–1440. doi:10.1287/mnsc.1080.0869

Eckerman, I. (2005). *The Bhopal saga: Causes and consequences of the world's largest industrial disaster*. Hyderabad: Universities Press.

Hearit, K. M. (2005). *Crisis management by apology: Corporate response to allegations of wrongdoing*. New York: Routledge.

Hiner, J. (2013, November 26). Understanding Snowden's impact on IT . . . in two minutes. *TechRepublic/U.S.* Retrieved from http://www.techrepublic.com/blog/tech-sanity-check/video-understanding-snowdens-impact-on-it-in-2-minutes/

International Confederation of Free Trade Unions & International Federation of Chemical, Energy, and General Workers Unions. (1985). *The report of the ICFTU-ICEF Mission* to study the causes and effects of the methyl isocyanate gas leak at the Union Carbide pesticide plant in Bhopal, India, on December 2nd/3rd 1984. Retrieved from http://www.bhopal.net/oldsite/documentlibrary/unionreport1985.html

Johnson, D., & Sellnow, T. L. (1995). Deliberative rhetoric as a step in organizational crisis management: Exxon as a case study. *Communication Reports, 8,* 54–60.

Kelley-Romano, S., & Westgate, V. (2007). Blaming Bush: An analysis of political cartoons following Hurricane Katrina. *Journalism Studies, 8,* 755–773. doi:10.1080/14616700701504724

Knittel, S. (2013, October 11). Matthew Shepard fifteen years late—how his parents are keeping his memory alive—and creating a better world. *Seattle Gay News.* Retrieved from http://www.sgn.org/sgnnews41_41/page3.cfm

Littlefield, R. S., & Quenette, A. M. (2007). Crisis leadership and Hurricane Katrina: The portrayal of authority by the media in natural disasters. *Journal of Applied Communication Research, 35,* 26–47.

Ott, B. L., & Aoki, E. (2002). The politics of negotiating public tragedy: Media framing of the Matthew Shepard murder. *Rhetoric and Public Affairs, 5,* 483–505.

Ryan, H. R. (Ed.) (1988). *Oratorical encounters: Selected studies and sources of twentieth-century political accusations and apologies.* Westport, CT: Greenwood Press.

Sellnow, D. D. (2014). *The rhetorical power of popular culture: Considering mediated texts.* Thousand Oaks, CA: Sage.

Sellnow, T. L., Ulmer, R. R., Seeger, M. W., & Littlefield, R. S. (2009). *Effective risk communication: A message-centered approach.* New York: Springer.

Ware, B. L., & Linkugel, W. A. (1973). They spoke in defense of themselves: On the generic criticism of apologia. *Quarterly Journal of speech, 59*(3), 273–283.

Weick, K. E., & Sutcliffe, K. M. (2007). *Managing the unexpected: Resilient performance in an age of uncertainty* (2nd ed.). San Francisco, CA: Jossey-Bass.

CHAPTER 6

Comfort, L. (1994). Self organization in complex systems, *Journal of Public Administration Research and Theory, 4,* 393–410.

Demuth, J. L. (2002). *Countering terrorism: Lessons learned from natural and technological disasters.* Washington DC: National Academy of Sciences.

Dimitrov, V., & Woog, R. (2000). Making sense of social complexity through strange attractors. In J. Lamp Altmann, P. E. D. Love, P. Mandal, R. Smith, & M. Warren (Eds.), *Proceedings of the International Conference on Systems Thinking and Management.* Geelong: Deakin University.

Fernandez, S., Barbera, J. A., & van Drop, J. R. (2006). Spontaneous volunteer response to disasters: The benefits and consequences of good intentions. *Journal of Emergency Management, 4*(5), 57–68.

Hariman, R., & Lucaites, J. L. (2007). *No caption needed: Iconic photographs, public culture, and liberal democracy.* Chicago: University of Chicago Press.

Littlefield, R. S., & Quenette, A. M. (2007). Crisis leadership and Hurricane Katrina: The portrayal of authority by the media in natural disasters. *Journal of Applied Communication Research, 35*(1), 26–47.

Norris, F. H., Stevens, S., Pfefferbaum, B., Wyche, K. F., & Pfefferbaum, R. L. (2008). Community resilience as a metaphor, theory, set of capacities, and strategy for disaster readiness. *American Journal of Community Psychology, 41*(1–2), 127–150.

Obama, B. (2012, July 22). *Remarks by the president after hospital visit.* White House. Retrieved from https://www.whitehouse.gov/the-press-office/2012/07/22/remarks -president-after-hospital-visit

Reierson, J. L., Sellnow, T. L., & Ulmer, R. R. (2009). Complexities of crisis renewal over time: Learning from the case of tainted Odwalla apple juice. *Communication Studies, 60,* 114–129.

Seeger, M. W. (1986). CEO performances: Lee Iacocca and the case of Chrysler. *Southern Speech Communication Journal, 52*(1), 52–68.

Seeger, M. W., & Griffin Padgett, D. R. (2010). From image restoration to renewal: Approaches to understanding postcrisis communication. *Review of Communication, 10*(2), 127–141.

Seeger, M., & Ulmer, R. (2002). A post-crisis discourse of renewal: The cases of Malden Mills and Cole Hardwoods. *Journal of Applied Communication Research, 30*(2), 126–142.

Seeger, M. W., Ulmer, R. R., Novak, J. M., & Sellnow, T. (2005). Post-crisis discourse and organizational change, failure and renewal. *Journal of Organizational Change Management, 18*(1), 78–95.

Sellnow, T. L., & Seeger, M. W. (2013). *Theorizing crisis communication* (vol. 4). Hoboken, NJ: Wiley.

Toelken, K., Seeger, M. W., & Batteau, A. (2005). Learning and renewal following threat and crisis: The experience of a computer services firm in response to Y2K and 9/11. In B. Van de Walle & B. Carle (Eds.), *Proceedings of the Second International ISCRAM Conference* (pp. 43–51). Brussels: Belgium ISCRAM.

Ulmer, R. R., Seeger, M. W., & Sellnow, T. L. (2007). Post-crisis communication and renewal: Expanding the parameters of post-crisis discourse. *Public Relations Review, 33*(2), 130–134.

Ulmer, R. R., Sellnow, T. L., & Seeger, M. W. (2010). *Effective crisis communication: Moving from crisis to opportunity.* Thousand Oaks, CA: Sage.

Ulmer, R. R., Sellnow, T. L., & Seeger, M.W. (2011). *Effective crisis communication: Moving from crisis to opportunity* (2nd ed.). Thousand Oaks, CA: Sage.

CHAPTER 7

Anthony, K. E., & Sellnow, T. L. (2011). Information acquisition, perception, preference, and convergence by Gulf Coast residents in the aftermath of the Hurricane Katrina crisis. *Argumentation and Advocacy, 48,* 81–96.

Berns, N. (2009). Contesting the victim card: Closure discourse and emotion in death penalty rhetoric. *Sociological Quarterly, 50,* 383–406.

Best, J. (1997). Victimization and the victim industry. *Society, 34*(4), 9–17.

Bourk, M. (2011, November). "A Makara-like wave came crashing": Sri Lankan narratives of the Boxing Day tsunami. *Media International Australia, Incorporating Culture and Policy, ,* no. 141, 49-57.

Brunswick to reactivate outdoor sirens. (2014, July 28). WKYC.com. Retrieved from http://www.wkyc.com/story/news/local/medina-county/2014/07/28/brunswick-siren -reactivation/13302467/

Burke, K. (1973). The rhetorical situation. *Communication: Ethical and Moral Issues, 10,* 263–275.

Coombs, W. T. (1999). Information and compassion in crisis responses: A test of their effects. *Journal of Public Relations, 11*(2), 125–142.

DART Center for Journalism and Trauma. (2003). *Tragedies and journalism: A guide for more effective coverage.* New York, NY: DART Center for Journalism and Trauma, Columbia University. Retrieved from http://dartcenter.org/files/en_tnj_0.pdf

Davis, K. (2013). RI fire code changes since The Station fire. *Turn to 10.* Retrieved from http://turnto10.com/archive/ri-fire-code-changes-since-the-station-fire

Dong, D., Chang, T., & Chen, D. (2008). Reporting AIDS and the invisible victims in China: Official knowledge as news in the *People's Daily,* 1986–2002. *Journal of Health Communication, 13,* 357-374.

"First statement from Ebola patient: 'I am growing stronger.'" *NBC News.* Retrieved from: http://www.nbcnews.com/storyline/ebola-virus-outbreak/first-statement-ebola-patient-i-am-growing-stronger-n176271

Kassing, J. W., & Armstrong, T. A., (2002). Someone's going to hear about this: Examining the association between dissent-triggering events and employees' dissent expression. *Management Communication Quarterly, 16,* 39–65.

King, E. G., & deYoung, M. (2008). Imag (in) ing September 11 Ward Churchill, frame contestation, and media hegemony. *Journal of Communication Inquiry, 32*(2), 123–139.

Marcus, A. A., & Goodman, R. S. (1991). Victims and shareholders: The dilemmas of presenting corporate policy during a crisis. *Academy of Management Journal, 34,* 281–305.

Marshall, C., & Pienaar, K. (2008). "You are not alone": The discursive construction of the "suffering victim" identity on *The Oprah Winfrey Show. Southern American Linguistics and Applied Language Studies, 26*(4), 525–546. doi:10.2989/SALALS.2008.26.4.9.681

Millner, A. G., Veil, S. R., & Sellnow, T. L. (2011). Proxy communication in crisis response. *Public Relations Review, 37,* 74–76. doi:10.1016/j.pubrev.2010.10.005

Newton, J. H. (2005). Visual ethics theory. In K. Smith, S. Moriarty, G. Barbatsis, & K. Kenney (Eds.), *Handbook of visual communication: Theory, methods, and media* (pp. 429–444). Mahwah, NJ: Erlbaum.

Prasad, A., & Prasad, (2001). (Un)Willing to resist? The discursive production of local workplace opposition. *Studies in Organizations and Societies, 7,* 105–125.

Shannahan, K. J., Hopkins, L. C., & Raymond, M. A. (2013). Depictions of self-*inflicted* versus blameless victims for nonprofits employing print advertisements. *Journal of Advertising, 41,* 55-74. doi:10.2753/JOA0091-3367410304

Smith, F. L. Coffelt, T. A., Rives, A. P., & Sollitto, M. (2012). The voice of victims: Positive response to a natural disaster cycle. *Qualitative Research Reports in Communication, 13,* 53-62.

Tan, C. (2014, September 4). Malaysia Airlines to be nationalized in a new form of "investment." *Asian Review.* Retrieved from http://asia.nikkei.com/magazine/20140904-TATA-GROUP/Business/Malaysia-Airlines-to-be-nationalized-in-new-form-of-investment

CHAPTER 8

Anker, E. (2005). Villains, victims and heroes: Melodrama, media, and September 11. *Journal of Communication, 55*(1), 22–37.

Bennett, S. (2004). Psychoanalytic reflections on heroism in a time of fallen heroes. *Journal of Mental and Nervous Diseases, 192*(3), 171-177.

CBSNews.Com Staff. (2001). *The day Reagan was shot.* CBSNews.com. Retrieved from http://www.cbsnews.com/news/the-day-reagan-was-shot/

Campbell, J. (1973). *The hero with a thousand faces.* Princeton, NJ: Princeton University Press.

Carnegie Hero Fund Commission. (2014). *Latest Carnegie Medal awardees*. Retrieved from http://carnegiehero.org/awardees/

Franco, Z. E., Blau, K., & Zimbardo, G. (2011). Heroism: A conceptual analysis and differentiation between heroic action and altruism, *Review of General Psychology* 15(2), 99–113.

Franco, Z., & Zimbardo, G. (2006). The banality of heroism. *Greater Good, 3*(2), 30–35.

Friedman, D. (2013, February 15). President Obama honors the six hero Newtown educators killed in the rampage at Sandy Hook Elementary School. *New York Daily News*. Retrieved from http://www.nydailynews.com/news/politics/obama-honors-newtown-heros-article-1.1265355#ixzz2urQjmGVr

Fraher, A. (2011). Hero-making as a defense against anxiety of responsibility and risk: A case study of US Airways flight 159. *Organisation and Social Dynamics, 11*(1), 59–78.

Goren, E. (2007). Societies' use of a hero following a national tragedy. *American Journal of Psychoanalysis, 67*, 37–52.

Monahan, B., & Gregory, C. (2001). *From Ground Zero to ground hero: Status appropriation and the FDNY*. Newark: University of Delaware Disaster Research Center. Retrieved from http://udspace.udel.edu/bitstream/handle/19716/705/PP315.pdf?sequence=1&origin=publication_detail

Schulman, R. (1996). Heroes, organizations and high reliability. *Journal of Contingencies and Crisis Management, 4*(2), 72–82.

Szalavitz, M. (2012). How disasters bring out our kindness In disasters, it's human nature to band together and be kind to one another in order to survive. *Time On Line*. Retrieved from http://healthland.time.com/2012/10/31/how-disasters-bring-out-our-kindness/

White House (2014). *The Presidential Citizens Medal criteria*. Retrieved from http://www.whitehouse.gov/citizensmedal/criteria

Zimbardo, G. (2011). Why the world needs heroes. *Europe's Journal of Psychology, 7*(3), 402–407.

CHAPTER 9

Autry, R. K. (2012). The monumental reconstruction of memory in South Africa: The Voortrekker Monument. *Theory, Culture, and Society, 29*(6), 146–164. doi:10.1177/0263276412438596

Azarian-Ceccato, N. (2010). Reverberations of the Armenian genocide: Narratives' intergenerational transmission and the task of not forgetting. *Narrative Inquiry, 20*(1), 106–123. doi:10.1075/ni.20.1.06aza

Baptist, K. W. (2013). Reenchanting memorial landscapes: Lessons from the roadside. *Landscape Journal, 32*, 35–50.

Blair, C., Jeppeson, M. S., & Pucci, E., Jr. (1991). Public memorializing in postmodernity: The Vietnam Veterans Memorial as prototype. *Quarterly Journal of Speech, 77*, 263–288.

Blair, C., & Michel, N. (2000). Reproducing civil rights tactics: The rhetorical performances of the Civil Rights Memorial. *Rhetoric Society Quarterly, 30*(2), 31–55.

Bloxham, D. (2005). *The great game of genocide: Imperialism, nationalism, and the destruction of the Ottoman Armenians*. New York, NY: Oxford University Press.

Bradford, V. (2010). *Public forgetting: The rhetoric and politics of beginning again*. University Park: Pennsylvania State University Press.

Eyre, A. (2007). Remembering: Community commemoration after disaster. In H. Rodriguez, E. L. Quarantelli, & R. R. Dynes (Eds.), *Handbook of disaster research* (pp. 441–455). New York, NY: Springer.

Hasian, M. Jr. (2004). Remembering and forgetting the "Final Solution": A rhetorical pilgrimage through the U.S. Holocaust Memorial Museum. *Critical Studies in Media Communication, 21*, 63–92.

Jones, C. (2007). The first displays: D.C. and S.F., 1987. *Rhetoric and Public Affairs, 10*, 580–594.

Jones, M. (2011). *Points of departure: Roadside memorial Polaroids*. Lexington, KY: Jargon Society.

Kitch, C. (2002). "A death in the American family": Myth, memory, and national values in the media mourning of John F. Kennedy, Jr. *Journalism and Mass Communication Quarterly, 79*(2), 294–309.

Littlefield, R. S., Reierson, J., Cowden, K., Stowman, S., & Long Feather, C. (2009). A case study of the Red Lake, Minnesota, school shooting: Intercultural learning in the renewal process. *Communication, Culture and Critique, 2*, 361–381. doi:10.1111/j.1753-9137.2009.01043.x

Liu, B. F., & Pompper, D. (2012). The crisis with no name: Defining the interplay of culture, ethnicity, and race on organizational issue and media outcomes. *Journal of Applied Communication Research, 40*, 127–146.

Marschall, S. (2006). Visualizing memories: The Hector Pieterson Memorial in Soweto. *Visual Anthropology, 19*, 145–169.

Mayo, J. M. (1988). *War memorials as political landscape: The American experience and beyond*. New York: Praeger.

Nielson, R. (2011, February 9). DOT will allow roadside memorials. *Athens Banner Herald*. Retrieved from http://onlineathens.com/stories/020911/new_782876027.shtml

Perelman, C., & Olbrechts-Tyteca, L. (1969). *The new rhetoric: A treatise on argumentation*. London: University of Notre Dame Press.

Seeger, M. W., Sellnow, T. L., & Ulmer, R. R. (2003). *Communication and organizational crisis*. Westport, CT: Praeger.

Smith, R., & Trimbur, J. (2003). Rhetorics of unity and disunity: The Worcester firefighters memorial service, *Rhetorical Society Quarterly, 33*(4), 7–24.

Stob, P. (2012). Lonely courage, commemorative confrontation, and communal therapy: William James remembers the Massachusetts 54th. *Quarterly Journal of Speech, 98*, 249–271. doi:10.1080/00335630.2012.691173

Sullivan, D. L. (1994). Exclusionary epideictic: NOVA's narrative excommunication of Fleischmann and Pons. *Science, Technology, and Human Values, 19*(3), 283–306.

Suter, K. (2010). Roadside memorials: Sacred places in a secular era. *Contemporary Review, 292*, 51–59.

Tay, R. (2009). Drivers' perceptions and reactions to roadside memorials. *Accident Analysis and Prevention, 41*, 663–669. doi:10.1016/j.aa2009.03.006

Vivian, B. (2006). Neoliberal epideictic: Rhetorical form and commemorative politics on September 11, 2002. *Quarterly Journal of Speech, 92*, 1–26.

Veil, S. R., Sellnow, T. L., & Heald, M. (2011). Memorializing crisis: The Oklahoma National Memorial as renewal discourse. *Journal of Applied Communication Research, 39*(2), 164–183.

White House. (2012, December 12). *Remarks by the president at Sandy Hook interfaith prayer vigil.* Retrieved from http://www.whitehouse.gov/the-press-office/2012/12/16/remarks-president-sandy-hook-interfaith-prayer-vigil

Zandberg, E., Meyers, O., & Neiger, M. (2012). Past continuous: Newsworthiness and the shaping of collective memory. *Critical Studies in Media Communication, 29,* 65–69.

CHAPTER 10

Anthony, K. E., Sellnow, T. L., & Millner, A. G. (2013). Message convergence as a message-centered approach to analyzing and improving risk communication. *Journal of Applied Communication Research, 41,* 346–364.

Benoit, W. L. (1995). *Accounts, excuses, and apologies: A theory of image restoration strategies.* Albany: State University Press of New York

Heath, R. L. (2004). Telling a story: A narrative approach to communication during crisis. In D. Millar & R. L. Heath (Eds.), *Responding to crisis: A rhetorical approach to crisis communication* (pp. 167–188). Mahwah, NJ: Erlbaum.

Liu, M., McIntyre, J. J., & Sellnow, T. L. (2008). Less ambiguity, more hope: The use of narrative in Chinese newspaper reports on the SARS crisis. In M. W. Seeger, T. L. Sellnow, & R. R. Ulmer (Eds.), *Crisis communication and the public health* (pp. 111–130). Cresskill, NJ: Hampton Press.

Park, C. L., & Folkman, S. (1997). Meaning in the context of stress and coping. *Review of General Psychology, 1*(2), 115–144.

Perelman, C., & Olbrechts-Tyteca, L. (1969). *The new rhetoric: A treatise on argumentation* .London: University of Notre Dame Press.

Perelman, C. (1979). *The new rhetoric and the humanities: Essays on rhetoric and its applications.* Dordrecht, Holland: D. Reidel.

Presidential Commission on the Space Shuttle Challenger Accident. (1986). *Report of the Presidential Commission on the Space Shuttle Challenger Accident.* Retrieved from http://history.nasa.gov/rogersrep/genindex.htm

Sellnow, T. L., Ulmer, R. R., Seeger, M. W., & Littlefield, R. S. (2009). *Effective risk communication: A message-centered approach.* New York, NY: Springer.

Venette, S. J., Sellnow, T. L., & Lang, A. (2003). Metanarration's role in restructuring perceptions of crisis: NHTSA's failure in the Ford-Firestone crisis. *Journal of Business Communication, 40*(3), 219–236.

Weick, K. E. (1993). The collapse of sensemaking in organizations: The Mann Gulch disaster. *Administrative Science Quarterly, 38,* 628–652.

CHAPTER 11

Bales, R. F. (2002). *The Great Chicago Fire and the myth of Mrs. O'Leary's cow.* Jefferson, NC: McFarland.

Barden, M. (2014, May 29). Sandy Hook father on gun violence: "It's not too late to protect your children" time. *Time.* Retrieved from http://time.com/138756/santa-barbara-shooting-sandy-hook-gun-violence/

Barsky, L., Trainor, J., & Torres, M. (2006). *Disaster realities in the aftermath of Hurricane Katrina: Revisiting the looting myth* (Natural Hazards Center Quick Response Report,84).

Birkland, T. A. (1998). Focusing events, mobilization, and agenda setting. *Journal of Public Policy, 18*(1), 53–74.

Carr, D. (2005, September 19). More horrible than truth: News reports. *New York Times.* Retrieved from http://www.nytimes.com/2005/09/19/business/media/19carr.html?pagewanted=all

Centers for Disease Control and Prevention. (2014). *Pandemic influenza storybook.* Atlanta, GA: Centers for Disease Control and Prevention. Retrieved from http://www.cdc.gov/publications/panflu/

Day, J. M. (1991). Role taking revisited: Narrative and cognitive developmental interpretations of moral growth. *Journal of Moral Education, 20*(3), 305–315.

Dowling, J., & Pfeffer, J. (1975). Organizational legitimacy: Social values and organizational behavior. *Pacific Sociological Review, 18,* 122–136.

Gerbner, G., Gross, L., Morgan, M., & Signorielli, N. (1980). The "mainstreaming" of America: Violence profile no. 11. *Journal of Communication, 30*(3), 10–29.

Kasperson, R. E., Renn, O., Slovic, Brown, H. S., Emel, J., Goble, R., & Ratick, S. (1988). The social amplification of risk: A conceptual framework. *Risk Analysis, 8*(2), 177–187.

Ott, M., Shaw, M. F., Danila, R. N., & Lynfield, R. (2007). Lessons learned from the 1918–1919 influenza pandemic in Minneapolis and St. Paul, Minnesota. *Public Health Reports, 122*(6), 803–810. Retrieved from http://www.ncbi.nlm.nih.gov/pmc/articles/PMC1997248/

Quarantelli, E. L. (1994). *Looting and antisocial behavior in disasters.* Newark: Disaster Research Center, University of Delaware. Retrieved from http://dspace.udel.edu/handle/19716/590

Sandy Hook Promise (2014). *About Sandy Hook Promise.* Retrieved from http://www2.sandyhookpromise.org

Seeger, M. W., & Ulmer, R. R. (2003). Explaining Enron communication and responsible leadership. *Management Communication Quarterly, 17*(1), 58–84.

Smith, C. (1995). *Urban disorder and the shape of belief: The Great Chicago Fire, the Haymarket bomb, and the model town of Pullman.* Chicago: University of Chicago Press.

Tappan, M. B., & Brown, L. M. (1989). Stories told and lessons learned: Toward a narrative approach to moral development and moral education. *Harvard Educational Review, 59*(2), 182–206.

Tierney, K. (2003). Disaster beliefs and institutional interests: Recycling disaster myths in the aftermath of 9-11. *Research in Social Problems and Public Policy, 11,* 33–51.

Turner, B. A. (1976). The organizational and interorganizational development of disasters. *Administrative Science Quarterly, 21*(3) 378–397.

Wilkins, L. (1984, August). Media coverage of a blizzard: Is the message helplessness? Paper presented at the Association for Education in Journalism and Mass Communication Conference, Gainesville, FL.

Wilkins, L., & Patterson, (1987). Risk analysis and the construction of news. *Journal of Communication, 37*(3), 80–92.

Index

CPSIA information can be obtained
at www.ICGtesting.com
Printed in the USA
LVHW031834160719
624281LV00006B/921/P

9 780804 799515